UpSizing
The Road to Zero Emissions
More Jobs, More Income and No Pollution

Gunter Pauli

The goal is zero: zero accidents, zero waste, zero emissions.

Edgar S. Woolard, Jr, Former Chairman, DuPont

With early success stories from Fiji, Namibia and Colombia highlighted in this book, Gunter Pauli demonstrates that it is not anymore a question *if* Zero Emissions works or not, but rather *when* will it be implemented all around the world.

Sarwono Kusumaatmadja, Chair,
United Nations Convention on Biodiversity 1996

ZERI demonstrates that productivity increases can be combined with job creation.

Ingvar Carlsson, Prime Minister of Sweden

Zero Emissions will be the standard for industry in the 21st century.

1996 White Book on the Environment,
The Environment Agency, Japan

ZERI . . . one of the most exciting initiatives the United Nations University has taken thus far.

Professor Hans J.A. van Ginkel,
Rector of the United Nations University

Acknowledgements

To produce three books in three years is only possible when one enjoys innumerable dialogues with a considerable number of concerned minds, ready generously to share and receive input. During my 30 trips around the world over the past 36 months, I have enjoyed all that, and much more.

The skeleton for this book was written in the Raffles Hotel in Singapore in August 1996. Then, I decided to retire for a few days and structure my thoughts only two months after my previous book, *Breakthroughs*, had been published. The post-midnight discussions with Joan Klar, Carolyn Tyler and Jim Channon in Ubud, Bali, in March 1997, brought clarity to the concepts of UpSizing and Generative Science, which had been simmering for a couple years. A couple of long flights over the Pacific with Dan Mapes and Fritjof Capra opened up the sky on Immunity Management as early as March 1996. These three concepts are the core contribution of this book to the reader, and they build on the Zero Emissions theory and methodology which I first started to develop five years ago. Arnold Thaler brought focus to the message: higher productivity, more jobs and less pollution. In the end, that is what this book is all about.

The students, professors, executives, politicians, pedagogues, activists and thousands of motivated individuals from China, Japan, Indonesia, Malaysia, Brazil, Colombia, Mexico, Kuwait, Namibia, Tanzania, England, Italy, Spain, Sweden, Botswana, Zambia, Zimbabwe, Fiji and many other countries gave me a chance to present, test and improve the methodology of UpSizing, fine-tune the concept of Zero Emissions and convert the concepts into a no-nonsense approach, which demonstrates that making more with less while generating jobs and slashing pollution is not only feasible, but can be designed by anyone.

The open ears and mind of the President of Namibia, HE Dr Sam Nujoma, from the State House meetings to lunch and dinners in Etosha, set the stage for the first commercial operationalisation of Zero Emissions and UpSizing.

The platform created by the State Minister of the Environment from Indonesia, and the Chairman of the UN Biodiversity Convention in 1996, HE Sarwono Kusumaatmadja, offered a chance to reach out to the business community of one of the potentially greatest economies. It was Linda Garland who had the vision to put us together in Ubud, Bali, in June 1995. Lester Brown and the Worldwatch Institute provided most of the facts and figures unaccredited with footnotes. This data has been sourced from various editions of *State of the World* and *Vital Signs*, published annually in the UK by Earthscan. The work of John Stuart and the team at Greenleaf Publishing proved invaluable in producing this book.

The interactions and field visits throughout Africa with Keto Mshigeni, this exceptional crusader for his continent, brought back my enthusiasm for Africa. I am convinced that Africa has a great future, if only the rest of the world would start to believe it. Without this scientist, who quotes as easily from the Bible as from his encyclopaedia of botany, I would never have ventured to imagine a strategy for the developing world along the lines that we are now proposing.

The determination and the quality of work of George Chan convinced me that 'too much is still not enough'. He is truly committed to reaching the unreached. George is relentless and, even when in pain, he cannot stop. Even without a contract or pay, he does not rest. He has no time to waste. I know that George has suffered much on his road to prove his opponents were wrong. George is a remarkable gentleman, who deserves to receive an OBE or CBE very soon, if only the British would recognise this Mauritius-born Chinese, who served the British Army in the Second World War, risked his life for the Union Jack and now has to apply for a visa to visit his sons, who graduated—like him—from Imperial College in London. This personal commitment of George in all he does makes him one of the unsung heroes in the quest for poverty alleviation and sustainable livelihoods, respecting nature, learning from nature, emulating nature.

The unconditional support of the Rector of the United Nations University, Heitor Gurgulino de Souza, and the Director of the Institute of Advanced Studies, Tarcisio Della Senta, was remarkable. I wonder if I would have had so much patience with an unorthodox, creative mind that seems to have a lack of respect for strict United Nations rules? I certainly did not make life easy for them. But I would definitely not have been able to prove that the UN system can be converted into a great mechanism to contribute to the betterment of the world, unless the rector believed in my chances of success and the value of my proposals. With several pilot units up and running less than three years from the start of the programme, we have moved a few mountains and guided the horses to the water trough. I am so glad to see they are drinking now.

Of course, there would have been no chance of maintaining the energy in all these endeavours without my brother in spirits, Kay Nishi. If he only knew how much he made possible. It is rare to find someone who shares so many concerns and ideals. It must be something to do with the fact that we were both born in the Year of Mozart ('56). There must be something in the stars spelling out the convergence of minds and the desire for achievements along much the same lines of interest. It seems that, at the age of 40, this is only the beginning.

Since my previous book, *Breakthroughs*, first appeared in Spanish in April 1996, my two boys Carl-Olaf and Laurenz-Frederik have learned to read, write, swim, ski and skate. While none of my recent work has been translated into their native language—since no one is a prophet in their own country—my books are now available in 12 languages. I am certain that it will not be long before they will teach their father more about the reality of life than he had ever imagined. For this, I have to thank Ingrid.

Thank you all my real friends for making that possible. And a very special thanks to my opponents and self-declared enemies for putting so many obstacles on the road. These were converted into a doubling of energy. The roadblocks were great catalysts. And those who do not feel like sharing love will not be met with hatred, but with my indifference. The world needs and deserves the best. Here is a small contribution from me to all of you!

Gunter Pauli
Chateau d'Oex, Switzerland
March 1998

Foreword

I became involved in supporting ZERI and its very energetic and committed Founder/Director Gunter Pauli for several reasons.

The concept of Zero Emissions is a radical but easily understood concept which is addressing one of the major flaws in our current market economies—waste. The logic of ZERI builds on recent achievements well known in business: zero defects, zero inventory, zero accidents—in short, a drive to enhance human and resource productivity while reducing/eliminating waste. If waste is seen as a measure of inefficiency in the use of resources, then ZERI should be the mission of every business. Oversimplified? Maybe, but why not? The world is stuck in an economic system characterised by both waste and innovation. If we take on ZERI as an objective, it will enhance the forces of innovation and certainly reduce waste. In business today the concept of 'eco-efficiency' is the management norm of any well-run company. ZERI is the logical end-result of eco-efficiency.

Secondly, ZERI is also drawing out of our research establishments new thinking on how to use our resources more completely. The focus to date has been on organic resources and optimal use of biomass. When one reflects on the massive wastage of biomass in all industrial processes today, the search for new uses of those wastes and new products through research makes a huge amount of good sense—particularly in a world where population is growing massively and waste at existing levels of generation cannot be handled.

Thirdly, ZERI is making an important contribution in adapting research to projects on a human scale. My association with ZERI is particularly focused on taking their research findings and trying to build these findings into business opportunities for people—particularly people on the margins of the economy. Unless we find solutions for the economically disenfranchised, there will never be sustainable development or human dignity for the bulk of the world's people.

Finally, I support ZERI for the same reasons I support Factor 10, Factor 4 and the few other initiatives that are addressing the core issues around sustainable development. In 1992 at the conclusion of the Earth Summit in Rio, Maurice Strong warned that the greatest threat to the major result of that Conference—*Agenda 21*—was inertia. Sadly, very prophetic words. Never has a written document become archival so quickly. The reality is that none of our governments is prepared to lead. Our international institutions are simply creatures of those governments. Therefore, it must be citizens, business leaders and others such as the people behind ZERI who will force the changes.

J. Hugh Faulkner
Executive Chairman of
Sustainable Project Management

Foreword

WHEN WE LOOK CLOSELY at ecosystems, we indeed see that living organisms do not sell products or services, but they do all produce something. They produce waste, just as we do, individually and in our human organisations. But in an ecosystem the waste is passed on. What is waste for one species is food for another, so that within the ecosystem virtually all wastes are continually being recycled. This is what we can do in our human organisations to mirror nature's patterns of organisation. We can redesign our businesses and our industries—in fact, we *must* redesign them—so that the waste of one industry will be a resource for the next.

To make this work, these industries need to be clustered geographically to form a network of transactions. In these industrial clusters, every business organisation would be embedded in an 'ecology of organisations', in which the waste of any one organisation would be a resource for another. In such a sustainable industrial system, the total outflow of each organisation—its products and wastes—would be perceived and treated as resources cycling through the system.

Such ecological clusters of industries have recently been initiated in several parts of the world under the auspices of ZERI—the Zero Emissions Research Initiative. In this book, Gunter Pauli, the founder of ZERI, gives us the first detailed account of the thinking that led him to this pioneering initiative, and provides ample illustrations of how the programme is now carried out in many places around the world.

Fritjof Capra

Introduction

I must admit, I considered myself a pioneer, only to realise that I was not. Worse, I was naïve and ignorant. When I took responsibility for the construction of the first ecological factory in Europe, I pretended to be able to change the world by setting an example. I had the arrogance to believe I knew what I was doing: promoting environmentally friendly detergent derived from tropical vegetable oils. One day I hit a brick wall and realised that the extracts my company was using represented less than 5% of the total biomass generated by the palm and coconut plantations that produce the oils. While I may have made a marginal contribution to reducing the contamination of detergents in a few European rivers, I had to accept responsibility for massive amounts of waste, generated through my demand for this biodegradable surfactant. Most of the waste was simply incinerated. I just did not know. I was a *Homo non sapiens*.

I concluded that I could only be a real pioneer if I found a way of using all the biomass, not just the 5% of immediate interest to my industry, but also the 95% waste, which, as I later found out, is, in fact, not waste at all, and therefore should not have been discarded. I was no better an example of an ecologically aware businessman than those who mine and extract virgin raw materials and then dump whatever is not needed. The mere fact that I used renewable sources while others used non-renewable ones did not give me any right to call myself a pioneer. This realisation was a wake-up call and is described both in this book and its predecessor, *Breakthroughs*.

After four years of reflection, I now believe that, after a decade of downsizing, the era of UpSizing has arrived. There is no doubt that, after tearing enterprises apart in search of hidden assets, company executives are keen to raise their productivity dramatically in a very different fashion. After years of reducing labour costs in an effort to generate more wealth for shareholders, corporate strategists can now hire people to generate more value-added for all their stakeholders, in addition, of course, for shareholders. After years of due diligence studies assessing risks and identifying possible problems, the newest types of due diligence studies highlight instead great opportunities. After teaching students year after year to focus on core business strategies, business schools are now teaching students how to master a portfolio of businesses together. After decades of losing its credibility, and even its legitimacy in the eyes of the public, business is finally starting to concern itself with community development, as well as wealth generation. After years of the rich getting richer and the poor getting poorer, the rich and the poor are both being given a chance to be better off, to an extent neither had ever imagined.

How can we succeed? By marrying the impatient art of management with the depth of science. This book proposes new approaches to both. And, while that is nothing new, the context has changed. A new management concept called 'Immunity Management' can be the basis for inspiring corporate strategists. For so long, business executives have mirrored their organisations in relation to the brain and the nervous system. Now, Harvard and INSEAD will hopefully start to teach managerial concepts based on the immune system and the genes. This does not mean the brain is dead; it means that there are more and better things to achieve with management concepts that mirror the immune system and genes—highly decentralised but with immediate access to all information. A new science, 'Generative Science', will support and offer insights into how different disciplines— as diverse as biology, economics, engineering, chemistry and physics— are complementary, and how these can succeed in merging the core agendas of corporations and entrepreneurs with those of society: secure food and water for all; healthcare; shelter; sufficient energy; and a platform for the generation of jobs that build a society founded on the quality of life.

But management strategies and a solid scientific basis are not enough. The approach needs to be practical. It must be applicable to any business in order to be replicable. This book therefore includes a straightforward methodology everyone can use, try, apply and perfect. The methodology of UpSizing is focused and pragmatic. The present system may be the best we have at the moment, but the world can do much better, and needs to do better urgently. This book demonstrates that competition is not about doing as good as the others on the market—it is about doing much better. This book is about the best we know: UpSizing.

This is not about growing big, or becoming lean, or cleaning up our waste. It is about generating more diversity, not just protecting it. It is about creating more jobs, not fewer. It is not about building conglomerates imitating General Electric under Jack Welch, or designing a success strategy for another Daewoo or Mitsubishi based on comfortable government protection. It is about a new approach to business in the next millennium.

The application of the art of Immunity Management, the concept of UpSizing and principles of Generative Science will offer the theory, the insights and the tools to achieve a most colourful revolution. This is not a revolution that will shackle or restrict entrepreneurship. This is a revolution that will empower business to achieve its goals, while allowing many others to join the drive towards the generation of value-added for all stakeholders in society. It is not just a green revolution, offering more food for the needy. It is a revolution in which all colours of the rainbow will be involved: red; yellow; blue; brown; and, of course, black—the bottom line.

The driving force of the book is that humankind—despite green consumerism and recycling—still does not realise how wasteful it is. When humankind fully realises it can do so much more with what the earth produces, we will be on the verge of a revolution. There is no need to restrain growth. There is no reason to be a doomsday thinker and warn of impending crises or sound alarms—as long as we recognise that the present system can be radically improved. Today is only a very preliminary version of the world to be and the future to see. Humankind can embark on strong economic growth without depleting the ozone layer, exhausting the ecosystem or changing the climate. But it depends on a change in our perceptions of reality.

The drive towards greater environmental protection is a start, but is certainly not enough. Cleaner production, responsible care, reduce–re-use–recycle or '3R', Factor 4 and Factor 10, Industrial Ecology and Industrial Metabolism are all fine first steps towards industry taking nature into account. Now we need industry to take both society *and* nature into account.

Business should link different interests, merge the agendas and envision the impact of its actions today on future generations. Business would become more profitable as a result, and investors would learn how to assess the risks of doing more of the same, or supporting the pioneers down the road of UpSizing. There is no doubt that it will entail risks, and mistakes will be made. Some of the first steps will be tough, and some will fail. New companies will emerge and succeed, others will go under, but the risk is worth taking.

This book will have succeeded if it encourages a few to venture along the lines that my teams at the Zero Emissions Research Initiative (ZERI) in Japan, the South Pacific, Latin America and Africa have been venturing along for the past four years. We need more people who are prepared to risk failure to demonstrate how the future can be shaped by the real *Homo sapiens*—the person that knows!

Chapter 1
The *Homo non sapiens*
Those Who Should Know How to Create Jobs, Increase Productivity and Eliminate Pollution

Every politician and corporate executive should know that it is possible to improve the productivity of an enterprise, while generating more jobs and dramatically reducing pollution. This may appear a bold claim to the proponents of downsizing with their focus on the productivity of labour— how to produce more with less people. Management has taken pride in recent years in turning over higher and higher levels of capital per employee. The creation of wealth for shareholders is now equated with slashing jobs— as if labour productivity is the only type of productivity one could target. Yet, creating wealth for a few, while perpetuating poverty and misery for many (there will about one billion people looking for a job on this planet at the turn of the millennium) is neither ethical nor productive. In fact, the obsession with labour productivity and downsizing is an incomplete and inadequate drive towards competitiveness. It ignores, to a very large extent, the productivity of raw materials.

While there are several personalities arguing in favour of resource productivity today,[1] the best role model for high levels of resource productivity is not hard to find. It is all around us. Nature already has the answers. It is time for our industrial engineers to wake up to the reality that production and processing methods should be based on first respecting, then emulating, nature. This is not a utopian pursuit, simply common sense. Humankind is the only species on the planet capable of generating waste no one wants: huge amounts of waste, often toxic and often harmful not just to human beings but to nature itself. It is a case of slow self-destruction.

---

1. Ernst Ulrich von Weizsäcker, Amory B. Lovins and L. Hunter Lovins, *Factor Four: Doubling Wealth, Halving Resource Use* (London: Earthscan, 1997); Friedrich Schmidt-Bleek and Paul Weaver (eds.), *Factor 10: Manifesto for a Sustainable Planet* (Sheffield, UK: Greenleaf Publishing, 1998).

Whoever said that they wanted dioxins? No one. On the contrary, a well-informed consumer would refuse to go near them. So why does industry continue to manufacture chlorinated plastics, which generate dioxins as a by-product? There is no buyer for this by-product. Similarly, no one offers a price for nuclear waste: indeed, those who generate this waste are prepared to pay a lot of money to anyone just for storing it, and there are few takers, a dwindling species. So why do governments and power industries continue to generate energy in this way? No one is in favour of the presence of heavy metals in our water, in the soil or in the air. So why does the car industry continue to produce metallic paints that discharge heavy metals into the atmosphere? The list can go on and on. When we seriously think about the amount of waste and toxins produced by industry, we begin to wonder: who designed it this way? It is not logical.

While the dangers of dioxins, asbestos, nuclear waste and heavy metals have been well documented, much adverse data on existing products and processes remains a secret from the consumer. The precautionary principle is much touted and yet rarely practised. One example is the case of optical brighteners in detergents. A whiter-than-white shirt is only possible when detergent-makers add a benzene-ring-based chemical. It attaches to the clothes and becomes energised in light, thus offsetting the greying of the shirt over time with a bluing colour, making it look brighter than white. But, if the buyer of the product does not know there are potentially toxic side-effects such as allergies, and when the manufacturer has no idea either—which is true, in some cases—then both are suffering from a lack of knowledge and understanding of the real impact of the industrial revolution on society.[2]

Adam Smith said in *The Wealth of Nations*, first published in 1776, that total and free access to information is a precondition for the functioning of the market system.[3] Yet there was no free market of any information until the Internet arrived and penetrated 100 million households and businesses. And, as long as information about the detrimental impact of products and processes remains unavailable to the consumer, it is impossible for them to make intelligent decisions. As long as there is no information on how waste can be converted into value-added ingredients, it will not be possible for industry to imagine better ways of manufacturing. The arrival of the Internet can change all of that, making it impossible to remain uninformed. The time of the *Homo sapiens* is about to arrive.

---

2. The University of Cologne led the research in Germany on the potential toxicity of optical brighteners. German law now prohibits the use of optical brighteners in hospital linen.

3. Adam Smith, *The Wealth of Nations: An Inquiry into the Nature and Causes* (Boston, MA: The Modern Library, 1991 [1776]).

But now, as the new millennium approaches, humankind is not the *Homo sapiens* it has pretended to be for over 5,000 years. Humankind still remains a *Homo non sapiens*. He—and it mostly has been a he—could *not* have known the adverse impacts of his activities—otherwise, he would have manufactured and produced in a totally different manner. Industry has often demonstrated that it neither knows what it is doing, nor cares, because its priorities are fast returns on investments and maintaining a focus on the core activities of the company.

The message of UpSizing is that these core activities are not an end in themselves, as so many corporate strategists believe, but a beginning. There is a need for diversification and co-operation, for more from less, for UpSizing.

Zero Emissions and the Total Productivity of Raw Materials

To operationalise UpSizing, we must stop expecting the earth to produce more, but start doing more with what the earth produces. Less than 5% of agro-forestry output is effectively used, with, on average, some 95% discarded. If we adopted an economic system that used this 95%—even 100%—we would be able to satisfy as much as 20 times more material needs without expecting the earth to produce more. We would also have created a huge job-making machine, have made industries more productive and have eliminated huge waste-streams. We would be much nearer to a world of zero emissions.

If we adopted the methodology of Zero Emissions and Zero Waste (explained in detail later in this book), we would immediately see the start of the process of UpSizing. Why?

The Zero Emissions Research Initiative (ZERI) founded by the author at the United Nations University in Tokyo in 1994 has devoted its initial efforts to small-scale demonstration projects in order to provide replicable test cases for others to emulate. Success has been rapid and the experiences from pilot projects positive. A growing number of companies worldwide, including DuPont in the USA and Ebara Corporation in Japan, are now publicly committed to achieving the ultimate target of zero waste. The objective of ZERI is simple: to eliminate the concept of waste. When waste is created, it should be re-used as an input for another process in order to produce value-added. New businesses, producing new products and services, are born as industrial activities emulate nature and cluster around each other, the by-product of one becoming the raw material—the food—for another. The overall productivity of the economy is increased in terms of capital, labour *and* raw materials. Zero emissions is the ultimate and final objective, but UpSizing is the immediate result.

Consider the tree. This structure is not only cellulose, the base material for pulp and paper—our current core activity—but much more. The cellulose represents only 20% in the case of softwood and not more than 30% in the case of a hardwood.[4] Yet today, the rest—mainly lignin and hemicellulose, euphemistically called 'black liquor'—is considered waste, mainly incinerated, and recovered as a biofuel.

The hemicellulose—some 30% of the residue—is basically the food of the tree and, when hydrolysed (by adding hydrogen molecules), becomes a new biochemical, xylan, with hugely interesting properties.[5] For example, when further processed it can produce a natural sweetener, xylitol, which is 50% sweeter than sugar, does not create plaque on teeth, and is low in calories. It does not take a marketing expert to appreciate that this is a saleable product waiting to be discovered.

Our major source of sugar is sugar cane, a plant that produces a sweetener that is widely used in food. However, it is well known that sugar is the main cause of dental plaque, leading to decay. In addition, this sweetener is high in calories. Sugar represents a mere 17% of the weight of the biomass of the sugar cane plant; the remaining 83% is discarded as 'bagasse'[6]—the generic term for everything that is left after the sugar has been extracted. Bagasse is often incinerated and is therefore a contributor to global warming. Why is no one interested in the sugars from trees? Furthermore, why is there no interest in bagasse, a substance far more interesting than the small fraction singled out as the main commercial product.

For example: the fibre in the waste bagasse, representing almost 50% of the residual biomass, could be recovered in the form of organic cement additives, used as a strengthener when manufacturing cement board. Even better, the fibres could be used for the paper production instead of harvesting hardwoods which take at least 50 years to grow.[7] Sugar cane yields quality fibres once a year: a huge improvement in efficiency. It could make sense to valorise sugar cane for its fibres, but only when it has been exploited for *all* its value-added. At the very least, biochemicals such as lipids, ethanol

---

4. G. Pauli, J. Gravitis *et al.*, 'The Zero Emissions Research Initiative: Separating Non-Wood Forest Products into Value Added Materials', in *Proceedings of the 9th World Forestry Congress*, Antalya, Turkey, 13–22 October 1997, p. 26.

5. *Ibid.*

6. G. Pauli and J. Gravitis, 'Environmental Management of Plantations through a Zero Emissions Approach: Plantation Management for the Twenty-First Century', in E. Pushparajah (ed.), *Proceedings of the International Planters' Conference on Plantation Management for the Twenty-First Century*, Kuala Lumpur, Malaysia, 21–22 May 1997, pp. 193-207.

7. *Ibid.*

and furfural should be recovered and used.[8] They provide great base materials for the manufacture of detergents, water softeners and even plastics—and these derivatives are highly biodegradable.

Moving back to the tree, lignin—the organic cement that holds the tree's fibres together and which has a high calorific value—can also be extracted, prior to the production of cellulose, and used as a clean fuel. It can also be used as a natural glue[9]—an alternative to the synthetic glues called epoxies which require formaldehyde, a potentially carcinogenic compound—to convert waste fibres into fibre-board.[10]

Today we see sustainable forestry as a goal to aim for. Schemes such as the certification of sustainable forests by organisations such as the Forest Stewardship Council are gaining momentum and manufacturers and retailers are clamouring to be involved. But 70% of the raw material for pulp and paper is treated as waste, no matter how 'sustainable' the forestry management practices are. How sustainable is this? When major reforestation projects are undertaken and logging is carried out, a total use of biomass should be borne in mind. Biotechnology companies today are attempting to manipulate tree DNA and redesign seeds to produce a tree with more cellulose. While that is not necessarily such a bad idea, there remains little focus on how to take advantage of all the unused elements—a more profound challenge altogether. We need the engineers to develop the process technologies and the investors to make it happen. After all, producing three marketable products—from the cellulose, hemicellulose and lignin—instead of just one, thereby improving revenues, reducing pollution and creating jobs should not be too much of a hard sell.

The world in the late twentieth century is facing a number of crises. A major conference in Rome in late 1996 organised by the United Nations Food and Agriculture Organisation (FAO) confirmed that over 800 million people do not have access to the most basic needs in terms of food, water, energy, healthcare, shelter and jobs.[11] And, while the earth's population increases by around 80 million each year, a further challenge is how to

---

8. See Dr Fernando de Mattos Oliveira, 'The Sugar Cane Industry towards Zero Emissions', in Keto Mshigeni and Gunter Pauli (eds.), *Proceedings of the 2nd Annual UNU World Congress on Zero Emissions,* Chattanooga, TN, 29–31 May 1996 (Tokyo: United Nations University, 1997), pp. 195-96.
9. Pauli, Gravitis *et al.*, 'The Zero Emissions Research Initiative'.
10. J. Gravitis and A. Kokorevics, 'Characterization of Water Sorption of Wood Cellulose and Lignin by Fractal Process', in *Abstract Book of the 5th Chemical Congress of North America*, Cansun, Mexico, 11–15 November 1997, p. 363.
11. Remarks made by the Secretary-General of the United Nations Food and Agriculture Organisation (FAO) in his opening speech to the World Food Summit, 13–17 November 1996, Rome.

respond to the shift in demand from a new emerging middle class. Asia alone is likely to add over the period 1990–2021 an estimated 400 million middle-class consumers to the world.[12] Their appetites will have a pervasive effect on the world economy. Why?

These new middle-class consumers in Asia will have the purchasing power to buy what they want. For example, they will have a dollar a day to buy a newspaper. Great for the pulp and paper business. They will have the cash to buy a chicken four to five times a week, exploding the world market price for chicken feed. These middle-class consumers will be prepared to pay one dollar for a beer. That will secure a solid income for the barley farmers: for two dollars, the Americans expect a six-pack! If each Chinese person were to drink one extra beer per week, the whole harvest of barley from Australia would have to be purchased by the traders in Shanghai and Beijing just to satisfy demand. The purchasing power that Europe has built up over the previous century will be replicated in just one-third of the time. How should the world respond to that?

The developed and industrialised world, in particular Europe, has another problem to face: unemployment. The European Union has an official rate of joblessness of 10.9%. This has recently fallen slightly, but the situation remains critical. In some regions of Spain such as Andalucia, the rate is more than 32%. And, if one considers youth unemployment, the picture becomes even gloomier. In southern Italy, 66% of under-25s are unemployed in Campania. We have a generation for which society appears to have no use.[13] If one includes those sent on training schemes, put on pre-pension at the prime age of 50, those who decide to become self-employed instead of under-employed in a useless job and those who will just withdraw from the job market altogether, probably one in four able people on the planet are being told that no one needs their intelligence, creativity, motivation and strong desire to work. Politicians, both nationally and supranationally, are talking at great length about solving unemployment—ironically at a time when downsizing is thriving as a corporate strategy.

It has become clear that, if business is to respond to the needs of society, without suffering from potential runaway inflation and excessive demand for products—a scenario in which consumers will compete heavily for very scarce resources—industry has to stop manufacturing in the way it has

---

12. ZERI has estimated this figure based on the following assumptions. China, India, Pakistan and Indonesia will have an estimated total population of 3 billion by 2010. If we assume that 15% of that population will belong to the middle class, we arrive at a figure of 400 million.

13. See Eurostat, *Statistics in Focus, Regions no. 3/97: Unemployment in the Regions of the European Union in 1996* (Luxembourg: Eurostat, Statistical Office of the European Communities, 1997).

done for the past hundred years. Different products and different sources for the products that our societies crave must be tested and operationalised. This should not manifest itself as a plundering of biodiversity but as a rationalisation of the illogical agro-industrial practices long established. And there is so much to rationalise! At a time in our history when, because of global warming, the use of petrochemicals is being questioned, it is time to open our eyes to what nature can show us about the useful and usually renewable resources we discard.

Homo non sapiens and Environmental Management

Today, businesses in industrialised countries argue that many strategies are in place to improve environmental performance: cleaner production; responsible care programmes; the polluter pays principle; eco-efficiency; life-cycle analysis (LCA); and voluntary certification of their environmental management systems under ISO 14001. The current paradigm is one of incremental change. All the initiatives are moving in the right direction, but they are moving very slowly. Engaging in cleaner production is a very valuable first step, but it is only a first step: cleaner is never completely clean; in fact, it is often still very dirty. And undertaking LCAs not only takes time, it remains inexact. A much more thorough analysis, in terms of both scope and content, is needed. Environmental management within the paradigm of incremental change is the environmental management of *Homo non sapiens*. In fact, one could argue further that it is the environmental management of the rich *Homo non sapiens*. Why?

Consider the 'polluter pays principle'. Many companies are in agreement with environmentalists in support of this premise. But not too many of its adherents are SMEs. The polluter pays principle, in effect, can be translated to mean that the 'rich can afford to pollute'.

Nature deals with waste materials in a very different manner. Just observe a tree in a forest. Each year the tree sheds its leaves. These instruments of photosynthesis have become useless and drop from the trees' branches. Just imagine if nature had designed its ecosystem according to the polluter pays principle. The tree would be required to pick up all the leaves and deposit this waste in a landfill, or treat its leaves on-site prior to discharge. This, of course, is ridiculous. The tree could not transport or treat its leaves in such a manner. More importantly, even if the tree were, by some extraordinary effort, to succeed, it would deprive the microsystem of flora and fauna that live off the discarded leaves. Without a thriving ecosystem around the roots of the tree, others would be deprived of food.

Fortunately, nature does not apply the polluter pays principle. Nature has organised a fragile but very well-balanced ecosystem around the tree. When the leaves fall, fungi, mushrooms, earthworms, insects, bacteria and the like happily convert this annual mass of fibres and hemicellulose into humus. Nature has clustered many activities of innumerable micro-organisms and fungi around the tree. And whatever is waste for one is food for many others— each extracting what is best for them and leaving behind new residues for the next.

How far does the *Homo non sapiens* have to travel to emulate such a system? Consider the following example. When we wanted the rivers in Europe to be cleaner, we opted for green detergents, which feature a fast-degradable active ingredient. While certainly this was to be applauded, we did not stop to think about the fact that the fatty acids needed to make these kinds of soap are derived from coconut and palm oils, which are obtained by milling coconut and palm fruits, thousands of miles away from the market. With the green consumer boom that followed the Rio Earth Summit in 1992, the market for such products grew exponentially. LCAs were presented by manufacturers to show the environmental advantages of their products, but not one of these explained that the biochemical extraction from the palm or coconut only represents a fraction—not even 5%—of the biomass the tree generates each year.[14] No LCA was ever made for the remaining 95%. In other words, while European rivers could become cleaner, this was only feasible by generating more waste in the developing countries, whatever the LCA of the detergent says.

Examine the difference with regard to the petrochemical-derived surfactant LAS (linear alkylbenzene sulphonate), a traditional cleansing ingredient. LAS suffers from a very poor rating in terms of biodegradation, causing foaming in rivers; but at least it is part of a process where almost 100% of the (non-renewable) raw material is used. Which ingredient is the more environmentally benign? Aren't the green consumers of Europe simply being hoodwinked? Their domestic environmental problems are, in effect, being exported to developing countries. Neither product should be classified as environmentally benign. While the ideal was to substitute petrochemicals with products from renewable resources, it is clear that the marginal extraction of an active ingredient from a renewable resource and the subsequent generation of more waste in the country of origin is not a solution either. The optimum solution is to emulate nature—in the same way that, by finding uses for secondary and waste products, our scientists have engineered systems to use all elements of non-renewable resources such as petrochemicals.

---

14. Based on data from the Palm Oil Research Institute of Malaysia (PORIM).

The Fractionation of Renewable Resources

How is it possible that a non-renewable, synthetic raw material can perform better in terms of price than a natural and renewable material which can be regenerated every year? The answer is simple. We have engineered a distillation and fractionation process for petroleum that permits the use of all the molecules derived from this non-renewable resource, while we have never designed a system that permits the similar separation of *all* the valuable components from renewable resources. As a result, we use only a small percentage of biomass and simply throw the rest away.

There will only be an optimal solution for the environment *and* the economy when everyone concerned understands how *all* the biomass can be re-used—not just a fraction for the detergent—and how this can be converted into an engine for growth in the host country of the plantation. It is the imitation of nature's clustering that can become the core idea for a new economy based on the concepts of Zero Emissions and UpSizing.

A brief study undertaken by a ZERI team has demonstrated that at least ten new industries could be built around the core business of palm oil mills.[15] Concentrating on just the lauric ether sulphate (LES) from the plantation's biomass for the detergents is a bad idea: it lacks vision, disregards basic biology and neglects facts that botanists have known for decades.

Consider what we could achieve if we could design a production and extraction system that recovers all the available proteins, vitamins, anti-oxidants and betacarotene from the world's agro-industrial processes. If we could do this, the cost and sales price of these valuable materials would fall, making them more accessible to those in most need.

Today, one of the world's largest potential sources for vitamin E is simply destroyed in the process of extracting coconut or palm oil. While Americans and Europeans are prepared to pay $US65,000 per ton for anti-oxidants, the industrial processes are designed in such a way that the richest sources of these vitamins are discarded. Coconut oil is rich in vitamin E, but the extraction is preceded by a drying system, which converts the coconut into copra, and which also destroys all vitamins and anti-oxidants. The copra method goes back to the days when the raw material of the coconut fruit was shipped to Europe for processing. Since fresh coconuts would rot, a drying system was invented: dried coconuts could be shipped anywhere. Coconuts have not been shipped to Europe for the extraction of

---

15. J. Gravitis, 'Clustering of New Industries around Tropical Biomass: Bamboo, Palm Oil and Pineapple Based on a Comparative Scientific Analysis', in Keto Mshigeni (ed.), *Proceedings of the 3rd World Congress on Zero Emissions, Jakarta, Indonesia, 31 July–2 August 1997* (Geneva: ZERI Foundation, 1998).

oil for over half a century, but their processing is still based on the old drying system.

Similarly, palm oil is rich in betacarotene, but the use of a steaming process that aims to eliminate enzymes and insects also results in the elimination of all betacarotene and vitamins. As a result, both palm and coconut oil, rich in vitamins, betacarotene and anti-oxidants, produce nothing. A minor adaptation in the steaming process, simply reducing the steaming to a lower temperature, can offer these mills a handsome additional revenue. Reducing the temperature can also save energy, reducing costs. And the world will have increased access to cheap raw materials for much-needed healthcare.

Consider what an estimated five million hectares of palm plantations around the world could generate. Each plantation produces between 25 and 40 tons of biomass waste per hectare per annum,[16] so, in all, the plantations generate some 200 million tons of biowaste per year. This is equivalent to a massive petrochemical refinery. The potential for the biorefinery exists, and it exists not in the North, but in the South: in those countries with the richest natural resources, now holding the key to a successful strategy to help eradicate poverty.

Consider another example: the case of sisal fibre, perhaps the strongest fibre produced by nature. Sisal was once the core ingredient in the production of strong ropes and fishing nets. The price of this natural fibre has been driven down to around $US200 per ton[17] and still it is not able to withstand competition from synthetic fibre. Sales revenues hardly cover the cost of manufacturing. Why? Sisal fibre producers use only 2% of the biomass of their resource;[18] there are currently no value-added products valorised from the original plant material. The rest—98%—is considered to be waste and discarded. Compare this with the production of synthetic fibres which are, in essence, value-added products from the fractionation of petroleum, a resource virtually all elements of which have had a value-added invented for them.

It is time for the *Homo non sapiens* to stand aside. In 1996–97, it was demonstrated in studies at Dar es Salaam University with funding by UNESCO that citric acid and lactic acid could be fermented from the residual biomass after the extraction of the sisal fibre.[19] In other words, a major

---

16. Data obtained from PORIM, *op. cit.*
17. A recent market price obtained from the Tanzanian Sisal Authority (TSA).
18. Francis Nkuba, 'The Sisal Industry in Tanzania', in *Proceedings of the 2nd UNU Congress on Zero Emissions*.
19. Dr Keto Mshigeni, 'Zero Emissions Projects in Tanzania', in *Proceedings of the 2nd UNU Congress on Zero Emissions*.

new possible revenue stream had been found, potentially much more important than the fibres themselves. The cost of sisal fibre production can, in fact, be fully covered by the extraction of the value-added components: an average of another $US3,000 is generated per ton of citric acid. The income from the fibre could even decrease from $US200 to $US100 per ton, a level at which the sisal fibre can out-compete the synthetic one in both performance and price. An outcome can be envisioned in which the total revenue for the sisal farmer will increase and the processing of sisal will regain its competitive position against synthetic fibres.

Generative Science

The *Homo non sapiens* is a linear thinker, a subscriber to the Darwinian theory, 'the survival of the fittest'. The interpretation of this principle has led to a gross misunderstanding of how nature actually works. In nature, species do not survive because they are the fittest; species survive because they work together, collaborating in the generation of food, energy and shelter, permitting the re-use of everything that is produced within the system so that all can develop and grow. Survival is possible thanks to the co-operation and development of many species, at first sight totally unrelated but in fact all part of the network and the system. Human beings could learn from nature, not by striving to be the strongest but by seeking collaboration across races and cultures, respecting the difference, and recognising that only by co-operation will they succeed in converting limited resources into an abundance for all.

Rational science is based on cause and effect and usually leads to singular processes, searching for one product, combining numerous components extracted from different raw materials. This rationale, based on Cartesian thinking,[20] has led to a situation where the end is achieved with the most incomplete use of the means. Much waste and much pollution have been the result. While we are all familiar with the argument that the means justifies the end, the further use of the means is rarely questioned. This book proposes a new science—Generative Science—which asks this question again and again, until the further use of the means is saturated. In Generative Science, everything is produced in a thoughtful endeavour with a conscious regard for the potentially harmful effects from emissions, effluents and other by-products which will all be reused to eliminate their adverse

---

20. René Descartes developed this method of analytical thinking, breaking up complex phenomena into pieces to understand the behaviour of the whole from the properties of the parts.

impact. Generative Science undertakes a creative effort to ensure that nothing is wasted—it calls for a further use of both the means and the end.

Generative Science proceeds on the assumption that, in any transformation of a resource, all by-products will be studied for their value-added potential. The subsequent results are likewise examined for process excesses, which will continue to boost returns autocatalytically through a complex network of feedback loops. One process builds on another, resulting in a cluster of industrial processes to be operationalised by the engineers. Generative Science always asks the question: what do we really want and need? If materials are produced in a process and they are not desired for a particular end-product, the process is questioned and opened up for improvements and re-engineering. If emissions to water, air or soil are similarly produced, the same questions apply. This is the basis of a systems approach to science.

When a pulping mill needs 100 tons of water to produce one ton of paper; when it sometimes takes 160 tons of water to recycle a ton of paper;[21] or when we need ten litres of water to ferment one litre of beer, we should question how such waste came to be engineered. When we only extract 8% of the nutrients from barley and discard 92%,[22] it makes no sense at all to pretend that this is efficient. If rates of consumption are going to continue to grow in this wasteful manner, the conclusions of the most pessimistic think-tanks may still come to pass.[23]

Immunity Management

Nature operates in a decentralised manner, practical, pragmatic and with great intelligence, accumulated after millions of years of experience. Most, if not all of the time, nature has systems in place to respond not only to its own basic needs, but also to those of humanity as well. For humanity, these can be defined not as cars, video recorders, television sets or annual holidays, but as the core necessities of water, food, shelter, healthcare, energy and jobs.

---

21. Data reproduced from the presentation by Helge Eklund, President of Södra Cell, at the First Annual UNU World Congress on Zero Emissions, Tokyo, 5–7 April 1995 (proceedings unpublished).
22. Dr Li Wenhua, 'Feasibility Study on the Application of the Integrated Biosystem Concept of Zero Emissions to the Beer Brewing Industry' (unpublished report by the Chinese Academy of Engineering Sciences, Beijing, presented to the United Nations University, August 1995).
23. See, for example, Donella Meadows, Denis Meadows, Jørgen Randers and William Behrens, *Limits to Growth* (London: Earth Island, 1972).

If one goes through the process of understanding the great wonders of nature, one arrives at Generative Science. And when humanity understands how nature is diverse, responsive and intelligent, it will want to imitate the best of nature. Nature has designed and operates the most fascinating management system: the immune system. And studying the immune system—one of the most impressive systems ever developed—offers a tremendous opportunity to improve the performance of all the components of Generative Science. The immune system is based on a perfect sharing of information. It presupposes that all the players are intelligent, so all new information is shared with everyone. This is remarkable, and leads us to rethink how one can envision a future market system.

There has been much written about bottom-up management, consensus decisions and participative systems within a flat organisation. But which system is as efficient as the immune system, where each cell (and we have billions in our body) has all the information it needs to distinguish, in seconds, the good from the bad among the three million bacteria we introduce into our body each time we inhale? And since there are an estimated five billion possible bacteria, this unimaginable task could never be performed even by a supercomputer. Our body works like a super-super-super-computer and processes all this information with so much ease that it sounds like science fiction. We tend to forget the small miracles happening every millisecond within our own bodies.

And it is not just the human immune system that astounds. Consider what happens to the sea star. Just cut the sea star in three pieces and, after a few weeks, there will be three sea stars. This is the incredible strength of the immune system of a simple living creature on the sea shore. The immune system is therefore the best source we can imagine for a new management philosophy to achieve UpSizing. From one business, empowered with a commitment toward Zero Emissions and equipped with an understanding of Generative Science, other businesses will surely spring. And therefore a core component of Generative Science is immunology, in particular its implications for management and computer science.

Conclusion

This book is about a new management, **Immunity Management**, which is based on a new science, **Generative Science**, structured around the pragmatic methodology of **Zero Emissions**. If you use it all, nothing will be wasted. It outlines strategies for poverty alleviation, as well as a new approach for dramatically improving cashflow and productivity. It aims to demonstrate that, if humankind expects the earth to produce more, the earth may very well collapse. But, if humankind does more with what the earth produces, then it is likely to succeed in responding to the basic needs for food, water, healthcare, shelter, energy and jobs.

This book is enthused about the changes that are taking place and the concrete results being achieved in Africa, Asia, Latin America, the Pacific and Europe. It does not pretend to offer a menu to follow, but it does outline a practical and pragmatic methodology that allows all of us to understand how we could start **UpSizing** business after years of downsizing. It is possible to increase productivity, generate more jobs, reduce pollution and respond to the needs of society. And, if we doubt it and classify this as utopia, then my advice is to go and see for yourself in Vichada, Colombia; Suva, Fiji; Tsumeb, Namibia; Gotland, Sweden; the Lake Districts of Eastern Africa and Japan, where the first grains of success have been planted for many to follow and imitate.

Chapter 2
About Darwin and Entropy

One of the scientific conclusions that most dominated the late nineteenth century was Darwin's evolutionary theory, summarised by the slogan: 'the survival of the fittest'. A scientific concept that has been popularised in the late twentieth century is the law of entropy. The thinking of today's generation has been very much influenced by both, and it seems that the time has now come to question each one.

Darwin's evolutionary theory has generated much debate, and continues to elicit vigorous exchanges, with both opposition and admiration for his vision. One thing is certain: the concept of the survival of the fittest is well known all over the world. Humankind now considers itself to be one of the 'fittest' species, and therefore can order the other living creatures to shape its own present well-being. The survival of the fittest is a theory with many components that appear logical. But there is no scientific proof: it is just a fine hypothesis.

The main shortcoming in its popular interpretation is that evolutionary theory studies individual species in isolation, searching for a logic behind the evolution of a specific type. Which one of the lion cubs survives? Of course, the strongest one will become the lion king, the weakest will soon die. Which wild beast will survive the voracious appetite of the leopard? The fastest one, while the weakest will be spotted and killed. There is no doubt that this logic holds up: the fittest does survive. But this analysis does not consider nature as a system; it only considers one species at a time.

It is well established that all elements of fauna and flora in nature do not function in an isolated fashion. On the contrary, it is a system—an ecosystem—in which all elements relate to each other in an interdependent manner. Water availability influences a species's digestive system; temperature determines the skin types; altitude and pressure determine blood circulation; insect types and bats relate to the bird and rodent species;

the tree types define the varieties of spores and mushrooms prevalent; and the mushrooms have an impact on the bacteria. It is an endless cycle of cause and effect—typical for any dynamic system—and the change in one component will have an impact on all others. The system is interactive, rich in feedback loops, responsive, and always looking to attain an optimal use of energy, food and shelter.

Thus, to state, as Darwin did, that the types of species that survive are the strongest is an over-simplification. Survival in nature depends on the species integration with the system. Any species that opts out of the system risks extinction over time, whatever its strength or intelligence—or it will cause the extinction of others if its opt-out prejudices the environment of others. This seems to be the predicament facing humankind today. Humanity has, to a great degree, decided to opt out of the ecosystem, considering itself smarter and stronger than other species and wishing to use the system for its sole comfort and advantage. This cannot work.

In nature, bacteria, enzymes, mushrooms, earthworms, insects, birds, bees, bats, rodents, deer, bushes and trees—just to take a dozen living species in the forest—all depend on each other. It is only by co-operating in a tightly knit fashion that they have a chance of surviving, an opportunity to develop and generate an ever-improving system in which all evolve.

The tree can only survive when there is sufficient mineral-rich humus in the soil around the root system. Its capacity to absorb nutrients is enhanced by bacteria and enzymes located around the tips of the roots, which are fed by the leaves of the tree, blended with a rich variety of biochemicals produced, digested and regenerated by all the other players.

The survival of species in nature depends on this interdependence and collaboration. It is a co-operation across species, and knowledge is not centralised in a single brain: it is highly decentralised, with each making decisions guided by principles that ultimately have more than self-interest and self-survival in mind. The objective is to re-use all the components of nature as food, so that the waste for one is food for another. What is most fascinating is the spirit of teamwork evident among the most diverse species. The ecosystem is one that demonstrates tremendous tolerance for diversity, and actually needs such differences to ensure that each element draws the best and most valuable from the resources it provides.

The diversity of systems and the diversity within the system is the wealth of nature. The only enzymes capable of breaking down lignocellulose, the fibres from the trees and grasses, are those from fungi. If there were no fungi, there would be no chance of converting this material into carbohydrates. The maintenance of alkalinity in water is possible thanks to the continuous generation of bird droppings. If the birds cannot find any algae—which allows their digestive system to access specific minerals—the alkalinity will decay over time and the blooming of algae types that thrive in acid waters will take over. When humans pump so much pollution into the air that it causes rainfall around the world to be permanently converted into acid rain, we destabilise the whole ecosystem. And, when the changes humans impose are permanent, the system will collapse, or operate at a much lower level of optimal uses. The system will accumulate wastes, since the fragile interaction has been disrupted. The famous case of algae blooming in rivers was the result of dumping massive amounts of phosphates. Today, some 70% of German forests are dying due to a permanent flow of acid rain and a continuous dumping of metal particles which accumulate in the root system of trees and make them sick, eventually killing them, and ultimately wrecking the ecosystem. One component's demise leads to ultimate collapse. This does not necessarily lead to complete desertification, but will result in pests on the one hand—because excessive food streams are generated—and the loss of species on the other. And whatever science humankind has developed, it will have a hard time reconstructing what it destroyed.

'Survival of the fittest' should be replaced by a new maxim: 'evolution through interdependence and co-operation'. Nature offers a single platform for tolerance, respect for diversity, and efficiency whereby nothing is wasted. One component's contribution leads to wealth for all. It does not necessarily lead to paradise, because nature has its own disasters and upsets. But the system will always succeed in optimising the generation of food and energy, which will result in a wholly efficient system enabling each species to develop, and by doing so make it possible for others to do so too. Nature does not know death as such: there is no end of the cycle *per se*, because the end for one is the beginning for another. Nature does not apply cradle-to-grave thinking; it is cradle-to-cradle that dominates the logic. Nature has a circular, not a linear concept of time, and thus death is never a reason for depression and sorrow, but an ultimate act to permit life for the next cycle.

The Law of Entropy

This leads to a second criticism of science: the law of entropy. This law is simultaneously complex and simple. It prescribes that all on earth will move from a state of order to a state of disorder, confusion and disorganisation. Entropy is easy to understand. A child looks in the mirror and sees a fresh young shiny skin and over the years this skin turns wrinkled and dry. What the old man who once was a child sees in the mirror at the age of 85 is entropy. The system—this body in general and the skin in particular—

disintegrates (starting from order) and leads to ultimate collapse (disorder). There is no doubt that entropy is a fact of life for that one person. But this logic only holds when the time factor under consideration is a linear one. It is based on the cradle-to-grave concept: that there is a time of birth and a time of death, with life after death in heaven (for the religious), not on earth. Within this framework, the law of entropy is actually the law of **degeneration**, the evolution towards ever-more inefficient systems.

But that is contradictory to our new maxim, 'evolution through inter-dependence and co-operation'. As we know, in nature there is no grave, life never ends, and whatever is waste for one is food for the other. Wherever life for one ends, life for another starts. The cycle of generating energy and food continues thanks to the unlimited supply of solar energy and the ingenious system of photosynthesis, enzymes, proteins and amino acids. Of course, one can argue that the supply of solar energy is limited in time, but at least that is some millions of years ahead. The law of entropy should be replaced by the law of **regeneration**. The present law does not make sense for the world we need to create.

Western cultures have never been prepared to consider nature in this way, because Western societies have been inspired by a linear concept of time: that is, whatever we do not do in our lifetime is lost forever. This is one of the reasons for stress in the Western system: one of the factors that contributes to the Western desire to accumulate wealth—and consume much of nature's wealth—in a lifetime. Oriental, and especially Pacific cultures have a circular concept of time. That is why reincarnation is such an important element in many religions. That is why there is no need to pressure ourselves to outperform, since a lost opportunity today will almost certainly come back, if not in this life, then in a next life—perhaps not as a human being, but as another species.

When the concept of time is linear, cultures produce linear laws, and these become the truths within that culture. The laws of evolution and entropy are typical creations of the logic that only functions within the linear paradigm that has created these laws.

The present paradigm sets forth that the universe is a mechanical system composed of elementary building blocks; life in society is a competitive struggle for existence; there is unlimited material progress that can be achieved through economic and technological growth; and humans consider themselves above and beyond nature. This cannot continue. We need a paradigm shift: a new paradigm that views the world as an integrated whole, rather than a dissociated collection of parts. A paradigm that, while recognising that all phenomena are fundamentally interdependent, also recognises that individuals and societies are ultimately dependent on the cyclical processes of nature within which all elements relate to each other in an interdependent manner. The new paradigm is reflected in the new values and new form of thinking as summarised by Fritjof Capra in his book *The Web of Life*,[24] which argues that the world is a complex system—a web, or a web of webs, combining many networks. The network of networks represents life.

While the new paradigm is not in vogue universally, it is clear that a shift is about to take place. And more is certain to happen in the decades ahead, as societies shed some of the rules and laws based on the paradigms of the past: reflections of the world of the *Homo non sapiens*. The world of the *Homo sapiens* is one where entropy is gone and progress is based on co-operation and respect for diversity. It is a world worth working for.

The law of entropy does not make sense for the world we need to create. It leads to consumerism, over-exploitation of natural resources and lacks the vision necessary to preserve the planet for future generations. Therefore, a new science needs to emerge: Generative Science, which respects the logic of the past, but offers the vision within which a new paradigm for the future can be created.

---

24. Fritjof Capra, *The Web of Life: A New Understanding of Living Systems* (London: Harper-Collins, 1997).

Chapter 3
The Principles of Generative Science

The time has come to develop this new theoretical framework, this new backbone for science: the Generative Sciences. The theory of Generative Science is new, under development and open for refinement—just like any other science that has emerged in recent history. But the fundamentals are clear: Generative Sciences are driven by the underlying desire to grow and develop, to generate and regenerate. The popular interpretation of this cycle is the concept of 'cradle-to-cradle', instead of the misconceived 'cradle-to-grave'.

Science has progressed a lot over the past 500 years. But this progress seems to depend on the situation whereby we learn more and more about less and less until we know everything about nothing. The era of specialisation and quantification has made us lose sight of the total picture. Newton, Bacon, Galileo and Descartes have made tremendous contributions, and had a enormous influence on the shaping of present society's thinking. Galileo imposed the practice that only what could be measured and quantified was to be considered scientific. This excluded qualitative considerations from science. Descartes proposed that the world is a perfect machine and could be understood by exact mathematical models. Newton stated that all physical phenomena can be reduced to the properties of hard and solid material particles. Thus, modern science was born. Since we have been educated along those principles, it indeed seems logical to us. Since science is so number-oriented, it is no surprise that numbers count in our society. And since the details are so complex, we often lose sight of the totality.

In the Western world, it was actually Goethe and Kant who first encouraged us to take a holistic view. Goethe saw organisms as wholes. Kant introduced the concept that the whole exists by means of the parts; the parts exist both because of and in order to sustain the whole. He introduced the understanding that life organisms are self-reproducing. The reality is that every junior school child will learn about Newton, and everyone in secondary school will have heard about—and maybe studied—Descartes and Galileo—but it will take an undergraduate to access the writings of Immanuel Kant. Even today, our educational system is not sharing the views and the insights of those who formed the basis of systems thinking, a generative thinking. So it is no surprise, when Kant is so sparsely shared, that only advanced students will discover Ilya Prigogine, Erich Jantsch and Fritjof Capra.[25]

There are, in fact, few cultures that have resisted this Newtonian and Cartesian thinking; it is dominant from Japan to North America to Europe to Australia. However, whereas the original African, Australian and American cultures were devastated through their exposure to Western societal organisation, the Asians assimilated many elements but continued to maintain a strong character of their own. The Asian cultures never separated from their circular concept of time, allowing for the regeneration of everyone, at some time.

For Westerners, there is a strong desire to accumulate personal wealth because our concept of time is a straight line. Whatever has happened is gone forever, and can never be repeated. Hence, our debate about whether history repeats itself, and whether we are prepared to learn from history. The Asian cultures have a different perspective. Since their concept of time is circular, opportunities to do better always exist. The future of the next generation is also your future. There is never a lost opportunity, because every opportunity will eventually return.

Until a century ago, Pacific cultures had never been exposed to the Western mechanistic, reductionist and atomic form of thinking, and they have never been absorbed by it since. The strength of their cultural backbone has never cracked and, today, many in the West search for inspiration and balance in Asian-originated religions and lifestyles. We find an exceptionally fertile ground for the paradigm of the future in the Pacific cultures (see Table 1).

This circular concept of time, the integration of quality and intuition, prepares the ground for the new Generative Science. This is a science that aims to generate wealth for all—and not only for the human species. If

---

25. See for example, Isabelle Stengers and Ilya Prigogine, *The End of Certainty: Time, Chaos and the New Laws of Nature* (New York: The Free Press, 1997); Erich Jantsch, *Self-Organizing Universe: Scientific and Human Implications of the Emerging Paradigm of Evolution* (Oxford, UK: Pergamon, 1980); Fritjof Capra, *The Tao of Physics: An Exploration of the Parallels between Modern Physics and Eastern Mysticism* (Boston, MA: Shambhala Publications, rev. edn, 1991); and Fritjof Capra, *The Turning Point: Science, Society and the Rising Culture* (New York: Bantam Doubleday Dell, reissued edn, 1988).

	Western	**Pacific**
Strategy	Clearly defined intentions Expeditious line of action Very useful for production Through large groups and co-ordinated tasks	Keep all members of the group in touch with adventure, clarify collective values so everyone is part of the team.
Time	Synchronise events; it is predictable, metered and everyone knows it. Useful for organisation of multiple and inter-related actions. Essence of efficiency.	Time is in the now; it is spontaneous. Useful for direct energy-based events such as tribal gatherings. It heightens the awareness of the moment.
Organisation	Based on creating a product or service for the market. Organisation is structured around actions; reporting structure reflects responsibility and accountability from the bottom to the top; can be tailored to adjust span of control.	Based on creating a culture with authentic relationships and meaningful traditions. Culture is organised around seasonal activities, based on nature. Individual roles and identity are highlighted.
Decision style	Decisions are determined by resources and time. Choices are presented one by one in agenda. Timely outcomes are priority. Reporting to the leaders	Tribal decisions are based on bone-deep conviction, gut-feeling, experience and wisdom. Content is developed organically by the first pass around the group. Time is not important, energy field becomes palpable.
Attire	Dress to accommodate work, functions and societal roles. Shops stock uniform sets. Business dress looks smart but bind the body at neck, chest, waist, hip and feet. Special cleaning is needed for most. Adornment displays wealth.	Dress based on tradition, more variety and colour. The fit and comfort are more important. Adornment reflects their special interest. Usually more elegant if less tailored.
Language	Words are the tool of choice. Diagrams and visuals used to assemble complex messages into whole system. Monotonal and exact sounds are the norm as to distinguish the choice of words in unbiased way. Excitable delivery is reserved for TV and actors.	Sounds and gestures more than words. Transmission must be exciting instead of just informative. Tonal patterns energise and evoke responses. Energy level is kept up like trying to keep a balloon from landing.
Basics	Three basics are reading, writing and arithmetic, One cannot function in society without these. Intelligence is grounded in these cognitive tools and, therefore, without them, one is not considered intelligent.	Primary set of awareness is more physically centred. The three basics are breathing, sensing and moving. The intelligence test would be hunting, fishing, shelter-building and farming. These basics create an experience-based partnership with nature.
Religion	God has been organised as a part of a holy order that originates from a place called heaven, in contrast to earth. What is represented as God's word is considered the truth. God brings truth and justice if one attends to the principles expressed in scripture.	Attempt to realise God within one's own being. God is here, not there. The focus is first on one's emotional state and then practice is to take it out into the village in a radiant way.

Table 1: *Western versus Pacific Paradigm*

Source: Based on the work by Jim Channon entitled
Pacific Passage (internal document; Hawaii, USA, 1997)

we accept that we are fundamentally part of the earth, and therefore of nature, and we depend on cycles that we do not control, then we have to imagine a way of generating sufficient quality of life so that all can live and develop in a humane way. We know that, today, we are not capable of providing even the minimum in terms of food, water, shelter, energy, healthcare and jobs for everyone on the planet. Our choice is either to accept that people continue to live in an inhumane fashion, or to recognise that we have to combine, merge, develop, improve and enthuse the global community to develop and fine-tune the theory and practice of Generative Science.

What are its Principles?

1. Generative Science aims to respond to the basic needs of humankind in terms of food, water, shelter, healthcare, energy and jobs. Its objective is to secure not only the preservation of the wealth of nature, but also enhance the further development of the biosphere. It is, by definition, generative.

2. Generative Science starts from the premise that humankind respects nature. It aims to learn from nature and dedicate its energy to the eradication of poverty and the continuous improvement of living conditions on earth in harmony with nature.

3. Generative Science accepts the principle that humankind cannot expect the earth to produce more. Humankind must do more with what the earth produces.

4. Generative Science builds on systems that permit the merging of agendas, which foresee an ultimately positive and complex chain of causes and effects. According to Generative Science, increased levels of production, productivity and profitability go hand in hand with an increased number of jobs, reduced pollution and reduced material consumption, and even the recovery of biodiversity.

5. In Generative Science, everything is produced in a thoughtful endeavour with a conscious regard for the lost opportunities whenever all the components of a material are not used. It carefully considers both harmful and harmless effects from emissions, effluents and other by-products. Generative Science undertakes a creative effort to ensure that nothing is wasted.

6. Generative Science proceeds on the assumption that in any transformation of a resource, all by-products will be studied for an additional

and well-considered value-added. This will be undertaken in an integrated fashion, clustering human activities, industries and natural processes that share material cycles.

7. The subsequent results of the re-use as value-added study are similarly examined for process excesses that will continue to boost returns autocatalytically through a complex, but very enriching network of feedback loops. One process builds on another and a cluster of complementary processes is born.

8. Generative Science is based on the principles of ecological systems where the concept of networks and the community are central.

9. Generative Science always asks the question: what do we really want and need? If materials are produced in a process and they are not desirable for a particular end-product, then the process is questioned, improved and re-engineered until there is no waste—and zero emissions has been achieved.

10. Generative Science depends on a management concept based on the immune system. It considers every core element of the system intelligent.

11. Generative Science promotes an information-sharing system that allows everyone to have access to all information at all times, and the freedom to act on that information as they deem appropriate at that time and place.

12. Generative Science proposes a leadership based on the capacity to initiate, guide and maintain dialogue among the knowledge-carriers in the community. Leadership is founded on the desire to secure a zero-conflict environment, where everyone is continuously benefiting from the fruits of progress.

13. Generative Science is an integrative science, building on the findings of botany, biology, agriculture, forestry and marine sciences—to name a few—furthering understanding through to chemistry, mathematics and physics, enhancing the use of computer sciences, engineering and economics, not forgetting history, geography, social and political sciences.

14. Generative Science does not search for traditional scientific proof for each step it undertakes. It combines intuition with traditional know-how and technologies: an intelligence accumulated by cultures from all around the world over millennia.

15. Generative Science starts from the embedded intelligence of nature, and searches for the maximisation of wealth of natural resources to all species on earth. It seeks to design a system that achieves the highest conversion of one resource into a food for another.

16. Generative Science follows a circular concept of time, whereby everything and everyone will have a new chance in the future.

17. Generative Science accepts that the system is always in flux. Changes are inevitable—even preferable—as this generates creativity and improves the system's adaptability to ever-occurring transformations beyond its control. The system is an open system.

18. Generative Science recognises it will never achieve perfection: the system is always up for improvement. It accepts that it will make mistakes and therefore will demonstrate a high level of tolerance.

19. Generative Science recognises the importance of each contribution, whatever its size or source. The system moves towards higher levels of productivity, deeper satisfaction and greater value, thanks to the participation of all.

20. Generative Science recognises the concept of joy. If an activity is challenging, and constantly attempting to achieve improvements, then it is enjoyable.

While these foundations are only the starting point, and certainly require further refinement and completion, the key is to be concrete and precise. The requirements are therefore to be philosophical, theoretical, pragmatic and action-oriented. It is pragmatism and action that guide this book from here on.

Chapter 4
The Revolutions We Have All Been Waiting For

Business and society must respond to the needs of people for water, food, healthcare, shelter, energy and jobs. The population explosion is adding stress to a system which even today is unable to provide even the most basic services to some 800 million people in the world. With an additional 80–90 million people joining the human race each year, the challenge is becoming increasingly unmanageable. Asia alone is responsible for some 54 million additional consumers on the globe this year. In order to respond to this increasing number of citizens, the earth needs to produce an additional 28 million tons of grain, or 78,000 tons per day.

Scientists and agronomists succeeded in achieving the First Green Revolution. Thanks to irrigation, the application of fertilisers, pesticides and the selection of high-performance seeds, productivity has risen dramatically. Irrigated land increased 2.5-fold between 1950 and 1990, expanding from 94 to 248 million hectares, two-thirds of which are to be found in Asia. World fertiliser consumption increased from 14 million tons in 1950 to a staggering 146 million tons in 1990. The increase in irrigation and the use of fertilisers led to the dramatic increase in output. World grain harvests have increased over 40 years from 631 million tons to 1,780 million tons. World production of beef has nearly tripled from 24 to 62 million tons, and the world's fish catch has increased more than fourfold from 19 to 85 million tons. The yield per hectare demonstrates the results over the 40-year period, with yields rising from 1.06 tons per hectare to 2.52 tons.

Scientists agree that we cannot expect a further threefold increase in the productivity of land to satisfy growing demand. The growing demand we face is not due simply to the numbers of people on the planet, but to the growing wealth and expectations of those people: 400 million middle-class consumers are expected to emerge in Asia alone over the next 25–30 years.[26]

---

26. ZERI estimate (see Chapter 1).

These are the consumers who are moving up a food chain characterised by the inefficient conversion of proteins and amino acids into food for humans. A chicken needs 2.2 kilos of grain to generate a kilo of chicken; cattle need 7 kilos of cereals to produce of one kilo of meat.

Indians currently only consume one-quarter of the amount of grain and wheat that Americans consume—and only 30 eggs and three kilos of meat a year, extremely low compared with the American average of 174 eggs per annum and 123 kilos of meat. New consumers moving up the food chain will have a major impact on the food security in the world. The consumption of eggs is increasing by 15% a year in India, to 300 million eggs in 1995, doubling to 600 million in 2000, and then 1.2 billion in 2005. This growth in egg consumption will be one of the factors that will drive the demand for chicken feed and cereals to the limits of production. Furthermore, with competing sources demanding access to a limited supply, prices will rise and, while the rich will be able to pay, the poor will not have the purchasing power to compete.

The Rise and Fall of the First Green Revolution

The time has come to realise that the going will get tough. With an additional 90 million people on the planet each year, we have to produce more food every day. The demand for water, shelter, healthcare, education and jobs will rise exponentially. We know this—but we do not know how to cope with the situation.

We are fooling ourselves if we expect that the present trends in food production and land productivity will continue for another 40 years, as the World Bank and the FAO are actually suggesting.[27] When, after the Second World War, demand for natural resources increased, there was massive room for expansion. Land was available, water was still in abundance, fertilisers were easily produced and technologies were ready to be put to use. Old technologies, around for over a century, finally found widespread application.

The discovery that nutrients removed from the soil could be replaced in mineral form was made by Justus von Leibig, the German agricultural chemist back in 1847. The basic principles of genetics that are used in

---

27. See Lester R. Brown and Linda Starke, *Tough Choices: Facing the Challenge of Food Scarcity* (The Worldwatch Environmental Alert Series; New York: W.W. Norton, 1996).

plant breeding were developed by Gregor Mendel, the Austrian monk who undertook his landmark research in the 1860s. The genes incorporated in the high-yielding dwarf wheats and rices that were at the heart of the Green Revolution in Asia in the mid-1960s were first isolated by Japanese scientists and incorporated into indigenous wheat and rice varieties in the 1880s. The hybridisation of corn that has contributed to a fourfold increase in corn yield per hectare in the United States was first commercialised before 1930. The development of irrigation goes back several thousand of years.

The fact is that there has not been a technological advance since the mid-twentieth century that would lead to a quantum leap in world food production similar to that associated with any of the basic technological advances outlined above: the basis for the Green Revolution. And this includes biotechnologies. What is the potential for biotechnology to create varieties that will yield much more than those developed by plant breeders using more conventional techniques? No one knows. Biotechnology has been around for more than 20 years, but it has yet to produce a single commercially successful, high-yielding variety of wheat, corn or rice. Genetically modified crops approved in the US have achieved 10%–20% improvements in yields. This is not enough. And while companies such as Monsanto claim that biotechnology can allow crops to be grown in climates and conditions where, because of pests, this was previously impossible, we remain unconvinced. What are the long-term implications for the ecosystem? Could this be another case of the *Homo non sapiens*?

Moreover, the basic conditions that made the first Green Revolution possible are being undermined: excessive irrigation has led to the depletion of water resources; the aquifers are losing their capacity to regenerate water; and, worse, we are quickly tapping all the water available from fossil underground water tables, which, when used up, will not be able to provide a droplet of water. Over-irrigation in other areas has led to a rise in water tables, with the result that the natural minerals present in any water concentrate excessively in the topsoil, and the high salt concentrations render the land less productive. While irrigation has its merits, ubiquitous misuse makes it ineffective, sometimes forever.

Each increase in the use of fertiliser guarantees a rise in yields, until this correlation stops. The total amount of fertiliser increased from 14 million tons in 1950 to 146 million tons in 1990. Farmers know that applying more fertilisers after a certain threshold has been reached will not generate any additional produce. And that maximum level has now been reached in many countries, including the world's largest exporting regions: the United States, Europe and Canada. Further breakthroughs in genetic engineering and seed selection are certain to improve yields, but, while scientists agree that an additional 25% yield in rice is possible with the introduction of new varieties,[28] no one dares to predict that the overall yield can be increased by a factor of three.

Therefore, a new revolution is needed: one that attempts to do more with the same, based on facts, clear opportunities and immediate results. The world is facing pressing problems, and we must take a creative and innovative approach to achieve a real breakthrough. We must recognise that there is no biological system that evolves along a straight line, and simply to draw a straight line into the future, based on the trends of the past and the expected improvement in technologies, is the wrong way to proceed. That is why this book proposes a second Green Revolution: one that is feasible and practical, and which depends mainly on a shift in our state of mind.

The Magic of Big Numbers

We know we need to produce much more, and offer many additional products and services with the resources we have. But a brief look at some of the data from China and India should convince us that the figures just do not add up. If the Chinese were to consume on average one beer per day, this would match the consumption of the Japanese, Germans and half of the Americans, and would lead to the Chinese cornering the world market for barley. The prices for barley and hops would rise twofold, fivefold. How many fold? We do not know. However, it has been predicted that, if all the Chinese were to drink only one extra beer a week, the price for barley could double.[29] Since there are already some 300 million Chinese with the disposable income to pay up to US$3 a day for a beer, the affluent middle class of the world are likely to have to compete for these limited raw materials. The total harvest of barley will be needed just to satisfy the thirst of the Chinese.

But beer not only requires barley and hops, it also needs considerable amounts of water. There are 300 cities in China suffering from a shortage of water. This situation is not unique to China: nearly all the world's megacities, from Tokyo to Sao Paolo, Nairobi to Barcelona, face the troubling reality of a shortage of drinking water. To produce one litre of beer requires an average of ten litres of water, and numerous breweries devour water at a rate of 30 litres per litre of beer.[30] Producing and consuming millions

---

28. Data supplied to ZERI Internet conference by the International Rice Research Institute (IRRI), Philippines, 1996.
29. Wenhua, 'Feasibility Study on the Integrated Biosystem Concept'.
30. *Ibid.*

of hectolitres of beer would require the diversion of water from agriculture and urban consumption. Since the purchasing power of the emerging middle class is stronger, the money available to buy the beer will outcompete the budget of the city authorities or the capacity of the farmer to secure enough water for their needs. Beer has become not just a thirst-quencher, but a status symbol all around the world. The fact is that, around Beijing, farmers have been forbidden to irrigate their crop land since the city faces a water shortage. By contrast, beer brewers and fast-food outlets always secure a licence to continue operations, whatever the water supply conditions.

The Chinese are moving up the food chain, not only in terms of beer. Their desire for meat has a major impact on the world demand for grain. The consumption of red meat has risen from 1.1 million tons to 4.4 millions tons in just six years.[31] Since seven kilos of grain are needed to produce one kilo of 'cow', the Chinese will divert just over 30 million tons of corn and soya to meat production. Since China does not have rangelands like America, where cattle can be sent to graze, there is a major additional pressure on the market for corn and soyfeed. Supply simply will not be able to follow demand.

India offers another case in point. If India maintains its present 15% growth for its chicken broiler industry, it will double the number of chickens every five years, from 300 million in 1995 to 600 million in 2000, and 2.4 billion in 2010. Since one chicken weighs on average four kilograms, and with a conversion of two kilograms of feed into one kilo of chicken, India alone will need 19.2 million tons of chicken feed, some 5% of today's world grain harvest. There is no genetically engineered or cloned chicken that could defy this arithmetic. Something else is needed.

The End of the Concept of Waste

In order to have any chance of meeting the explosion in demand that we face, there is the need for a new philosophy in how we view natural resources. We cannot continue to produce, consume and discard as wastefully as we do today. The challenge of feeding the world is not only a challenge of production; it is also a challenge of consumption. Sustainable Development has been defined as producing and consuming in such a way that you do not jeopardise the ability of future generations to satisfy their

---

31. Lester R. Brown *et al.*, *Vital Signs 1998: The Environmental Trends that are Shaping Our Future* (New York: W.W. Norton, 1998).

needs.[32] We are currently a million miles away from achieving this capability. Production and consumption patterns in our society lead inexorably towards entropy. Sustainable production should be redefined as using and extracting components from raw materials in such a way that nothing will be wasted, and everything will be used. If humankind decided to take this route—the Zero Emissions route—then we would start to close the loop and evolve into a society based on the principles of interdependence and co-operation and a law of regeneration.

The human species is the only species on earth capable of generating waste. When we harvest maize, we basically only harvest the corn grains; the rest is considered waste. When we harvest coconuts for their oil, we only use the oil; the rest is considered waste. When we fish in the oceans, some 30% of all fish caught are of no value to the fishermen and thrown back dead into the sea. When we ferment barley and hops into beer, we only extract 8% of the sugars; the fibres and the protein are considered waste, and given free of charge to cattle farmers. When we make a so-called 'green' detergent from the fatty acids from palm oil, we only use 5% of the biomass from the plantation; the rest is waste. When we log trees for their cellulose, we only extract a maximum of 30% of the hardwood's biomass; the rest is incinerated as black liquor, a cocktail of natural and synthetic chemicals. Humankind cannot claim it has designed an efficient system of manufacturing; on the contrary, it has a most inefficient system in place—to the level of absurdity.

The list of waste-streams is long. It has been estimated that the agro-industries generate an estimated two billion tons of biomass waste each year. A major portion of this is incinerated; nearly all is discarded since it is considered to have no value. A small percentage is now recovered for re-use as soil additives and fertilisers. This is a good step in the right direction, but still 999 steps short of meeting the target of zero waste. There are few agro-products that we use for more than 30% of the biomass. We satisfy most of our needs by extracting the one component we require, and discard the rest. Why?

From Linear Thinking to Systems Building

We are linear thinkers, practitioners of the simple rule of input–output. We apply a simple logic: Cartesian, in fact. Whatever cannot be used in the main product is considered waste. This is fundamentally wrong—and

---

32. World Commission on Environment and Development (WCED), *Our Common Future* (New York: Oxford University Press, 1987).

the problems start with our educational system. We lack basic understanding of how the system of nature works, even after centuries of research. The training of economists and future managers in particular suffers from the desire to oversimplify reality, to focus on the inputs needed to make one output, calculate costs, define sales prices, implement a marketing strategy—and unfortunately disregard nearly everything else: people, environment, health and the most efficient system of production, nature. The public relations department will alleviate the situation when problems do emerge, offer sponsorships and sign research contracts. If the worst comes to the worst, there is still an army of lawyers ready to be deployed, in the first place to attack and in the worst case to defend. The tobacco industry certainly offers a most discouraging example of how industry tries to avoid its responsibilities to society. Unfortunately, this sector is not an exception.

The problem is not just a matter of attitudes: the prevailing model of management systems also creates problems. The concept of the core business strategy which has stood at the centre of corporate strategy since the 1980s has done more harm to nature than any oil spill or nuclear disaster. Today of course, the stock market and thus the shareholders value executives who can target narrowly defined markets, downsize and focus their strengths on one business. They have no idea that a different approach, based on the materials cycle point of view, can identify for industry millions of tons of waste materials which could generate additional revenues and jobs by serving as value-added inputs for other industries.

The Second Green Revolution

In order to improve yields in world agriculture by the massive amounts necessary, we need a second Green Revolution: a revolution based on utilising what we waste, correcting gross inefficiencies and creating greater diversity.

Take the case of forestry. Why does the industry fell a tree? To produce cellulose with which we make paper. Only between 20% and 30% of the woody mass of a tree is cellulose; the rest is a variety of biochemicals, some of which are not only very useful, but also very valuable. But the present state of the art in pulping technology does not consider the potential of the main components: after all, cellulose represents a maximum 30%, and the chemical cocktail—the black liquor— leaving the pulp mill is incinerated. This is applauded as a contribution to the preservation of the environment. Indeed, the argument goes, instead of having to use fossil fuels, a 'renewable' energy source is being tapped. But the only efficient energy source in the black liquor is the lignin, and the rest is more or less useless as a source of calories. Where there is a use—from the biochemical point of view—it is currently ignored. A due diligence report along the lines of 'zero emissions' or 'nothing will be wasted' would quickly identify products and processes capable of recovering the valuable components.

Moreover, when developing countries, most of them in the tropics, are searching for local sources of cellulose, international consultants nearly always suggest the species they know: pine trees and eucalyptus. But neither tree is native, which is a problem in itself. Worse, the introduction of these species ignores the tremendous sources of fibres that are already in abundance. For example, the guadua—a type of bamboo—is an excellent provider of lignocellulose, but it is considered useless as a source of cellulose since its yield of fibres of the quality needed for paper is insufficient when using the advanced extraction technologies for pine and eucalyptus. However, when alternative extraction techniques such as vacuum evaporation, steam explosion or enzyme extraction are used—outdated and inefficient according to the experts—the situation and yield changes dramatically.

The natural fibres from the tropics, in abundance in bamboo, rattan and sugar cane, are of considerable value, and their use goes beyond the making of paper. Research has confirmed[33] that these organic fibres are an excellent substitute for damaging inorganic fibres such as asbestos, which continues to be produced in developing countries even when banned elsewhere. When a cement producer blends bamboo fibre, free of sugars, with cement to manufacture a cement board, as has happened in Japan, it not only creates a construction material of value with a longer useful life, and better resistance to humidity, more importantly, it is offsetting its discharge of carbon dioxide by fixing a major portion of it. And by planting the bamboo—to secure a continuous supply of green fibrous material—on a brownfield site suffering from rampant soil contamination, the cement factory also contributes to soil bioremediation.

If we were to think in terms of systems, then we would take a very different view on manufacturing, forestry, plantations and agriculture. Instead of considering the tree as the source of cellulose, or the palm plantation as the producer of vegetable oils, we could start looking at these millions of hectares of vegetation as the 'chemical' industries of the twenty-first century. The biorefinery would be born. For the first time, we would be able to see natural products out-competing synthetic ones. Why? Because instead of only using a fraction of the raw material, we will use it all. Finally, we will be able to flood the market with the materials urgently needed to respond to the needs of society in terms of food, shelter and healthcare and we will also be able to do this in a sustainable manner. These

---

33. Gravitis, 'Clustering of New Industries'.

products will be cheap. The time has come to learn from the petrochemical industry, perhaps the best system thinkers and practitioners the industrial world has found.[34] It is a travesty that their approach has never been applied to renewable resource processing.

The End of Segregation

The shift from linear to systems thinking is not only needed in industry—society at large also needs to evolve in that direction. Such a change would necessarily affect the thinking of the green movement, would have an impact on city planning, would change the way we live at home, would require us to rethink policy-making and, not least, would require business and industry to undertake a fundamental redesign of its operations.

Today, linear thinking is found in our land use planning. Our planners felt there was a need to segregate industry from urban living areas, and concentrate commercial activities in one area, preferably outside the immediate city boundaries, where there is little or no public transport. Agriculture is usually even further away from the city, as isolated as possible. The days of securing food for the city within the city walls have long gone. But this means that, when a brewery wishes to dispose of its spent grain as cattle feed, it has to transport it over long distances, at high cost. If, for example, mushroom farming could be established next to the beer brewery—and it can as we will see—then we would have a most efficient production facility generating one ton of mushrooms for each four tons of spent grain.[35] But the zoning laws in OECD countries—products of our linear thinking—prohibit farming activities in an industrial zone.

The water a brewery discharges is warm and alkaline. Environmental legislation in most OECD countries prescribes that the water is first cooled off, then made pH-neutral by adding acid chemicals before it is discharged.

---

34. This is not to say that we have maximised our re-use of non-renewable resources. Far from it. However, corporations are continuing to make breakthroughs. EBARA Corporation, one of Japan's leading engineering companies, recently opened a production unit in China that converts waste gases from a coal-fired power station into fertilisers. BP, a recent convert to acceptance that global warming is actually happening, identified hundreds of potential re-uses of CO_2. One of the options currently under consideration is the production of synthetic fibres by re-using CO_2 and ammonia. Neste, the Finnish chemical giant, has undertaken research into how to combine ammonia (NH_3) with CO_2 to produce synthetic cellulose, the raw material for rayon, a high-quality textile used in the automotive and aeronautical industries.

35. See P.G. Miles and S.T. Chang, *Mushroom Biology: Concise Basics and Current Development* (Singapore: World Scientific Publishing, 1997).

This is another clear case of linear thinking. There are beneficial micro-algae (spirulina) which thrive in alkaline waters, and alkaline water is rare due to the amount of acid rain pouring down from the sky in most industrialised regions. The alkaline water does not need to be treated and discharged at all. It could be re-used: for example, in fish farming. If we captured warm water in a permanent basin, it would allow the farming of warm-water fish such as tilapia in Sweden or Canada, unfeasible if one had to heat the water for just that purpose. A milk-powder-processing plant could also be converted into a fish-farming operation by making use of the warm waste-water and the suspended protein, which, while waste for one, is great feed for the fish.

Linear thinking has been translated into rules and legislation that do not make sense as soon as one recognises the logic and the efficiency of complex systems: in particular when one understands how nature functions. If we are to set in motion a second Green Revolution based on the principles of Generative Science, utilising the art of Immunity Management and targeting a zero-emissions society, we will need to UpSize. And to do that we will need to redesign many of our linear truths. We need to emulate nature and cluster our industrial and agricultural activities in order to use what we currently consider unusable. We have not yet understood how to design such a system. In order to do so, we must understand the basics of biology and examine the rainbow of revolutions that will be part of the second Green Revolution: the brown revolution of the mushrooms; the red revolution of the earthworms; the blue revolution of fish farming; the yellow revolution of the desert; and the black revolution of the bottom line.

Chapter 5

The Bottom Line

From Mushrooms to Earthworms

The word 'revolution' has often been misused. In its most widely used sense, it refers to the forcible overthrow of a government or social order. It can also be used to describe any fundamental change or reversal of conditions. When the application of agricultural sciences succeeded in raising output to a level to match the population explosion, it was called the 'Green Revolution'. Here, we are really talking about revolutions of perception, of insights. In a number of areas, organisations such as ZERI have undertaken pioneering work in highlighting how, by changing our perceptions, we can change the linear processes we have accepted as the norm, and produce much more with much less by clustering activities and cascading waste-streams. Taken together, these examples bring us closer to the rainbow of revolutions which together can comprise the second Green Revolution. Some of the actors in our colourful scenario may at first appear surprising. But consider.

When spent grain is used as a substrate for mushroom farming and earthworm cultivation, a cost of disposal is converted into a revenue stream. When the waste substrate from the mushroom farming is used as cattle feed or for further earthworm farming, it is once more generating revenues. When the waste from the earthworm farming is sold off as humus, it also makes additional cash. When the waste from the chickens and the cattle is used in a digester to generate biogas, it offers free energy. And when the sludge from the digester is further mineralised in algae ponds, and finally used as fish feed, the cycle of cascading wastes and generating revenues has resulted in a fascinating loop. It is making more money with little additional investments. It is generating more food and energy with no extra raw materials. It is a real breakthrough for humankind—which has never seen this type of clustering and cascading before.

The most critical is the Brown Revolution, since it precedes most of the other processes. Therefore, let us review in more detail how the mushroom is changing the way we look at food and health in the years to come.

The Brown Revolution

Breakthroughs depend on utilising several components of the system that nature has put in place—and there are few that can match the performance of fungi. The big fungi consist of the world of mushrooms, the value of which should be reassessed in all our designs for the future. The small and the big fungi have the same function, to break down fibres and live off the energy that such separation generates; the only difference is that most fungi are too small for the eye to see. Mushrooms are still considered exotic, expensive and sometimes dangerous. While mushrooms remain an upmarket commodity for many, they used to be common food for the poor. In southern Africa, for example, mushrooms were an everyday staple, bridging the gap between the autumn cereals harvest and the carry-over stocks of the previous year. But increasing urbanisation and the excessive use of wood as a fuel has dramatically reduced the quantity of naturally occurring mushrooms.

If we were increasingly to industrialise the production of mushrooms, using massive amounts of waste fibres, we could very well transform the food market—in much the same way that chicken producers have over the past hundred years. Whereas a chicken on the table was an exquisite dinner 20 years ago, today it is on the common person's plate. The productivity of mushrooms is already mushrooming and the inputs—in an over-simplified mode—are limited to a lignocellulosic substrate, steam, spores and an appropriate shelter.

Only 50 years ago, one square metre would yield five kilos of white button mushrooms in 12 weeks. Today, the same type of fungus will yield 60 kilos in only six weeks. If we wish to feed the world, and aim to eliminate poverty and malnutrition, there are few solutions that carry the same prospects as the mushroom. And there are few commodities that thrive on such cheap and abundant raw materials as these macro-fungi.

The great advantage is that mushrooms derive their energy mainly from lignocellulose, a macromolecule available in abundance. About one-third of all the biomass on the planet is lignocellulose, commonly referred to as 'fibres'. This material is often considered waste in our industrial processing of agricultural and forestry products, the fibres being abundant in the straw from wheat, corn or rice. Fibres are also the core component of bagasse, the product left over from the extraction of sugar from sugar cane; they represent some 70% of the residue from the malt after brewing beer or whisky. The leftovers from processing vegetable oils from coconuts, palm or olives are also mainly fibres and, whenever a weed such as water hyacinth or bamboo takes over a plot of land, then there is again abundant generation of fibres. Fibres are everywhere, and therefore mushrooms can thrive everywhere—in cold, temperate, sub-tropical or tropical climates.

Trees and plants build up large, long and strong structures. To succeed in their growth process, the flora blend three major components: cellulose, lignin and hemicellulose. The cellulose is the building block, the material that offers the backbone and the structure. The lignin is the cement and the glue that holds the construction material together. As the tree or the plant needs to stand up against wind, temperature changes and rain, fibres develop where there is a good blend of lignin and cellulose in the cell walls of the plant to help it withstand the pressures of erosion and time. To ensure more success, nature added into its design some anti-enzymatic and anti-oxidising compounds such as vitamin E, which make it very difficult for anything to break down the core structure of the plant or tree. Next to these construction materials, cement and protecting shields, a third component dominates any plant or tree: the hemicellulose. This is the food of the tree, rich in sugars, which is converted into more cellulose and lignin combinations through the process of photosynthesis.

Most of the living species in the world live on sugars, carbohydrates and proteins. But mushrooms are a different breed. These species derive their energy from the separation of the lignin from the cellulose. Indeed, mushrooms are the only species capable of separating lignin from cellulose and converting the components into carbohydrates. Mushrooms are not parasites. Parasites derive their energy from living systems, whereas mushrooms produce a wide range of enzymes that degrade agricultural material. They thrive on what would be classified as dead material. The small fungi and large mushrooms help the world by digesting these millions of tons of waste which would otherwise overwhelm the planet.

Thus, mushrooms play a central role in the recycling of carbon and other minerals found in agro-industrial and forest waste such as sugar cane bagasse, cereal straws, coconut, palm and coffee plantation debris, cotton residues, water hyacinth and bamboo. There are simply no limits. In our so-called efficient industrial age, the large majority of wastes from agro-industrial processing are left unused, and either incinerated or even landfilled. Increasingly, the lignocellulosic residues are used as a soil additive where fungi then degrade the material over time. These waste-streams constitute a potentially very valuable resource, and can be re-used for the production of edible food for humankind. However, today, only the rural poor and the traditional Chinese agro-industrial system utilise fibres for this purpose.

Interestingly enough, we know more about the fibres that the mushrooms consume than we know about the mushrooms themselves. Over the past few decades, nutritional and health experts have reminded us of the need to consume fibre. Most grass-, vegetable- and plant-eating animals, and human beings, only extract the sugars and the proteins from the green mass. The rest is excreted. It is recommended that we eat more fibre because we eat too much processed food—which eliminates fibres in the processing. Fibres pass through our digestive system. In our alimentary canal, they absorb numerous strings of bacteria which could cause health problems such as *E. coli* and salmonella which are then excreted from the body. So, we know we need fibres, but we also know we cannot digest them. That is why numerous species of mushrooms thrive on dung, where all other elements apart from the fibres have been eliminated in the digestive process. And because bacteria such as *E. coli* do not thrive on mushrooms, they are eliminated from the system.

Fossil records indicate that mushrooms existed 130 million years ago, long before human beings emerged on earth. The first recorded farming of mushrooms dates back to the seventh century and their popularity spread from China, to India and to France. They were among the first cultivated crops, but underwent a mechanisation and professionalisation process only very late in the twentieth century. Today, only 20 out of the 5,000 edible mushrooms are commercially cultivated, and six have reached industrial scale. The scope for expansion is tremendous. We have not even seen the tip of the iceberg.

Thanks to the development of cultivation techniques, and an understanding of the specific conditions in which each of the mushrooms thrive, more and more species will be commercialised. The development of specific breeding techniques will lead to more uniformly cultivated mushrooms of stable yield. In Western countries, the most popular mushroom is the *champignon* or button mushroom (*Agaricus bisporus*). This mushroom now grows anywhere from temperate to tropical climates, with Taiwan becoming the third-largest producer. These champignons are the unsung hero of the first food revolution—increasing productivity by a factor of over 20 over 50 years. The straw mushroom (*Volvariella volvacea*) is likely to follow the same pattern and become the fastest-growing edible foodstuff on earth: the time required from spawning to harvesting is only eight to ten days. This mushroom thrives in the tropics in temperatures in excess of 30°C. Mushrooms therefore offer a chance to respond naturally—without cloning or genetic modification—to the growing needs for food in the world—and with very little water consumption. If the challenge is to provide food, water and healthcare to the poor, or even for an optimal diet for the rich, it is impossible to imagine how to provide for well-balanced nutrition without relying heavily on mushrooms.

Mushrooms are impressive producers of protein and vitamins. With technical advances, the cultivation of edible mushrooms has spread all over

the world. Since mushrooms can be grown under different climatological conditions, and on waste from agriculture and industries, they can help
to solve problems ranging from child malnutrition to resource recovery.
Mushrooms need very little nitrogen, so fertiliser is not needed, since the
optimum ratio of carbon to nitrogen atoms is up to 60 carbon for one
nitrogen. Annual production is growing steadily at double-digit rates. Today,
it is estimated that the world market for edible mushrooms stands at $US9
billion![36]

Fibres represent a great food for mushrooms, which thrive when the
lignocellulose is blended with a few key ingredients such as chalk, rice
bran or even cotton waste. Large areas of Africa are now struggling to deal
with the pest, the water hyacinth. In Chapter 11 we will see how this plant
can be harvested and blended with, for example, waste cotton to make
an excellent substrate for mushrooms. And, after growing mushrooms, the
residue of the water hyacinths can be used as cattle feed. Mushrooms thrive
on the waste in the forests, and could also thrive on many more wastes
that humankind does not know what to do with.

The Brown Revolution has only just begun. With appetites in the West
clearly tilting towards healthy food, mushrooms will become a core component of everyday diets. Not only are mushrooms nutritious, the massive re-use of waste materials in their cultivation could make them very,
very cheap. Shiitake were once so expensive that only the Japanese could
afford them. Now, shiitake could become the new chicken of the food staple.

The production of mushrooms will explode, maintaining a healthy 15%
per annum growth rate for 20 years.[37] Their quality and variety will further increase as the public becomes aware of this great product of the
earth's biodiversity. In the Pacific North-West of North America, covering
British Columbia, Washington and Oregon, some 40 varieties of mushroom
are offered commercially through the supermarkets. The white button mushroom, a crop mainly farmed in Pennsylvania, is quickly losing popularity.
The market is discovering the quality of chanterelles, straw mushrooms,
shiitake, mayetake and numerous other exotic species unheard of by the
public at large only a decade ago.

It has also now discovered that mushrooms can serve as a basis for a
new pharmaceutical industry to treat conditions such as cancer.[38] While

---

36. Miles and Chang, *Mushroom Biology*, p. 119. See also S.L. Ge, 'Principal Species
    of Mushrooms Exported in 1996', in *National Edible Fungi Information Bulletin*
    (Beijing: Government of the People's Republic of China, 1997), p. 10.
37. Miles and Chang, *Mushroom Biology*, p. 119.
38. The Chinese have been using mushroom extracts as medicines for centuries.
    See also Miles and Chang, *Mushroom Biology*, p. 9, and S.H. Pai, S.C. Jong and
    D.W. Lo, 'Uses of Mushrooms', in *Bioindustry* 1 (1990), pp. 126-31.

the price of the mushroom is highest when sold as fresh produce, a good price is also obtained for mushrooms sold to the pharmaceutical industry. The value of this trade worldwide is now estimated at $US3.6 billion. The capacity of mushrooms to recover minerals from the soil or from its substrate is remarkable.

When the combination of waste from cotton mills, water hyacinths and seaweed extraction was proposed as a substrate for mushroom farming in Africa, many renowned world experts argued it was not feasible. But one of the world's leading experts on mushrooms, Professor Dr S.T. Chang, was not only prepared to put his name to it, he also undertook to train key people in Africa to put the project into practice in the framework of a Zero Emissions Research Initiative. Perceptions and opinions quickly changed. The core materials were cheap, even free, and the results have been impressive, as we will see in Chapter 11.

It is interesting to note how entrepreneurs in the tropics tried to enter the mushroom business. They first attempted to produce champignons. These mushrooms are not native to the tropics and their cultivation is only possible when climate controls are added at great expense. Most farms, with the exception of those in Taiwan and China cannot compete with imports. African and Latin American entrepreneurs first searched for better substrates on which to grow the mushrooms, shifting from the cheap local bagasse to high-quality material. With a conversion rate of 7%–19% of the bagasse into mushroom weight, it was not very productive. The 'professional' substrate would yield up to 60% mushrooms, but at a price.

When local cultivation could not withstand the competition of importation, labour was usually blamed for the lack of productivity. Management sought financing to introduce automation schemes to raise output per worker. But with minimum wages varying between two and ten dollars a day, labour costs were not really the problem. The maintenance cost of technology-intensive systems is expensive and cannot count on a good domestic support system. Finally, when everything else failed, an effort would be made quickly to introduce the latest technologies, such as automatic climate controls and harvesting systems. The result was often bankruptcy.

It is clear that when people in the tropics do not understand the mushrooms of the tropics, flourishing in that great biodiversity, then there is no way to convert these multiple sources of protein into a mainstream food staple. The tropics need to exploit their own biodiversity, including the vast wealth of tropical mushrooms: only then will the revolution materialise.

The use of mushrooms can be expanded from feeding people to feeding cattle, to health food and pharmaceuticals. Other cultivated mushrooms, known as *mycorrhizal* fungi, can be used as conditioners, preparing highly acidic soil for reforestation. This is what happened at the Colombian environmental research establishment 'Las Gaviotas': a success story described later in this book. The bottom-line result of all this is that, without exception, new industries can emerge, in particular in the tropics, where conditions are so favourable to undertaking such innovations. The Brown Revolution can thrive on innumerable materials we now classify as wastes in our agricultural processes. And where the Brown Revolution occurs, other revolutions will follow.

The Red Revolution

The Red Revolution has nothing to do with communism. It is about the earthworm, and is labelled 'red' because the predominant species we now farm and promote worldwide as a means of regenerating humus is the red Californian earthworm—a monoculture of worms. Yet there are 3,500 known species of earthworm around the globe. Each climate, each eco-system has its own species, all of which are unique producers of enzymes and efficient aerators of soil. This species of fauna converts waste into food, extracts all types of vegetable protein and converts these into ani-mal protein—which in itself is the preferred food of many other species, in particular birds. Chickens prefer earthworms for breakfast, lunch and dinner. With a conversion rate of 2.2 kilos of earthworms into one kilo of chicken, the results are quite impressive. The waste the earthworm leaves behind is humus of exceptional quality.

Aristotle called worms 'the intestine of the earth'. He believed that the planet's soil was a living holistic organism, and he understood the role of the earthworms in its maintenance. Yet, even as recently as the late nine-teenth century, it was thought that, because worms were found around plant roots, they ate roots, retarding growth and even destroying plant life. It was therefore recommended that worms be killed. It was not until Charles Darwin's book, *The Formation of Vegetable Mould through the Action of Worms with Observations on their Habits*, was published in 1881 that the earthworm was rehabilitated. Darwin wrote 'Earthworms prepare the ground in an excellent manner for the growth of fibrous-rooted plants and their seedlings of all kinds.' The major contribution of Darwin is perhaps not his theory of the survival of the fittest but his breakthrough vision that the earthworm could indeed be seen as a critical component in life on earth. Darwin's book heralded the beginning of investigations into earth-worms. There is still much to be learned, but what we already know is remarkable.

Worms are subject to so few diseases that one could say, in effect, that they catch none at all. The bacteria fostered in their gut are produced in such overwhelming numbers that disease-producing bacteria find life very difficult in an earthworm environment. Furthermore, antibiotics are found naturally in the environment created by earthworms. Soil fungi-like bacteria (*actinomycetes*) produce antibiotics (*streptomycin*) and, when earthworms are present, the production increases dramatically. Most disease-producing bacteria require an oxygen-free (anaerobic) environment, whereas the environment created by earthworms is oxygen-rich (aerobic). Earthworms do not kill the bacteria: they create an environment in which their numbers are substantially reduced.

Creating a healthy environment, with reduced numbers of bacteria, is a unique contribution. But that is only the beginning. Earthworms do not operate single-handedly. Soil with a good population of earthworms will also have a large population of bacteria, viruses, fungi, insects, spiders and other biota related to the soil. A worm population of 500 per square metre at an average weight of one gram each represents five tons per hectare. In a healthy soil, the presence of earthworms encourages the development of a biomass that can reach a mass six times that of the worms, or 30 tons of biota. This represents 35 tons per hectare of living species just beneath your feet.[39]

Earthworms will eat half or more of their own weight daily and, as they do, will till, aerate and fertilise at a rate of more than 90 kilos of soil per square metre each year. This is a massive 900 tons of soil per hectare. Worms work 365 days of the year. It has been calculated that, in Europe, earthworms can deposit a 200 mm-thick layer of topsoil over 100 years. Swallowing soil is the earthworm's main way of moving about and they ingest about 50% of what they encounter. Worms break down the mat of decomposing plant material, thus permitting the easier entry of rainwater and oxygen in the soil. As the worms burrow through the soil, worm-populated soil becomes wet faster and deeper and holds the moisture longer. The tunnels are coated with mucus, which is rich in nitrates, and plant roots take advantage of the tunnels as an easy-growth channels. Rainwater flows through the channels, dissolving the nitrates from the mucus and spreading it through the soil.

Plants need nitrogen, and dead plant material has a ratio in excess of 20 carbon to 1 nitrogen. This cannot be absorbed by plants and the soil could therefore become acid, the soluble mineral locked up and the soil less fertile. Earthworms partly separate the carbon from the nitrogen in

---

39. See Ina Meyer, 'Integrated Earthworm Farming', in K. Mshigeni *et al.* (eds.), *New Hope for Sustainable Development in Africa: Zero Emissions and the Total Productivity of Raw Materials* (Windhoek, Namibia: University of Namibia; Tokyo: United Nations University, 1997).

their intestines. Most nitrogen is deposited in the soil as castings and as mucus lining. A proportion of the carbon is then dissipated through the worm's skin during respiration as carbon dioxide and the balance in the castings. Dead earthworms themselves are significant contributors of nitrogen to the soil, being 60%–70% protein, with a nitrogen content of around 12%.

Worms have a very simple and unsophisticated digestive system. Yet insoluble minerals are converted in soluble form, which is then available to plants. Even cellulose is partly broken down. The digestion is possible thanks to enzyme-producing bacteria and, when the castings are excreted, the bacteria and the enzymes are excreted along with them. The bacteria are soil-benevolent and continue the work in the soil they carried out in the intestine, i.e. converting minerals into a plant-available form, breaking down cellulose and making humus.

The marriage between bacteria and worms is a good illustration of harmony and co-operation in nature. The dense population of bacteria in the worm's intestine can exist only because of the worm's ability to absorb oxygen readily. In return, the bacteria not only take care of the digestion of their host's food, but actually become worm food themselves as they die off. Then, after being deposited in the soil by the worms, they break down cellulose into a form that can be ingested by the worms as food. The survival and development of species in nature depends on co-operation.

The earthworm makes so much more available to plant life: seven times phosphorus, six times nitrogen, three times magnesium, two times carbon and 50% more calcium. It does not mean that the worms produced this: they just make this available for consumption by the plants and other biota. Earthworms separate the materials so that they become useful. The earthworms tolerate different levels of acidity. Some worms will tolerate extremes of 3.5 and, with their production of calcium carbonate, they help neutralise acid soils. And when the earthworm castings are around, bacterial activity will increase by a factor of 100.[40]

Recent research has demonstrated that the earthworms are a critical component in soil remediation, destroying toxins and accumulating heavy metals which can then be separated out. The worms' ability to decontaminate soils polluted with heavy metals was first established in 1975 by a Welsh researcher, M.P. Ireland. He conducted trials on polluted mining sites in Wales and successfully extracted lead, zinc and calcium from the soil. The worms accumulated the metals and the concentration of the castings excreted by the worms after digestion contained less metals than the original contaminated soil, but the worms contained considerably more: 12 times more in the case of lead.

---

40. Meyer, 'Integrated Earthworm Farming'.

The research results motivated others to undertake trials on toxic heavy metals such as cadmium. Two polluted sites recorded concentrations of cadmium of 38 and 29 parts per million respectively. Worms extracted from these soils were found in both cases to have a concentration of 143 parts per million. Despite the difference in concentration of the cadmium in the soil, the worms had absorbed an identical amount into their bodies, and this suggests that some worms will absorb poisonous heavy metals until their presence becomes life-threatening, at which time they are able to stop.

Since there are—as indicated—some 3,500 different earthworms, it is necessary to choose the right worm for the job: in this case, the recovery of heavy metals. Some species have demonstrated an ability to absorb a specific type of waste, and should be used to remove lead, another for cadmium, another for chromium, and so on. The leading research centre on the application of earthworms for the cleaning of heavy-metal-contaminated soils, night soil and raw sewage is located in Pune, India. The Bhawalkar Earthworm Research Institute has designed toilets that convert human waste into valuable pathogen-free castings. The institute designed vermifilters which produce drinking-quality water from raw sewage. This continuous process is 100% worm-driven and provides both primary and secondary treatment: that is, the worm beds and filters successfully dispose of the solids by converting them into castings, and also purify the waste-water. The system works by simply trickle-feeding the raw sewage across a succession of specially designed worm beds by means of a rotating boom, after first grinding the solids into fine particles. The solids stick to the existing castings which form the filter medium and are eaten by the worms, forming more castings. The longer the system is in use, the more efficient it becomes.

The insights first made by Aristotle and then scientifically confirmed by Charles Darwin have now received a broader scientific interest. Now there is a better understanding on how what Aristotle called 'the gut of the earth's gut' is functioning. The enzymes from earthworms are now researched for their beneficial use in the purification of beverages and for the elimination of impurities and toxic substances. Even in the highly sterilised environments needed for vaccines, antibiotics are successfully purified by earthworm enzymes at a fraction of the cost of chemical purification. And natural colours that are often difficult to maintain and standardise are streamlined through a purification process based on earthworm enzymes. Just like the mushroom, we have only seen the beginning of the revolution so far.

It is high time that we acknowledged our shortcomings in understanding, and learned to follow the lead of the master: the humble earthworm. Or better, it is time we acquired a better understanding of this worker in the dark, the enzyme. Both the earthworm and the mushroom play a key role and, when we fully understand them, their impact on reducing waste and generating additional revenues—the essence of UpSizing—could be phenomenal.

The Blue Revolution

The blue revolution is fish farming. In nature—in the seas, oceans, lakes and rivers—there is never a need for anyone to feed the fish and aerate the water. The productivity levels are high, the quality is high and the diversity is enormous. Why does humankind have to resort to fish-farming techniques, cultivating a few species, administering expensive feed and adding oxygen? Why not produce as nature does? The answer, of course, at least from the point of view of a linear mind, is demand. The result of growing demand has been a chronic depletion of stocks in our oceans and an exponential growth in the numbers of fish farms. But why should the artificial monocultures that dominate such farms be assumed to be the best that we can do?

The process promoted by George Chan, an advisor to the ZERI project at the United Nations University, based on his Chinese expertise, is, in fact, the best that we have. He has demonstrated that an integrated approach that uses appropriate organic waste as food for fish succeeds in cultivating 15 tons of fish per hectare without needing to buy fish feed.[41] I have said we are talking about a revolution, but this is no revolution: it is just the way nature works. Nature feeds its fish very well. The drive towards monocultures in fish farming is as incomprehensible as the monocultures in agriculture that led to the generation of pests. While it could be sold to some as scientific, and while the result has been an increase of productivity, it certainly has little in common with the way nature secures food for many. George Chan combined six to eight different fish species, benthos, macrophytes, halophytes, zooplankton and phytoplankton in achieving these results.

When one studies fish farms around the world, it is clear that all need to aerate the pond with oxygen. This is costly, requiring both energy and infrastructure. In nature, not one lake is aerated! The use of species such as the big-headed carp in fish farms eliminates the need for aeration: this hard-working fish does the job by constantly swimming up and down, provided there is space to do so. The carp can get the job done in a three-

---

41. See *Proceedings of the 1st Training Workshop in Zero Emissions in the South Pacific*, Suva, Fiji, 5–9 May 1997 (Suva, Fiji: ZERI Foundation; Geneva: UNDP, 1998).

metre-deep pond, so it is better not to harvest him. In addition, all fish farms have to clean out their lakes about once a year in order to take out the accumulated waste on the bottom. The decomposing biomass consumes oxygen, thus decreasing the productivity of the fish farming. Nature never has to clean out lakes: nature takes care of the problem in its own way, with the mud carp and comparable fish in other climates cleaning the bottom. To use such fish would be far more efficient because it would increase the return on investment and cash flow since there would be no interruption to the production system. In addition, the mineralisation of the waste products on the bottom of a lake requires oxygen, and thus competes with the fishes' need to breathe.

The integrated systems designed by George Chan are a near-perfect copy of nature, and depend on over 500 years of accumulated expertise from the Chinese, where 50% of the world's fish farming has been successfully developed.

The industrialisation of fish farming has led to the everyday usage of hormonal treatment to change the sex of fish artificially to male. Females, carrying eggs, weigh less and are treated. In addition, because of the preference for monocultures, disease is an everyday possibility. Antibiotics are routinely used, raising prices and causing increasing concern among consumers who may well be at risk from excessive exposure. Most importantly, as we will see, polyculture fish farming can be established as part of a cluster in which the waste from one or more other processes can provide the feed for the operation.

The Yellow Revolution

In order to set up clusters of complementary activities, where the waste for one becomes the food for another, we need space. Until the current design for the ZERI integrated biosystem, developed by George Chan, is further refined and begins to miniaturise, we need lots of it. And yet, with desertification increasing due to a variety of factors, such as population growth, unsustainable farming practices and climate change, we are, as a planet, seeing reductions in the amount of land we can usefully farm.

The Yellow Revolution is the desert, as symbolised by the amazing 2,000-year-old plant, the *Welwitchia mirabilis*, indigenous to the Namib Desert—a largely inhospitable place—and which survives by harvesting fog that condenses on its leaves. So, in a place without water, the plant succeeds in finding some. The process is possible because Namibia experiences large amounts of fog along its coast due to the effect of a cold current. In Chile, a similar current also creates fog, which is recovered as potable water for humans or animals, or as the life-blood for agriculture where agriculture was previously impossible. As the fog comes inland from the sea, it is collected in gutters and finally in storage tanks.

In Hawaii, scientists have experimented with cold-root systems to promote crop growth. Cold water is pumped from deep seas and passed through simple agricultural piping at both root depth and ground level. At ground level, the cold water pipes produce condensation which keeps the soil moist enough to propagate selected crops.

In Namibia, ZERI research is examining how the process can be emulated. Cold water is already at surface level, and therefore deep-water pumping is not necessary. It may be possible to pump water from the coast to the desert using wind power, abundant along the Namibian coast. According to Keto Mshigeni, Namibia is optimistic that 'we shall be able to transform some parts of the Namib Desert into green productive lands'.[42]

The Black Revolution

The Black Revolution is the bottom line. The result of our rainbow of revolutions is that the bottom line improves. Uncompetitive companies, wasteful processes and expensive operations are converted into profitable, or more profitable ones thanks to the additional revenues that are generated. The creation of new value-added, based on waste from one process becoming food for another leads to a shift in the economics. This is the revolution that will sustain all others.

---

42. Keto Mshigeni, 'An Overview of the ZERI Africa Programme', in Mshigeni *et al.* (eds.), *New Hope for Sustainable Development in Africa*.

Chapter 6
Productivity and Jobs at Biorefineries

The first Green Revolution offered one solution to one problem. The demand for food increased, so the search for ways of increasing the production of proteins and sugars dominated the challenge of how to respond to the ever-growing appetite of an ever-growing population. Irrigation, seed selection, pesticides, fertilisers and herbicides represent the combined technologies that increased the yield. Humankind expected the earth to produce more.

The second Green Revolution does not pretend to address only the issue of food shortage through increasing the supply of protein and sugars. This new revolution addresses, fundamentally, all the problems of sustainable livelihoods. This revolution does not expect the earth to produce more. It recognises that the earth has come to its limits. It aims to do more with what the earth already produces. Complex solutions for complex problems.

If one is searching only for food from crop production, then the majority of what is produced cannot be used, and is simply left in the field or incinerated. But poverty alleviation requires more than just food, and so all that is produced should now be assessed for its best contribution to the challenge of providing shelter, energy, healthcare and, of course, jobs. This is the fundamental difference between the first revolution which started in the 1960s and the second, which is emerging along with the development of Generative Sciences, UpSizing and Zero Emissions.

The differences are clear. One leads to monocultures, genetic engineering, cloning and technologies which basically aim to **change the nature** of plant and animal life. The focus is on the exploitation of known resources, even when their transplantation to other parts of the world requires the introduction of non-native species (such as pine trees in the tropics). This production system is very sensitive to changes in the market, where the dependency on one commodity increases the risks of social instability whenever market conditions vary. The second Green Revolution will endeavour to use

First Green Revolution	Second Green Revolution
1. Addresses food problems	Addresses poverty alleviation
2. Searches for protein and sugars	Searches for uses for all elements
3. Monoculture	Clustering of industries
4. Produces more of the same	Does more with what is available
5. Genetic engineering	Integrated systems
6. Increased output	Biodiversity and total use
7. Mechanises, technology	Learns from nature
8. Changes nature	Mimics nature
9. Exploits known sources	Searches for the best sources
10. High level of standardisation	Combines multiple uses
11. Cloning is the name of the game	Biodiversity is enhanced
12. Sensitive to market changes and dependent on single commodities	Multiple markets and less dependent on a few markets

Table 2: *Comparison of the First and the Second Green Revolution*
Source: ZERI Foundation, Geneva

all elements, cluster industries, use integrated systems and aim to **mimic nature** and enhance biodiversity. There will be multiple markets for producers who will be far less prone to fluctuations in global market conditions (see Table 2).

There is no sector in the economy where the opportunity to convert from a monoculture to a multiple-use system could be so rapidly achieved than in the agro-forestry industry in general, and the plantation business in particular.

If plantation management were to opt for an innovative approach towards all the elements of the biomass generated by its crops and trees, the plantation business would be converted into an economic powerhouse of the twenty-first century, comparable to the petroleum industry of the twentieth century. It would be an engine for sustainable growth: indeed, one of the best potential platforms for socially equitable economic expansion. It is an ideal case for applying the concept of UpSizing, evolving from the cash crops of today to a major source for the generation of wealth, trade and jobs in the world economy, through diversification and the cascading of wastes. And the importance of plantations is increasing because their impact on the global environment reaches far beyond the use of water, fertilisers and pesticides. On the one hand, they have the unfortunate capacity to be huge sources of CO_2 emissions and air pollution, as happened during the disastrous Indonesian forest fires. On the other, they have the

Traditional	Zero Emissions
Linear approach	Systems approach
Core business	Clusters of industries
Yield of one crop	Value-added of the total biomass
Sideline of world economy	Forefront of the world economy

Table 3: *Traditional Plantation versus Twenty-First-Century Management*
Source: ZERI Foundation, Geneva

opportunity to position themselves as key carbon sinks—centres for the absorption of carbon dioxide—and they are the potential home of the **bio-refinery**.

Based on an innovative form of management, UpSizing and Zero Emissions (see Table 3), it is feasible to merge several agendas and position the plantation industries at the forefront of the global economy in terms of magnitude, technological innovation and political influence.

Core Business Strategies: Petroleum versus Natural Products

Plantations are still a prime example of 'core businesses'. After all, when you plant pineapples, you are in the pineapple business. When you harvest sisal for its fibres, you are in the fibre business. When you extract oil from the palm-fruit bunches or from the olives, you are in the vegetable or olive oil business. But this approach does not permit the valorisation of the total potential of the plantations.

If we were to hydrolyse all the macromolecules of the plantation in the same way as chemistry cracks petroleum into hundreds, even thousands of products, then the renewable resources of the biomass offered by the plantations would be in a position to eliminate synthetic materials within a decade. Unfortunately, we don't, and plantations remain very much as core-business operations.

Change requires a shift from a linear approach—searching for one product—to a systems approach—recovering all components as value-added. Instead of focusing on the core business, plantations should cluster several industries together (see Table 3). The yield of one component of the crop would then be less important than the total value-added generated by the total biomass. If this strategy is pursued, then the plantations will move from the sidelines of the world economy to centre-stage.

Research and Development Today

Research and development for the plantation industries focuses on how to increase the yield: how much more oil can be pressed from coconuts, olives and oil palm, with a given acreage; how many more coffee beans can be processed; how many more citrus fruits can be harvested using less water? This clear focus on yields and the productivity of the core product has stimulated the responsible use of water, fertilisers, pesticides and herbicides. The conservation of energy and materials has also become increasingly important as world commodity prices have spiralled downwards over the last decade. The careful seed selection and the cloning of pest-resistant varieties, sometimes the product of genetic engineering, has pushed the results beyond imagination.

While the success of this scientific approach, spearheaded by prominent institutions such as the Palm Oil Research Institute of Malaysia (PORIM), certainly cannot be disputed, the time may now have arrived to introduce a new focus. Indeed, while scientists agree that yields can be expected to go up even further, no one is expecting a continuation of the same dramatic improvements achieved in the first Green Revolution. Indeed, the current trend is to defend the advances already made.

There are increasing problems with pests that have become increasingly resistant to some of the previously effective chemical controlling agents. *La broca*, the pest affecting coffee plantations in Latin America, is gaining ground. Even when new pesticides are introduced and more stringent controls are implemented, the pests are adapting and returning. Coffee is not the only crop affected. The palm and coconut tree is attacked by fungi from within. The banana plantations have also been infested with pests and new varieties have had to be cloned rapidly to secure the survival of the industry. In fact, there are few plantations that are free of pests. Whenever a monoculture takes over a patch of land, pests will have a chance to invade and dominate.

Biodiversity, DDT and Slash and Burn

Plantations are certainly not praised for their contribution to the preservation of biodiversity. On the contrary, many varieties have been lost in the drive towards higher yields, and only now are scientists sometimes desperately searching for new and even ancient varieties, which would offer security against infestations of mildew, fungi and insects that have developed resistance, even immunity, against the harshest forms of chemical control. Plantations around the world are searching for more resistant

1960s Practice	1980s Substituted by	2000 In addition to all previous
Pesticides	Biological pest control	Re-use of all biomass in clusters
Spraying undergrowth	Plant nitrogen-fixing cover crops	Strategic planning of carbon sink
Fertilisers	Waste as soil enrichment	Establishment of tradable carbon rights
Monocultures	Seed bank expansion	Productivity through biomass re-use in other industries
Selection for high yield	Selection for pest-resistance	Cloning of biochemically rich varieties
Clean-clearing and burning	Zero burning	Search for value-added

Table 4: *Environmental Management of Plantations: A Chronology*
Source: ZERI Foundation, Geneva

varieties, even studying the DNA of long-lost plants and fruits in the tombs of ancient civilisations.

Plantations have evolved from consumers of DDT to test-beds for biological control. Chemical spraying was once the norm, but it has now increasingly become the last resort of defence. Today, plantations conserve the soil by planting species that will obviate the extraction of nutrients, while the growth cycle of these species will even plough nitrogen back into the fertile ground, enhancing the plantation and reducing the need for chemical fertilisers. Table 4 reviews the strategies of the past, the concepts that are now gaining ground and the progress that needs to be achieved in the future in order to achieve a truly competitive industry.

Plantations have been criticised for their clean-clearing, involving burning, to get the fields prepared for planting or replanting. Most responsible plantation companies owning large acreages across the globe are now self-imposing the no-burn option—meaning that none of the biomass waste will be incinerated. While this is still a relatively innovative approach, introduced among others by a Malaysian palm oil plantation company and the pineapple plantation industry, it is not yet mainstream. It has been suspected that plantations have been a major contributor to global warming due to the repeated release of carbon dioxide into the atmosphere through the burning practice. The re-use of this biomass as a fertiliser or a soil additive is a first step, though not enough. If a process can be identified that permits the generation of value-added, then it will quickly be embraced by plantations around the world. Further research and development funds to test scientific proposals are urgently needed.

How to Steer Plantations towards Sustainability

The key question is: how can we stimulate plantations to embark on a real sustainable strategy that goes beyond biological pest control, the safeguarding of biodiversity, and the non-incineration of biomass waste? What we have to do is ensure that plantations evolve into pioneers of environmentally sustainable development. We have to envisage a strategy to enable them to become examples of resource productivity. How can this be done?

As Edgar Woolard, ex-chairman of DuPont, has stated: 'Governments can regulate; NGOs can agitate. But only business can innovate.'[43] And, in order to move plantations towards real sustainability, numerous innovations are needed: in management; in technology; and in philosophy.

Many would stress the role of government in steering business toward sustainability. Excesses do need to be restrained. Governments must respond to the basic needs for food, water, healthcare and shelter—but they should refrain from going way beyond their main tasks. This is not a plea for a *laissez-faire* policy, *à la* Adam Smith. However, it is appropriate to point out that, for example, the introduction of quality management systems and the application of ISO 9000 standards was never imposed by law, nor demanded by NGOs. Business—including the plantation business—realised that, if they did not embark on a quality programme, they would lose their competitive position on the market. It was competition that drove industries to implement new management practices where quality stands central (Table 5). It is competition that is driving companies towards certification to the environmental management system standard, ISO 14001. And it is competition that will drive plantations towards the Zero Emissions management concept.

An Emerging Management Target: Zero Emissions

The concept of '**Zero Emissions**' is a new management instrument which emerged only a few years ago (Table 5). It is comparable to the Total Quality

---

43. Quote from Edgar Woolard from his keynote speech at the *2nd UNU Congress on Zero Emissions*.

Management concept	Target
Total Quality Management	zero defects
Just-in-Time	zero inventory
Total customer satisfaction	zero defections
Health and safety in the company	zero accidents
Total productivity of materials	zero emissions
Consensus-building	zero conflicts

Table 5: *Managing Zeros*
Source: ZERI Foundation, Geneva

Management (TQM) concept, without which no business can prosper today. Total quality equates to **zero defects**. Zero Emissions can also be compared with the Just-in-Time, or the **Zero Inventory** concept which clusters suppliers together around major assemblers, as is the case in the car industry. The concept of Zero Emissions is the continuation of the concept of total customer satisfaction, where no executive will rest until every customer comes back for more products: the target of **zero defections**. Just as no manager can tolerate one fatal accident (**zero accidents** or total safety) in his company, the ultimate objective of business must be **zero emissions**: nothing will be wasted. It is only when all materials are fully used that processing industries will have reached their highest potential.

Zero Emissions, as discussed earlier, basically means that 'nothing will be lost; all waste will be used as value-added'. These residues can either be re-used within the industry's own activities, or as a value-added input for other industries. It is an integrated approach and, as such, differs from the linear approach of the core business strategy.

This new management concept of Zero Emissions has the potential to reposition the plantation industries in the world economy. The application of the ZERI methodology, which will be described in Chapter 9, could have a profound effect on the plantation business. This methodology first searches for cleaner production practices. It then identifies the value-added that can be generated on the basis of the waste. The methodology will then prescribe the clusters of industries that could emerge; it can identify the technologies needed; and suggests the government policies that are necessary to support this approach. Table 6 highlights the results of such a methodological approach to the palm oil plantations.

Output type	Existing best practice	New uses under research
Crude palm oil	Raw material for palm oil refining	Palm diesel production
Trunk	Soil conditioner (zero burning technique)	Wood products (fibre-board, particle board, furniture), pulp/paper, animal feed, glucose, cellulose substrate, fuel, palm heart, activated carbon, polypropylene filler
Fronds	Soil conditioner	Vitamin E extraction, fibre-board, particle board, pulp/paper/paper board
Pericarp fibre (fibre around the fruit of the palm)	Fuel for mill	Fibre-board, mushroom-growing substrate, pulp/paper, roofing tiles/cement aggregate, sorption for heavy metal cations
Empty fruit bunch (EFB)	Mulch for soil application	Fibre-board, substrate for growing mushrooms, betacarotene production, solid fuel
Shells	Fuel for mill	Activated charcoal, cement aggregate, potting medium
Steriliser condensate	(see total palm oil mill effluent [POME])	Cellulose, single-cell protein substrate
Sludge	(see total POME)	Feed supplement
Hydrocyclone water	(see total POME)	(see total POME)
Total POME	Closed-tank or lagoon digestion to produce anaerobic slurry for fertiliser use, and biogas for heat/power generation	Ethanol/amino acid production
Washings	(see POME)	(see total POME)
Boiler ash	Fertiliser, detergent, landfill	–
Kernel	Kernel meal, animal feed	–
Crude palm kernel oil	Raw material for palm kernel oil refining	–

Table 6: *Existing Best Practice for Palm Oil Waste and Potential New Use*
Source: Teoh Cheng Hai, Golden Hope Plantations Bhd, Malaysia, 1996

Productivity of the Plantation

Plantations, like any other business, need to focus on further increases in productivity. Theoretically, there is always the chance to go beyond the limits. But the first Green Revolution has now reached the stage where a doubling or tripling of revenues for the plantation industry will only be possible when it targets the full use of the biomass it is producing.

The palm oil plantations in Indonesia, Malaysia, Colombia, Nigeria, Central America and Brazil generate an estimated 200 million tons of biomass per annum.[44] The sisal plantations in Tanzania alone generate over 10 million tons of biomass. These amounts are comparable to the volumes processed by the petrochemical industries. However, most of the plantations commercialise less than 10% of the green mass, trunks and fruits they generate each year. The palm oil represents approximately 9% of the biomass of the plantation over its lifetime; the sisal fibre is just about 2% per harvest;[45] sugar is some 17% of the cane. By any standard, this is not a very productive operation. On the contrary, there is huge potential for improvement and increased valorisation.

Within the main crop that is sought, little can be done. Coffee farmers in Colombia cannot double their yields with new varieties; the sugar plantations in el Valle del Cauca, Colombia, cannot harvest more than they do now. So how can the system be improved? By doing more with what the earth produces. This is a creative process that must go way beyond the existing best practice (Table 6).

Downcycling, Recycling and Generating Value-Added

Plantations are not discarding all waste materials from the field or the processing units. Many use the waste from the fruits as a soil additive or a fertiliser. But, how many by-products generate additional value that outstrips the costs of production and disposal? Very few indeed. How much do the coconut plantations in Sri Lanka or Ivory Coast receive for the fibre of the fruit that is used to wrap drainage pipes in Europe? How much do the sugar plantations in South Africa derive from the sales of bagasse to

---

44. These countries have a combined expanse of 5 million hectares of operational palm plantations. If we assume that each hectare generates up to 40 tons of waste per year, then the farming alone can generate 200 million tons. This does not take the waste from the factories into account.
45. Nkuba, 'The Sisal Industry in Tanzania'.

cattle farmers? What is the calorific value of the bamboo plantation waste in Indonesia? How much do the citrus farmers get for their seeds?

While we all underwrite initiatives and support the desire to re-use the waste as by-products, the question is how much value-added is and can be generated? All too often, the value is minimal and resembles more a 'downcycling'—getting rid of waste at a price cheaper than the straight-forward disposal—or a cheap recycling in the form of a fertiliser. Only if plantations can generate considerably more money from the additional harvesting and processing will these materials be used.

The volumes of biomass that plantations have to deal with are staggering. A palm oil plantation generates a minimum of 25 tons of biomass waste per hectare per year, so a 40,000 ha plantation, not unusual in Kalimantan, Indonesia, has to handle one million tons. This means that any further commercial utilisation of the biomass that can be identified represents a major additional opportunity.

The first requirement is the need to think beyond the core business. The second requirement is to identify the biochemical components, outside of the mainstream business of the plantation which would provide a unique competitive opportunity if and when extracted efficiently. A concrete example is the isolation of furfural from the African oil palm. The Latvian State Institute of Wood Chemistry has demonstrated furfural processing from biomass of the oil palm with its pilot units in Riga in a programme performed under contract with ZERI.[46]

Not many oil palm planters have even heard of furfural, so no one can blame them for their lack of vision. Furfural is a natural anti-enzymatic and efficient bactericide used, for example, in the paint industry as a solvent. It commands a higher price (US$1,350 per ton) on the market than palm oil (US$350–450). Biochemists found that the conversion of hemicellulose from the trunk of the tree into furfural was 17%-efficient at laboratory scale, a finding that calls for an investment study. If the laboratory success rate could be translated to the plantation, the result would put the oil palm plantation not only in the palm oil business, but also in the furfural business. Of course, if all plantations were to engage in this extraction, prices would drop, perhaps to half or even one-third of the present world market price. Today, furfural is available both in its synthetic and in its renewable form. The natural variety is likely to become cheaper

---

46. Professor Nikolas Vedernikov, Deputy Director of the Latvian State Institute for Wood Chemistry, has succeeded in producing furfural from a variety of 'waste' raw materials: corn cobs, rice hulls, cottonseed hulls and sunflower hulls. The technology has been commercially applied in six plants in the former Soviet Union. Twenty patents in 11 countries have been received.

than the petrochemical product, and could take over the market. The plantation will increase revenues.

The biochemical study of the sisal plant—a crop that is rapidly losing popularity due to the advent of synthetic ropes at a cheaper price—has confirmed that the bowel of the sisal plant can serve as an excellent basis for the fermentation of citric and lactic acid.[47] The price of citric acid is ten times higher than the price obtained for sisal fibres. The citric acid production process is a fermentation system. The tropical climate in Africa permits a solid-state fermentation, eliminating the need for the expensive steam widely used in Europe and America. Just imagine: the sisal fibre represents 2% of the biomass, and 10% of the bowel can be converted into citric acid, at ten times the value. It is possible to regain the competitive position for sisal fibres when additional revenue is generated from the production of the food additives.

These are just two concrete examples of the added value that can be extracted. But this is just the beginning. Consider the iodine from the seaweed plantations, the betacarotene from the avocado and marine algae, the vitamin E and anti-oxidants from the coconuts, palm oil and the seeds of citrus fruits. There is so much that can be extracted. Multidisciplinary research that goes beyond the boundaries of one sector will undoubtedly find numerous additional products for extraction and commercialisation. A comparative analysis, still admittedly at an early stage in development, will, for example, indicate that coconuts are much richer in vitamin E than palm oil, while palm oil is richer in betacarotene. The potential is vast; the need for a vision urgent. A further component deserves special attention: fibre.

Fibres

One of the most successful environmental programmes in the world has been the operationalisation of the recycling of paper. Countries around the world are dedicated to the recovery of used paper. The reason is simple: people are aware that trees are logged in order to supply cellulose, from which pulp and then paper are made. The Japanese recover over 50% of all used paper, while American states even legislate the minimum content of recycled fibres in newsprint. Demand for cellulose for the production of paper and packaging materials is increasing to meet increases in literacy and the improvement in living standards in Asia, Latin America and Africa. The need for fibres goes beyond pulp, paper and packaging. Cellulose is also used in construction materials, as an additive to cement, rendering

---

47. Mshigeni, 'Zero Emissions Projects in Tanzania'.

the cement board more resistant in tropical climates. A cement board factory in Thailand will need a 2,000 ha bamboo plantation in order to access the right blend of green mass to strengthen its cement.

For some reason, the world's plantations seem to neglect that they represent the largest source of cellulose in the world. Plantations have a massive capacity to generate cellulose. Any plantation, of whatever type, could be considered a cellulose factory. Most of them are located in the most productive areas, offering a quality that is comparable with the cellulose varieties found in the hard- and softwoods from Scandinavia or North America.

Therefore, it appears to make little sense to engage in the planting and harvesting of trees such as spruce and Douglas fir or pine—which need at least 20 years to grow—in regions where plantations are abundant, in order to supply the new centres of cellulose consumption—rapidly shifting to South-East Asia and Latin America—when the plantations already there could easily respond to the demand. The richest concentrations of cellulose are found in plantation crops such as bamboo, sugar cane, rattan, oil palm, banana and coconut trees.

Why is the extraction of cellulose from the plantation neglected? When Indonesia declared in 1996 that it plans the construction of 30 new pulp mills by the year 2010 with a capacity of 11.1 million tons,[48] it did not indicate from where it will acquire the cellulose. At a time when the harvesting of primary forests is prohibited, and the replanting of the cleared land will take years, the plantations offer the logical answer. If Indonesia were to engage in special forestry projects, then the plantation management is missing a unique opportunity to valorise its biomass. Indeed, the booming plantations on some of the 17,000 islands of Indonesia could become the key supplier of the cellulose in a variety of strengths and lengths that meet even the most demanding pulp buyers in the world. The full 11 million tons could be supplied by the 2.2 million hectares of oil palm plantations.

Implementing this strategy requires multidisciplinary research, in which the forestry experts cannot expect to take a lead. They have an existing business to defend. It is up to the plantation industry to take the lead and demonstrate the feasibility, both technically and economically, in order to move forward. And it is also up to the industry to identify the new technologies needed to facilitate their task and their challenge.

This is an environmental and economic opportunity of great significance. Moreover, it is the birth of a new industry, complementary to the plantations' original business: the oil from the palm or the coconut, or the sugar from the cane. This use of cellulose represents a major additional demand for biomass which is not exploited today. And, the value generated will

---

48. *Jakarta Post*, 15 August 1996, p. 3.

be much higher than the economic importance of using cellulose as a soil additive. Even at the rock bottom price of US$400 per ton, it amounts to extra annual revenue of between US$1,100 and US$1,700 per hectare.

Plantations as Carbon Sinks

As major cellulose producers, plantations could also be one of the earth's most efficient carbon sinks, capturing carbon from the air through photosynthesis and returning oxygen to the atmosphere. This basic function of the forests is mirrored by the plantations, and is performed in a very controllable and measurable fashion. The disposal of cellulose from plantations has been a major problem in the past. Indeed, most of it has been either ploughed back into the soil or even incinerated, contributing to carbon emissions.

If the fibres were re-used, it would not only generate additional business, it would also represent the creation of a massive carbon sink. The world is in urgent need of carbon sinks. Humankind is creating an excess of CO_2 around the globe and, as a result, scientists now fear that human-induced global warming is an imminent and real danger. The world is not sitting still: massive research efforts are being made, not the least by the Japanese, who wish to find the best technologies that can deal quickly with the threat caused by excessive emissions of CO_2. The Research Institute for Innovative Technologies for the Earth (RITE), located in Japan, has some US$80 million research funds per year and the Intergovernmental Panel on Climate Change (IPCC) is dedicating the minds of several thousand researchers around the world to this issue.

If only a fraction of that budget could be reserved for studying the carbon sink capacity of plantations through the commercial re-use of the cellulose, numerous win–win situations are possible—the capture of carbon and the production of valuable new products—the opportunity to generate new jobs, to expand trade and to generate investments.

Certification of Carbon Sinks

At this point in time, plantations could consider quantifying—through certified organisations—how much carbon dioxide they are effectively fixing, and how to increase it. Why? Because this back-up data could spur international interest in the role of the plantations, and secure funding for research. Longer term, it could even represent a key source of revenues. It is now extremely likely that a system of tradable rights for CO_2 emissions will be established when the next round of negotiations on the post-Kyoto protocol

Climate Change Convention convenes in Buenos Aires in November 1998. That means that each company will have a specific limited number of emission rights, and when they exceed those rights, management must either reduce emissions, which technically may not be feasible, or have to buy rights from those who either did not use them or who have captured carbon dioxide from the air.

The question 'which business are you in?' will be posed a few times in this book. And, while plantations may be willing to consider utilising new biochemical components that were not valorised before, entering into the business of tradable carbon dioxide rights may seem far-fetched today. But it will certainly not be theory for long. The Costa Rican government have pre-empted the likely agreement of a global system for carbon trading at the next round of negotiations on the Framework Convention on Climate Change. The country has already established an infrastructure for carbon trading based on the natural capital of Costa Rican rainforest. Costa Rica sold its first carbon credits (referred to as 'Certified Tradable Offsets' [CTOs] in the Kyoto Protocol) in early 1997, almost a year ahead of the Kyoto Protocol. The credits were certified by Société Générale de Surveillance (SGS), who have now established a centre of competence for the inspection, testing and verification of carbon offsets. Once purchased, the carbon credits allow the buyer the right to emit a specific amount of CO_2 certified as sequestered in Costa Rica. The Costa Rican government has used the income from the trades for sustainable forestry projects—paying farmers to adopt sustainable practices—and financing and conserving national parks.

It is only a matter of time before this becomes a global norm. Japan confirms that this is on the priority list for moving toward global environmental stewardship. The Japanese Energy Institute has studied in detail the possibilities of establishing such a system: the missing core element was the producers of the carbon sinks. Plantations: which business are you in?

Extended Life-Cycle Analysis in the Plantation Industries

The third challenge for the plantation industries (as well as for all industries) is to introduce full life-cycle analysis (LCA) into their operations. At present, the application of LCA is gaining ground in industrialised countries, permitting better insights into the impact of products on the environment. A thorough LCA takes years to establish, and often the data is missing to permit a full scan. While every effort is now being made to determine the life-cycle of a product from its cradle to its grave, there is a need to go further: a need for a new extended form that can be introduced in the next few years (see Figure 1). Few are better placed than the plantations to take the lead. Instead of conducting an LCA on the current core product—the palm oil or coconut—an effort should be made to examine the tree in its entirety.

Take the case of coconut fruit from plantations in the Philippines. When consumers in Japan become increasingly aware that detergents are a major uncontrollable cause of water pollution, as consumers in Europe did a decade ago, they may wish to substitute the very slowly degradable chemical tensides (water surface tension reduction agents) with fast-degradable vegetable-based water surface tension reducers. This is certainly to be applauded. The most popular vegetable surfactants are fatty acids derived from coconut oil and palm kernel oil. Lauric ether sulphate is particularly popular. An extended LCA of a coconut-based detergent looks straightforward. In fact, it is not.

While rivers in Japan or Europe may be cleaner thanks to the use of environmentally less detrimental raw materials from vegetable origin, there is a major flaw in the logic. The fatty acids from the coconut oil represent only 5% of the biomass generated annually from the plantation: nearly all the rest is being discarded. The conclusion does not at all favour the use of renewables—unless the practice of discarding the major part of the biomass is changed.

Traditional LCA focusing on the product and the ingredient

Extended LCA of the complete tree

Figure 1: *Extended Life-Cycle Analysis in the Plantation Industries*

The Philippine coconut plantation industry would have an interest in reminding the Japanese that, if they wish to have cleaner rivers, an extended life-cycle analysis could benefit the planters and the planet much more than just through the purchase of a commodity such as fatty acids. The coconut tree is not only the provider of oils and acids, it is also the supplier of cellulose. It is a source of biochemicals and clean fuels (such as lignin) which can be used in an efficient manner. The small fibres can be recovered in the form of particle boards; the coconut oil is rich in vitamin E. So, instead of having only one business, we see the emergence of five industries, all clustered around the coconut tree—while, at the same time, responding to the desire of the Japanese for better river quality.

This proposed extended life-cycle analysis potentially offers answers to many challenges. It is more than a tool for measuring environmental performance: it is an investment platform, a trade generator, a job machine.

ZERI has already undertaken biochemical assessments of the biomass from the oil palm in Malaysia and Indonesia, sisal in Tanzania, sugar cane plantation industries in Brazil, and pineapple plantations in Indonesia— and with success. The first vitamin E plant has been constructed by Golden Hope Plantations Bhd in Malaysia, which also hosts the first particle board production unit. Vitamin E is extracted from the crude palm oil. The particle board unit utilises waste fibres from the palm tree and palm fruit. Pilot plants for the extraction of furfural have now been constructed in Latvia. Other plantations—such as the olive oil plantations in Italy—are preparing to adopt this approach. These are important first steps and this methodology is expanding rapidly, since all the partners in the exercise realise that it offers a unique chance to merge numerous agendas: preservation of the environment, increased productivity of the biomass, creation of jobs, attraction of additional investments, expansion of trade and pursuit of innovative research and development programmes. Not least, it reduces the inherent risk in business pursuing a single product strategy.

Portfolio Approach

The clustering of industries around the biomass factory—the plantation— moves the business from a single-product enterprise which is subject to volatile changes in world commodity prices to a portfolio of products and derivatives, which are part of different business cycles and which therefore promise better stability in revenues. Throughout history, we have too often seen that over-production of one crop risks wiping out nearly all plantations, or that a synthetic substitute, such as synthetic rubber, eliminates fortunes in just a few years, as the city of Manoas in Brazil can testify.

A portfolio approach, based on biomass generated in the commercial exploitation of one species, will offer, in addition to the core crop, a set of other products that could challenge the petroleum derivatives in price and volume.

Conclusions

The design of the environmentally sustainable plantation of the twenty-first century is more than a strategy for preserving the environment. It will make plantations more competitive, both with each other and against substitute materials of synthetic origin. Being more competitive can be achieved by continuing to focus on higher levels of productivity. Now that yields of crops have almost reached their limit, plantations need to undertake the analyses that will unveil the opportunities for derivatives that can be extracted from the massive amounts of biomass which today remain worthless. This is a fertile ground for new investments, for job creation, for trade and for technological co-operation.

It requires a multidisciplinary approach. It can only succeed with co-operation across business sectors. For example, fibres from the plantation are re-used in the pulp industry: lignin as a binding agent and hemicellulose in the food industry. The Japanese government is certainly prepared to co-operate in such an analysis, and industry will be prepared to convert the findings into new industrial development schemes. The Zero Emissions concept has found fertile ground and, if the major planters around the world, backed by their governments, demanded it, several initiatives could be started in the short term.

Whereas downsizing attempts to produce more value for the core business with less people, UpSizing, when applied to the plantation business, demonstrates that we can produce more—much more—in many more ways, with many more people employed.

Chapter 7
Free Trade and Wealth for All

Traditional economics prescribes that trade depends on the efficient combination of labour, capital and raw materials—enhanced by storage, transportation and financing facilities. The role of trade in enhancing development is beyond doubt. Trade has the potential to increase consumers' purchasing power in rich and poor countries alike. Thanks to trade, buyers can access goods that are manufactured more economically and are of higher quality. Persistent trade deficits identify the weak areas of agriculture, industry and services. Trade surpluses highlight competitive industries. Trade may create unemployment for one, and a job for another. Trading centres have emerged over time at crossroads all over the world, leading to prosperity for cities and nations lacking natural resources, but strategically located and efficiently operated.

Trade may be catapulted by technological breakthroughs available to one, but inaccessible to another. The British Empire considered time and its measurement so strategic that it imposed the death penalty on watchmakers sharing their knowledge with the enemy.[49] Industrial espionage is nothing new; competition to own and control proprietary information was as important in Napoleon Bonaparte's time—when the need to preserve food on the front line led to the invention of the tin can in France and the glass jar in the United Kingdom—as it was in the Cold War. Nor is trade restricted to agricultural and industrial products: it is growing rapidly in services, intellectual property rights—and even the right to pollute or the capacity to generate oxygen.

On the one hand, trade neglects cultural identity and simply follows purchasing power. On the other, from the Silk Route to the Viking voyages, the exchange of goods has promoted cultural understanding, and

---

49. Peter Coveney and Roger Highfield, *The Arrow of Time: A Voyage through Science to Solve Time's Greatest Mystery* (New York: Fawcett Books, 1992).

allowed new techniques and products to be adopted. Spaghetti, an Italian 'original', was famously invented by the Chinese. The search for new trading routes drove the world to finance voyages that led to the discoveries of new continents and the creation of new nations. Trade has its heroes, such as Marco Polo; it has its 'villains', such as post-war Japan.

For some, trade in general, and free trade in particular, is a core component of development; others view it as an obstacle to development. Both camps can advance examples to support their position. The Japanese and Koreans protected their markets against any disruptive form of importation—and, even today, the world's richest nations remain highly protective of some market segments. Even the champions of free trade apply restrictions: the Jones Act in the US,[50] the Swiss trucking standards which effectively restrict access through the Alps on EU freight, and product safety measures in Japan.[51] Many products and services face barriers, some formal, some informal, and they almost always deprive consumers of access to cheaper, better products. Some forms of protection are, of course, necessary to safeguard the survival of cultural identity, artisan production or maintain environmental or social standards. This chapter does not offer a criticism of trade or question its role in development. Rather, it examines how trade can evolve in symbiosis with development by (1) suggesting how the present trading system can be restructured to accelerate economic development and reduce pollution simultaneously, and (2) identifying new strategies and trends that can help the existing system serve those who today benefit least from it.

In the process, it examines the importance of information, innovative ways to expand trade, systems to assure that small and medium-sized companies have their fair share in the continuing globalisation of trade, and strategies for survival against the onslaught from overly aggressive and powerful corporations. It also attempts to learn from history, while sharing ideas on how the core objectives of socially just and environmentally sustainable economic development—increased productivity, competitiveness, job creation and reduced pollution—can be met. All four must be considered simultaneously, and there must be no trade-off between any of them—otherwise free trade's ability to help meet the basic needs of society for food, water, shelter, healthcare, energy, transport and employment will be thwarted. If this happens, its legitimacy will be rightly questioned.

---

50. The Jones Act restricts the transportation of goods between two American port cities by ships that do not carry the American flag.
51. For example, the Japanese require that baseball bats manufactured in the US be tested to far higher standards than has ever been the case in the country of production, where baseball is a major sport.

Free Access to Information

As noted previously, Adam Smith stated in 1776 that the free and equitable exchange of goods and services is only possible when there is free and equitable access to information.[52] Unfortunately, information is not, and has never been, freely available. In fact, it has become a commodity, and access is a privilege, traditionally exploited by the few at the expense of the many—as the widespread abuse of 'insider information' confirms.

When one party to a transaction is well informed and the other is ignorant, the former can be regarded as exploiting the latter. Accordingly, the world's 'haves' and 'have nots' can be defined as those who have access to information and those who do not. The explosion of information services, the emergence of electronic databanks and the flourishing role of consultants, who gather, digest and interpret facts, figures and trends, have become major growth businesses at all levels. From the standpoint of *The Wealth of Nations*, therefore, free trade, generally speaking, is impossible unless it is accompanied by free and equitable trade in information. Therefore, it *is* currently impossible.

The only trading areas that come close to meeting this criterion are: (1) the currency markets trading in foreign exchange, linked by a web of complex electronic data and trading channels; (2) the commodity exchanges in Chicago, London and Singapore, which represent the meeting places for world trade in metals, pigs, coffee, eggs, chickens, fruit juices and, today, even recycled paper; (3) the stock exchanges, trading shares, warrants and options in stocks and bonds; and (4) the reinsurance markets where companies share their risks and premiums on concluded contracts.

In those markets, information is gathered from around the world and prices are determined according to fluctuations in supply and demand. But, interestingly, it is not hard facts and scientific analyses alone that determine decisions. 'Hunches', informed or otherwise, drive decision-making so much that, often, the facts are immaterial. Of course, microeconomic theory acknowledges that price is determined by expectations.[53] At the global level, it is *what may be* that sets prices, influences trade and determines investment flows. The expected rainfall, or lack or it, will determine the prices for wheat. El Niño *may* hit Australia, cause drought, reduce the harvest and push up wheat prices. The projected increase in beer consumption in China will drive up barley prices. The risk of sub-zero temperatures in the south of Brazil will send coffee prices soaring, then send

---

52. *The Wealth of Nations.*
53. Represented in the function p(E) by a capital E, where p = price and E = expectations.

them down again when the weather forecasters change their prediction. The mere fact that ministers of finance meet will send interest rates up or down just before they do so.

The oscillations of prices and rates are further influenced by the fact that only a small fraction of the trading deals concluded in commodities or currencies are ever consummated. The large majority of agreements simply do not materialise, but are offset by reverse contracts. There is much more money to be made by pretending to make a trade than in trading itself. This profit motive and the speculative nature of a market that is characterised by imperfect access to information leads, for example, to the situation where a ship loaded in Kuwait with 200,000 tons of crude oil can be bought and sold tenfold before reaching Rotterdam—during which time the captain is quite unaware about what has happened to his cargo.

Information and Intermediaries

This is, of course, a simplistic description of the world of commodities and futures exchanges. But it is basically a true one—and contrasts sharply with the reality of third-world economies, where, for instance, a farmer is preparing his cash crop for export. Apart from the fact that wealth is gained or lost without his knowledge, the farmer does not have anything like the access to market information that the first-world trader has. Indeed, the farmer's only expectation is to be able to feed his family.

But the problem of access to information is also a problem of intermediation. Before commodity exchanges can speculate, intermediaries handling the produce will take their first 'cut'. Since they have no interest in the farmer being well informed, they will only offer the minimum amount of information. Some will be inclined towards *dis*information.

Fortunately, the trend towards *dis*intermediation—as a result of the decentralising influence of advances in telecommunications—will change this situation dramatically. The introduction of rural phones in Sri Lanka in the last ten years has allowed coconut farmers to secure a 20% better sales price from their buying agents.[54] One call to the Colombo commodity exchange by the local co-operative achieved badly needed increases in revenues—not by getting the end-user (the consumer) to pay more, but simply by forcing the middleman to pay more. How? First, the farmers learned the price for the day, then they were told that a new market had emerged in Europe for waste coconut fibre, which could be re-used for

---

54. Personal visit, 1988.

wrapping drainage pipes in muddy fields. This provided a precious opportunity to generate additional revenues.

This is why plans to increase access to information are such a central component of global development strategies, and why training and capacity-building are so critical to agencies such as the United Nations Development Programme (UNDP). Simple information transmission systems, ranging from radio communications to basic computers, offering updates on core commodity prices, can make a major difference to the bargaining power of villagers.

But a more fundamental approach is needed to achieve a quantum leap in development and to open up the numerous additional opportunities for trade, particularly for those from the developing to the industrialised world.

The Emerging Middle Class

Demand for food, water, construction materials, healthcare and consumer products is increasing worldwide. The continuing population explosion is putting further pressure on our limited resources, while the emerging new middle class, particularly in Asia, is shifting consumption patterns towards a more inefficient use of raw materials. For instance, the typical middle-class family will now serve chicken and beef for dinner, prepared with butter, replacing the traditional rice, soya sauce and vegetable diet. Their bamboo houses will make way for energy-inefficient modern buildings of concrete, steel and aluminium: buildings that are also much less resistant to earthquakes.

This new middle class has the buying power to move products around the world. The poor may be in need, but since they do not have any purchasing clout in the trading marketplace, products will only move to them when aid and emergency assistance is provided.

If this trend continues, economic development in the twenty-first century will simply be an extension of the existing pattern of production, trade and consumption—and that will pose major challenges for the world. These challenges can be overcome through the application of the Zero Emissions and Generative Science concepts to achieve a new approach to production and processing, which will result in a much broader spectrum for agro-industrial development trade.

Homo non sapiens

This book has cited many examples of where components of our industrial system have been designed by those with no understanding of how nature works. Seaweed and detergents are two cases worth examining from the trade perspective.

Seaweed

When Japan, the US and Europe import dried baled seaweed from Africa, South-East Asia, the Pacific Islands and South America, it seems a straight-forward flow of goods. The seaweed is farmed along the coastal zones of Tanzania, the Philippines and Chile, dried on the beaches and sold to inter-national traders for processing in the North. The seaweed produces highly sought-after—and highly priced—alginates such as agar and carrageenan: core ingredients in the biopropagation and food industries. But seaweed is processed almost exclusively in the North. The so-called waste materials, mainly fibres with some trace minerals such as iodine and magnesium, are disposed of by dumping them back into the sea. Yet the iodine is highly valued in the developing world, and needed there to fight iodine deficiency disorders (IDD). Iodine is critical for the development of the brain: a few micrograms suffice, but a chronic lack of iodine leads to goitre and even mental retardation. In China alone, the World Health Organisation esti-mated that, in 1990, there were ten million people suffering from IDD. Western governments are aware of this health problem and have initiated priority aid programmes to produce and export potassium iodide as a food supplement.

This is a clear case of how the access to and integration of information into a real world of inter-related problems and opportunities could dra-matically enhance world trade and economic development. Processing the seaweed in, say, Tanzania or Namibia would leave over 50% of the biomass behind, and exporting the semi-refined agar and carrageenan would reduce freight charges and the energy requirements for the shipments. There would also be less unwanted waste for the North to dispose of. In addition, of course, Tanzania or Namibia would benefit: from better healthcare by rein-troducing the iodine into the food stream, from new industries, and from more jobs and additional revenues.

The information is available, but it is useful only if it is integrated into a clear, simple system. This would lead to a more efficient use of resources, higher generation of economic value-added, more effective preventative healthcare and more jobs: a vastly preferable alternative to subsidies and aid, and what development should be all about. It is a clear case of where official development aid (ODA) can be converted into official development investments (ODI), something the developing world has been urging for decades.

Today, the information is available but it is not integrated. One can find quotes for natural resources, but not for the value of the alleged waste products. Of course, the traders do not know about recovering waste and using it as a food or healthcare component. What is essential is that the information must be available in an easily accessible and integrated fashion.

Green Detergents

The emergence of green detergents illustrates another opportunity for integrated information systems and UpSizing trade.

The demand for ecological cleaning products has supported investments in palm oil plantations and the expansion of the international trade in fatty acids. The benefit is twofold: (1) an increase in international trade in renewable resources generates wealth in the country of export (which enjoys not only greater revenues but greater plant growth through enhanced photosynthesis); and (2) water quality is impacted positively in the importing countries.

However, a close look at the fatty acids shows that they represent less than 5% of the green mass generated each year by the plantation. As reported elsewhere in this book, 95% of the biomass from the plantation is discarded, and therefore generates no additional value. If consumers in the North knew that 95% of the raw material used for the product they are buying is wasted, they would probably conclude that importing a green detergent to clean up their water supplies was at the expense of the producing country.

If the information was made available in an integrated form, this waste-stream could be converted from a problem into an opportunity: 90% of what is considered waste could be recovered and transformed into marketable products, sold at competitive prices, without subsidies.

For example, extracting the vitamins, anti-oxidants and betacarotene in the palm oil would bring down prices for these valuable health products, boost demand and support new trade flows—and also make them accessible to more people. Using the lignin in the manufacture of formaldehyde-free medium-density fibre (MDF) board, a construction material in growing demand, would put manufacturers in a better position to compete and trade across the world. And the waste fibres generated by plantations could produce a cascade of products and by-products—to the point where the plantation is converted into a biorefinery: an engine for development and trade.

The new system would be in complete contrast to the present system of trade which generates massive amounts of waste in the country of export.

Agriculture and Trade: The Case of Sugar

Agriculture is one of the most protected markets in international trade. How can developing nations penetrate this sector of high value-added products and services? The tropics have clear advantages.

Consider the case of sugar. Sugar from sugar beets cannot compete with sugar from sugar cane. In addition, the world market for sugar is suffering from an over-supply—mainly because of a shift in consumer preference for a sweetener that does not damage teeth or add unwanted calories. The synthetic production of artificial sweeteners is adding to the pressures on sugar beets and sugar cane. But, in an evolving market, xylitol has been introduced: a natural sweetener, extracted from hydrolysed hemicellulose, the food of the tree. At present, it is mainly extracted from 'black liquor', the waste from pulp and paper mills. In the future, xylitol is expected to be widely available from the rich hemicellulose found in tropical zones.

This swinging back and forth by the markets causes continuous upheaval. The consumer has a preference, and, if the marketers take this into account, there is little future for either beet or cane sugar—even when the Japanese and the European Union (EU) continue to subsidise production, and create tariff barriers by pushing the price to the consumer up to US$6,000 a ton. If the policy-makers want to promote an enlightened trade agenda—one which is mindful of the health effects on consumers—they should promote investment in the further extraction of natural sweeteners.

Protectionism and the Swiss

In the same year that Adam Smith wrote *The Wealth of Nations*, Britain imposed a 100% tariff on watches imported from Switzerland. The justification was similar to the arguments heard today for building tariff barriers: 'to stop the exploitation of children in the mountains of Switzerland where the great design of the latest watch technologies of the Empire have been conspicuously copied as a result of espionage'.[55] Swiss watches either paid the duties or were confiscated. Britain was promoting free trade and industrialisation, while introducing protection against competition with both tariff and non-tariff barriers: it was forbidden to export both patents on watch technologies and the fine machinery tools needed to produce the parts.

The Swiss were undeterred. What the British never realised was that their policies actually led to the demise of their own watch industry, and also gave rise to several industries which today are still part and parcel of the backbone of the Swiss economy. The Swiss were forced to manufacture their own tools, and the precision work they displayed was superior to the standards prevalent in the market.

---

55. David S. Landes, *Revolution in Time: Clocks and the Making of the Modern World* (Cambridge, MA: Harvard University Press, 1985), pp. 236-37.

The emergence of the insurance industry is also interesting. Demand for Swiss watches continued to increase—and when there is demand, supply will find a way to meet it. The Swiss realised that exporting and paying duties would price their products out of the market, so they organised the smuggling of watches into Britain. Since the risk of being caught was judged to be only one in ten, the Swiss watchmakers paid a 10% fee to a central organisation which would reimburse 100% of the watch's production costs if the merchandise was caught and confiscated. Thus, the insurance industry in Switzerland was born. Over time, the Swiss called on their creativity to reduce the insurance premiums, lower costs and convert the benefits of the collective insurance service into profits.

This experience—which led to the emergence of the Swiss watchmaking, machinery tools and insurance industries—demonstrates that competitive advantage in industry and trade is mainly man-made, and not determined by geography and access to raw materials. It also reconfirms that competitive advantage is never permanent.

Japan and the Terms of Trade

After their crushing defeat in the Second World War, Japanese industry studied the markets with great care, then examined how they could play the system to their own advantage.

The Japanese quickly grasped the crucial importance of their 'purchasing power', a central concept in economics. In the 1950s, Japanese trading houses (*soga shoshas*) went into business everywhere in the world. Whereas, today, we acknowledge this strategy as a key success factor in Japan's export drive, we tend to forget that the prime function of the trading houses was to control imports into Japan: a function they still assume with considerable success. Foreign trade missions to Japan will always call on the trading houses for help with exporting there. It was only recently that some Western companies began handling their sales to the Japanese market themselves. For almost all products, the Japanese continue to control both imports and exports—making money on both sides of the trading game.

The logic behind Japan's import strategy was simple: if you are weak, you do not concentrate on your competitors' strengths, but focus on their biggest weaknesses. If you are David and pretend to be Goliath, you will most likely lose the fight. If you are David and act like him, you have every chance of winning. What is surprising is that, after 1945, the Americans never complemented their huge military presence in Japan with a similar business presence. Instead, the Japanese went to America and did good business. Their trading houses co-ordinated all the imports Japan needed, and established an impressive network of purchasing companies. When the *soga shoshas* controlled 80%–90% of US and European exports to Japan, it was easy for them to forge an entry into Western markets 20 years later, because, if someone controls the sales of a company, they have influence over their suppliers' buying. Then, it was up to the Japanese *keiretsu*—informal holding companies of complementary businesses—to deliver quality and deliver on time, all the time. And they did.

The message offered by the Japanese is clear: before any country embarks on an expensive export promotion strategy, establishing offices worldwide to facilitate sales, it is important to study how import offices can secure a first leveraging in the power game.

The Swiss and Japanese cases demonstrate that protectionism by one can be exploited by the other, even if smuggling is illegal. In addition, blocking direct entry to the market with non-tariff methods such as the controlling of imports through purchasing houses not only protects the market, it channels the majority of value-added to the importing country and creates the right kind of leverage to pursue export strategies afterwards. It is a strategy for development that worked two centuries and two decades ago and can be made to work in the future as well.

David versus Goliath

The majority of developing countries do not have leverage with the largest trading partners in the world. The EU, Japan and the US have the strength to impose their will on many other trading partners—and they do. The response from developing countries can only be effective when they behave like David. Demanding free trade for agricultural products from the Europeans and Japanese would be a daring but ultimately foolish strategy.

It is time to show how the request for market entry could succeed by taking the priorities of the North into account and combining the agenda items of the industrialised countries—such as the protection of biodiversity and pollution abatement, particularly reductions in CO_2 emissions in developing countries—with the South's priorities for increased output and more jobs.

Over-Supply and Over-Standardisation

Since it will take at least a decade or two before the markets for agricultural products are truly open, it is necessary to think and act creatively about how the agenda for the development of trade can be combined with an agenda for Sustainable Development. A liberalisation of the international food commodities market could have—initially—a devastating impact on many developing countries. The EU, for example, has not only been subsidising its own sugar beet cultivation, it has been subsidising production of sugar cane and has paid above-market rates to countries such as Mauritius and Fiji. The Japanese pay seven times the going market price for sugar from Okinawa. No wonder that sugar in the south of Japan is still harvested by hand. European Union policy on bananas—paying higher prices to Caribbean producers, even though the Brazilians and Colombians could deliver at a lower price—makes no economic sense. The Europeans stick to their support mechanisms, and have their reasons for doing so: to protect the fragile economies of some member states' former colonies. The Japanese still impose quotas on imported rice, even when their productivity is the world's highest. Their costs per ton are also the heaviest.

Free trade in bananas and sugar would be bad news for smaller countries. The current campaign by Caribbean nations to maintain preferential prices for bananas from the EU highlights the problems. Smallholding farmers would suffer from reduced revenues; landholders would have to consolidate; production would be further streamlined; and large professional and technical operations promoting scientific agriculture based on monocultures would increasingly dominate. Small farmers would lose their jobs because competing against the large monoculture producers would be difficult if not impossible. The present system favours highly focused enterprises, searching only for core businesses: exploiting just six varieties of cereals when nature offers more than 500. One of the few alternatives is to look for alternative crops.[56] Certainly, higher unemployment in the countryside—and in cities and towns, following the exodus there from rural areas—would not be a welcome development.

The world commodity markets are still characterised by over-supply and over-standardisation. The consumer has a choice—even in the developing countries, where they can buy *Nutrasweet*, brown or bleached sugar. Often, products are also over-standardised: the same is available everywhere, so it is difficult to differentiate one from another, even though producers and

---

56. It has been predicted by Oxfam (Claire Godfrey, *A Future for Caribbean Bananas: The Importance of Europe's Banana Market to the Caribbean* [London: Policy Dept, Oxfam, 1998]) that, when preferential rates for Caribbean bananas in the EU are ended, the resulting impacts on vulnerable single-commodity-dependent economies such as the Windward Islands will include mass poverty, high levels of unemployment and political instability. As confidence ebbs away, the only economic alternative for many will be the illegal cultivation of marijuana. *The Economist* (20 December 1997) has stated that, for St Vincent, marijuana is now the principal export crop.

clients alike are actually looking for differentiation for products responding to the specific needs and interests of a narrowly defined market segment.

There are two strategies to pursue: free trade in organic produce, and the sustainable exploitation of biodiversity.

Free Trade in Organic Produce

The market is increasingly demanding chemical-free products. In the US, demand for organic produce is growing at around 20% each year. Swissair, the Swiss national airline, has decided to offer organic food and healthy fruit juices. In the UK, the supermarket chain Sainsbury's recently offered its customers the opportunity to request new product lines and, in a survey called 'More choice because it's your choice', which attracted a quarter of a million responses in August 1997, the overwhelming result was a demand for more organic produce. In Japan, the demand for chemical-free food is rising rapidly, with over 200,000 households subscribing to a service to purchase ¥5,000 of organic fruits and vegetables each week. While it is inconceivable that OECD member states would permit across-the-board free trade in agro-produce, intermediate options may be possible. Those options would maintain tight control over the imports of products that could destabilise, say, rice farmers in Japan and milk producers in Europe—but would also allow entry for new products from the South, which would make use of the free trade system for the development of trade and for the environment, while at the same time contributing to poverty alleviation.

It would be an innovative step if the European, North American and Japanese governments were to agree to free trade in organic produce. It would mean that any produce that is guaranteed to have been cultivated without the use of chemicals could enjoy free, unlimited access to the market. The proposal is simple; the implementation pragmatic. This strategy would depend on a clear and agreed definition of what is meant by 'organic'. There are differing definitions; there will be varying standards. If governments would agree on the principle, a standard could be established making use of and streamlining existing government and non-governmental organisations' (NGO) programmes. A system for monitoring performance would then need to be put in place.

The advantages are clear. Consumers will pay a premium for organically produced goods—it is generally accepted that food that is certified as being organic fetches price premiums of between 50% and 200%.[57] Supply will follow demand, leading to more sustainable agriculture. This is a possible

---

57. See N. Robins and S. Roberts, 'Reaping the Benefits: Trade Opportunities for Developing Country Producers from Sustainable Production and Consumption', in *Greener Management International* 19 (Autumn 1997).

solution to the problems of the Caribbean banana producers. Farmers' associations in the Windward Islands are already trying to promote a 'Fair Trade' banana. Organic agriculture would fuel a demand for local compost, assisting the recovery of biomass waste from cities, reducing their waste-streams while at the same time reconnecting the urban and agricultural zones. Since large-scale operations are difficult to convert to organic agriculture, it would mainly be the smaller farmers who would reap most benefit. As a result, a programme promoting free trade in organic produce would counter-balance the pressure for large-scale agriculture—ensuring that those with limited land would be able to survive, indeed, carve out a new market niche. Since organic farmers generally need more manual labour, more job opportunities would be created in the rural areas.

It has been established among coffee farmers in Colombia that the poorest growers with marginal land are largely using organic techniques today. Because of their poverty, and their inability to buy fertilisers and pesticides, the soil has been cleansed of chemicals. Their products would be among the easiest to classify as organic, and to sell at a premium price.

Introducing free trade in organic produce would promote sustainable agriculture, generate additional revenues and develop small-scale farming. Political will is needed—and so is a clear, simple certification process: the massive bureaucracy surrounding the EU's recognition of imported organic goods is currently deterring many producers. It would be the beginning of a long process towards empowering smaller farmers. But more is needed. It is essential to establish direct contact between producers and consumers, eliminating detrimental intermediaries such as brokers and buyers. This disintermediation would ensure that more of the additional revenues generated by the opening of markets actually reaches the farmers.

Disintermediation

Large-scale and global distribution, it is argued, needs numerous middlemen: to process information, store the produce and combine the harvests of many smallholders to produce a volume attractive to international traders. True. But there is also a need to exploit the opportunities to be more efficient. To repeat: the market is characterised by over-supply. The mere fact of being able to supply goods of a certain quality at a certain price is not enough: to acquire and retain a share of the market requires finding a distribution channel that satisfies demand and reaches the consumer with the ideal profile.

The 'something extra' in a product could be the organic quality, the artisan-like manner of production, or a clarification of what the farmer can do with the funds obtained through direct trade. It comes down to per-sonalising trade in an era when everything is over-standardised. It is offer-ing the consumers in the North an insight into the catalytic effects of their purchasing decisions.

For example, when a local co-operative in Guatemala noticed the dwin-dling price for honey that traders were prepared to pay, they realised there was no future for their beehives. They produced just 11 containers a year, insufficient to represent any unique value or volume for the traders, even on the local market. The honey is 100% natural, organic and of excellent quality. But the majority of trading houses in North America were not inter-ested: this quality was not valued in monetary terms. Then, a church organ-isation facilitated a direct agreement with a medium-sized supermarket chain in Belgium. This chain of 40 stores agreed to buy the honey direct, and organise an annual quality inspection by third parties. The honey was repackaged in Belgium in a glass looking like a beehive, and marketed as 'Honey from the Maya Country'. The margins for the co-operative increased by a factor of three, and the supermarket chain had an exclusive product—which was accompanied by a small folder picturing the environment in which the bees thrived, and explaining how the product was delivered directly to the customer without the addition of any preservative.

Electronic Commerce

Trade is beneficial, but the question needs to be asked: beneficial to whom? When the price for coffee paid to the farmer is just 10% of the sale price paid by consumers, it is obvious that the farmer does not receive the biggest share of the value-added generated in the chain. One can either criticise the system or study it to identify ways of changing the balance of power, and find means of generating more value-added for the farmer.

The promotion of trade—especially trade in areas such as organic or small-scale production based unique commodities—could, in the future, take place through the Internet. This would generate additional trade, secure better margins and provide extra value-added to promote development where it is most needed: the rural areas.

In the past, this kind of direct marketing mainly depended on goodwill ambassadors. But, increasingly, the Internet will take over the function of commerce, connecting people and facilitating direct trade on a hitherto unimagined scale. The Internet is a growing electronic marketplace for everyone to exploit; and, with 50 million users in the industrialised coun-tries, it offers enormous market opportunities.

Electronic retailing was valued at less than a billion dollars worldwide in 1996; by 1997, it had jumped to US$2.2 billion—and by 2000, it is expected to reach US$12 billion. Tourism is set to become the biggest electronically traded business, while food and drinks will reach nearly US$300 million in the next few years. The average transaction price is now nearly US$200, and by 2000 it is still expected to remain as high as US$130.[58] Each transaction is therefore worth more than the minimum monthly wage in the 50 poorest countries in the world. Imagine what a few million dollars of direct trade would mean to the communities able to tap into these affluent markets—driven by a dynamic website, with payments guaranteed with credit cards, and reaching an estimated 50 million households.

Biodiversity and Marketing

Biodiversity is an issue of concern to many. The time has come to link the agenda of preserving and enhancing biodiversity with the issue of asking the industrialised countries to support free trade in organic produce. Marketing is a management tool for enhancing a company's competitive position. In the 1960s, Philip Kotler said that successful companies listen to what their clients want.[59] But, sometimes, clients do not know what they want.

If you have never taken a bath in some of the 1,000 different essential oils, it is impossible to savour the joy made possible by the sustainable exploitation of biodiversity. Colombia, well known for its drug trade, should become better known for its essential oils. They are extracted from leaves, flowers, wood or roots, and represent a growing business, with consumption increasing. Well-known cosmetics houses are trading in and distributing essential oils. But many processors of agro-forestry products do not even realise they have the potential to develop this business.

The opportunity for trade is there. If those committed to Sustainable Development had a vision of how trade could promote biodiversity, the protection of the earth's biodiversity could become a self-sustaining activity—instead of one that requires either subsidising or self-restraint in economic development. In Tokyo, 10 cl of geranium oil sells for US$50; even lemon grass, one of the more abundant oils, sells for US$20. Apart from

---

58. Gary R. Craft, *Electronic Payments, Commerce and On-Line Financial Services* (San Francisco: BancAmerica Robertson Stephens, Contract Market Survey, 1997).
59. Philip Kotler, *Marketing Management* (Englewood Cliffs, NJ: Prentice–Hall, 9th edn, 1996); *idem*, *Principles of Marketing* (Englewood Cliffs, NJ: Prentice–Hall, 7th edn, 1996).

cocaine, there are few products that generate such a price on the international market and offer such a high revenue potential.

Mushrooms, as cited elsewhere in this book, are further proof of the largely unexploited richness of biodiversity. The market for mushrooms has grown from US$5 billion to US$10 billion in export value in the past five years.[60] China has positioned itself as the world's leading producer and exporter both of edible mushrooms and for those destined for pharmaceutical uses. A targeted strategy to exploit the opportunities from the 1,000 unused tropical mushrooms would provide a sustainable food source—and boost world production and consumption, support the rediscovery of biodiversity, generate income and produce further opportunities for trade.

If the developing countries could unlock the real power of their biodiversity—as found in products such as essential oils and mushrooms—and if this was backed by some enlightened trade policies, it would create room for thousands of initiatives.

From Products to Services to Rights

The trade in services is growing like the trade in products. Since the double-digit growth in new services such as couriers, software, security and databanks is likely to be maintained, the opportunities for new forms of trade and development are legion. Examples include innovative services such as software engineering in India, which has the largest concentration of experts in the world, the information-processing centres in the Caribbean, where all airline tickets are accounted for, or the telemarketing hub in Jamaica where toll-free calls are re-routed to ensure a 24-hour-a-day service. The merging of computer and telecommunications technologies, combined with the miniaturisation of the hardware, is converting services into tradable items.

There is an additional new route towards developing trade: the international trade in rights. If properly negotiated, this will become a major source of revenues for developing nations—and just recognition for the contribution many countries are making to the global community.

The likely acceptance in Buenos Aires in November 1998 of a regime for the Tradable Rights in Carbon Dioxide Emissions certainly favours numerous developing countries, which will never reach their emissions limits. Countries such as Japan will need to acquire the CO_2 rights from these

---

60. Miles and Chang, *Mushroom Biology*.

countries, and will have to pay for them. The Latin American countries around the tropical rainforests have considered establishing an 'oxygen bank'—requesting those countries that are massive consumers of oxygen to contribute to funding Sustainable Development in their region, a massive net producer of oxygen. Other rights could also be traded. The trade in biodiversity rights could become an agenda item, whereby there is an active strategy to recover lost diversity in regions affected by decades of over-mining, over-fishing, over-logging and over-grazing. While species that have vanished permanently cannot be recovered, species that cease to exist in one area may find refuge in other regions, and could be reintroduced. The successful programme of the Las Gaviotas Environmental Research Centre has demonstrated what is possible and is discussed in detail in this book (Chapter 11).

Conclusion

The message is clear: an innovative and creative approach to the major environmental and developmental issues facing the world can be perfectly compatible with an active trade and investment promotion strategy.

Protectionism can have both good and bad points—and unforeseen impacts. What is certain is that, if industries around the world continue to pursue trade along the same lines as now, society will fall short of its objectives: economic, socially just and Sustainable Development for all partners. If, however, information is made widely available and integrated into a systematic model, it will be possible to translate new ideas and concepts into action. The leadership must come and it is most likely to come first from the periphery in both the industrialised and developing nations.

Chapter 8
The First Step and the Final Objective

The concept of recycling, re-using and implementing cleaner technologies for manufacturing industries has found wide support. In Japan, nearly 55% of all paper is recycled; the recycling of plastics across Europe is a legal requirement under the terms of the EU's Packaging Directive; the use of recycled fibre in newspapers is legislated in many American states; there are subsidies for American households to shift from their wasteful toilets and showers to highly water-efficient ones. The list of initiatives is long. But, while these initiatives have reduced the consumption of energy and water, and certainly increased the re-use of waste materials and the recycling of discarded materials, the results obtained are insufficient. Despite 20 years of paper recycling and the introduction of sustainable forest management, the rainforests continue to diminish and demand continues to rise for tropical forest products.

If societies want to achieve a sustainable community, which guarantees not only the competitiveness of its industries but, more importantly, provides the basics in terms of water, food and shelter for present and future generations, then a more innovative approach is needed. This approach will require the study of industrial design upstream: the identification of new processes and systems at raw material stage. The concepts of co-responsibility, the clustering of industries and UpSizing will become central to achieving this. The drive towards cleaner production provides the right mindset, but the objective must be zero waste and zero emissions if humanity is to succeed in UpSizing.

Can industry learn from nature? Can legislators agree rules and regulations based on how nature operates? We know that, if we rely on industry to reduce, re-use and recycle (3R) under its own steam, it will never succeed in ridding itself of all waste, and society will be forced—as now—to face the burden of dealing with whatever is left over that has no further value. While the 3R programme has much logic to it, and indeed has secured many incremental improvements in the use of materials, it is not only difficult to reach perfection, it is likely to be too costly. And if 3R does not pay for itself, it affects the competitive position of industry and will require subsidies. Subsidisation is a guarantee of failure over time, since the subsidies are borne by the consumer, either through increased prices on the market, or through increased taxes which are channelled to industry. Neither is advisable.

3R programmes have been implemented by the introduction of cleaner production technologies in order to minimise pollution. Scrubbers reduce the discharge of SO_x and NO_x into the atmosphere; the catalytic converter limits the toxic exhausts from the car; vacuum evaporation technologies recover the zinc from plated steel. But demand continues to rise and the supply of biomass and minerals cannot maintain pace. As a result, most prices increase and a growing proportion of society around the world is unlikely to be able to meet them. Moreover, while minimising pollution offers opportunities to reduce end-of-pipe expenses up to a point, going beyond that leads to costs beginning to outweigh savings. Achieving zero waste and eliminating all forms of pollution—in a world where many of the largest energy companies still refuse to accept that CO_2 emissions should be reduced at all because of perceived economic consequences—will be impossible within our present linear manufacturing and processing paradigm. The standard belief is that some form of pollution has to be tolerated if unreasonable costs are to be avoided (see Figure 2). And this is correct when one remains within a linear model. But, if industry were designed in accordance with a systems model, then there is no reason why Zero Emissions would be the most expensive option. On the contrary, it would become the cheapest and the most competitive option.

Produce According to Design and Demand

When you produce beer, you can extract only 8% of the nutrients from the barley. There is no way of improving the use of the fresh grain in terms of fibres and proteins. No technology can change this. But, if the brewery, which now needs 30 litres of water to produce one litre of beer, could reduce its water consumption to seven, or even five litres, then that would be an excellent application of the 3R programme and the use of cleaner technologies. However, all brewers agree that, while they must reduce the amount of waste-water, it is impossible to eliminate water altogether. Some residual amount of water will always be left over.

If the cost of water is high, the drive towards productivity of water will be strong, as is the case with the Namibian Brewers in the Tsumeb Desert

Conventional linear model

Zero Emissions model

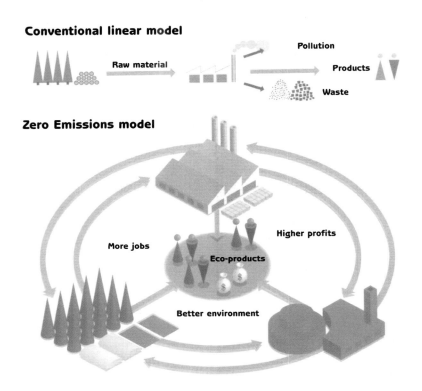

Figure 2: *Conventional Linear Model versus Zero Emissions Model*
Source: ZERI Foundation, Geneva

(see Chapter 11). If the cost of water is low, as in China, then a considerable amount of this vital resource will be wasted. Beyond a certain point, it is too costly to try to reduce, recycle and recover all the water—and impossible to justify the reduction of water consumption. This does not mean, however, that the water simply has to be discharged. Recovering the waste-water requires looking for solutions outside the brewery. It is here that the Zero Emissions concept finds its unique value. When the cost of improvement through cleaner production becomes too high, that is when the Zero Emissions concept starts. What are the possible uses for the waste-water? For example, do the conditions exist for fish farming to be established?

The same logic applies to the fatty acids used for green detergents. Making use of other materials—apart from the 5% of coconut biomass needed to produce the detergent—requires looking for solutions outside of the coconut plantation and the detergents business. While cleaner production will only look for solutions within the particular business, Zero Emissions will look for solutions in other industries: upstream, sidestream and downstream.

The First Step versus The Final Objective

Cleaner production, industrial ecology and the reduce–re-use–recycle programmes are important first steps in the process of steering business and society towards sustainability. But they cannot be the only steps. Sustainability can only be achieved if the final target is Zero Emissions—whereby the waste of one becomes the input for another, without exception. Zero Emissions has become the ultimate application of cleaner production and is the most advanced format of 3R. We now need an evolution of the managerial mindset that has embraced cleaner production: an evolution towards Zero Emissions.

Business is not standing idle. Systems are being developed to improve, and even certify, the way business integrates environment into its day-to-day management practice. The installation of effective environmental management systems or certification to ISO 14001 offers an excellent insight into the process of manufacturing. It is an effort to document clearly the enterprise's objectives in terms of environmental performance. Its procedures verify how the company achieves it own objectives and, hopefully, exceeds all environmental laws and regulations. It is a way of tracking performance targets and the process of moving towards clear goals in a predictable manner. Companies are required to document their efforts fully so that they are completely verifiable by third parties.

This is a major advance, but it remains a linear process. Looking at inputs and outputs and how these are treated within the framework of the law as well as the objectives of the company is as limited as studying the environmental performance of a tree in isolation from its ecosystem. By itself, the tree will never perform as well as the complete microsystem around it. The 3R-styled drive towards sustainability accepts that every process generates waste, and that it is not cost-effective to try to eliminate all residues and re-use them all within the process. By contrast, the drive towards Zero Emissions offers a framework for innovation and total use of all materials which, although they may have no value for one, will be of great value to another. It searches in a creative manner, through the output–input tables (see Chapter 9), for the best uses for outputs. This is a complex but productive exercise, since the precondition for success is marked not just by the desire to get rid of the waste, but by the objective of adding value to that waste.

This means that engineers will look for applications that may be far outside the domain of a single process and industry. For example, the production of vitamin E is not a primary objective, nor a logical consequence of milling oil from the palm fruit. But, when a detailed biochemical assessment is made of all the components of the palm oil biomass generated at a plantation,[61] vitamin E emerges as one of the most valuable unused components. Vitamin E has been recognised as a major potential component in the fight against cancer, so why are not all natural sources of this vitamin are being tapped?

The same biochemical analysis indicates that the leaves of the same oil palm tree are a rich source of furfural. 'Which business are you in: palm oil, vitamin E or furfural?'

So, the coconut or palm oil plantation could, in the future, be at the heart of clusters of secondary industries. Its waste, traditionally used as a fuel, is too valuable to burn. Incinerating the so-called waste amounts to the permanent destruction of commercially viable components. The plantation industry presently discards a massive amount of biomass considered to have no value. Instead, all residues that do not find any application within the palm oil plantations can be the basis for a whole new cluster of industries. Consider the scale: the palm plantations in the four largest production countries in the world generate an estimated 200 million tons of biomass waste per year! The re-use of it through a cluster of new-born industries is not the advent of a nascent cottage industry: it is the basis for new mainstream industries.

These industries will be the source of thousands of new jobs, while at the same time displacing existing production units which could never have access to such a volume of raw material with so little requirement for transportation, at such a low cost price in such a sustainable fashion. The first such known operational case is the Kalundborg industrial site in Denmark. There, waste has to be transported from one factory to the other over distances not further than 20 km, and it has been a much-applauded success. The design of integrated plants and intermediate material-separation production units will pipe residual components to other industries with such efficiency that it will not only target the ultimate elimination of all waste but will also create more competitive enterprises.

---

61. Gravitis, 'Clustering of New Industries'.

From Simple to Complex Systems

It is obvious that such developments require a highly complex and dynamic system. But the price of added complexity is a price worth paying since it leads to the generation of so much value-added. The sum of the parts far exceeds what a 3R programme or the introduction of cleaner technology can ever achieve. After all, there are few recycling programmes that generate additional value: most of them carry an extra sticker price, as paper recycling has demonstrated over the past decades, even when waste paper has been offered free of charge. The Zero Emissions programme leads to the clustering of industries that generate additional income, and can therefore be sustainable both in financial and technical terms.

Corporate strategists wonder if such a complex system can ever be achieved. However, it is not the first time that industry has searched for higher levels of efficiency through the concept of clustering. The Just-in-Time (JIT) programme led to the elimination of overstocking (and warehousing space), which locked up capital and required excessive amounts of space. JIT could only work when hundreds of companies collaborated and relocated. Even in a country such as Japan, where space is scarce and its cost is very high, dozens of suppliers of materials were forced to relocate so that they could meet the tight delivery standards imposed by the leading producers.

The cleaner production and 3R programmes have the here-and-now environment in mind, and rightly so. They aim to reduce harmful downstream effects and minimise waste. They hope that costs can be cut, in particular the costs of the disposal of waste and the growing burden of related ecotaxes. The focus is on water, energy and solid waste. Process engineers have established over the years detailed input–output tables, which offer a quick review of the chances of improving environmental performance (Table 7).

The Zero Emissions concept does not isolate the environment as the single target: it seeks to merge agendas. ZERI is analysing how new value-added can be generated, which new industries can be created upstream of outputs and how this will increase the total income. The use of the innovative output–input tables (described in Chapter 9) offers a methodology for multidisciplinary teams to find the creative solutions. ZERI does not aim to find solutions within a single industry: it clusters industries into complementary networks where the waste of one is food for another. If industry is to be converted into the prime agent for sustainable development, it must not be burdened with excessive additional expenses, which either reduce its competitiveness or impose an extra cost on the shoulders of the consumer. Zero Emissions is the target and UpSizing the process.

Cleaner Production and reduce–re-use–recycle	Zero Emissions or total productivity
1. The first step to take	The final objective
2 Reducing downstream effects	Create new industries upstream
3. Minimise waste	Value-added inputs
4. Reduce costs	Generate more income
5. Single process	Clustering of industries
6. Focus on waste, energy, water	Merging of agendas, including jobs
7. Focus on the issue of 'here and now'	Address the generic demand
8. Process based on input–output	Process based on output–input
9. Linear	Complex

Table 7: *Cleaner Production versus Zero Emissions*
Source: ZERI Foundation, Geneva

Merging the agendas includes social aspects as well. World unemployment is unacceptably high. Even Japan, traditionally immune, is experiencing record high levels. Countries such as Indonesia have to generate an estimated three million jobs per annum to keep the jobless rate at its present level. China has no option but to create some 10–12 million new vacancies each year.[62] The Zero Emissions concept has demonstrated that it is possible to increase the productivity of manufacturing systems while also generating additional jobs. It is a unique way of addressing one of the pressing problems of our time.

Paper in China:
A Comparison of Cleaner Production with Zero Emissions

The production of pulp and paper in China demonstrates the differences between, as well as the complementarity, of cleaner production, recycling and Zero Emissions. All three approaches are needed to bring China closer towards being a sustainable society. 3R is the first step, but Zero Emissions could ultimately ensure that the objective of sustainable economic and social development is achieved today without diminishing the ability of future generations in China to do the same.

---

62. See Bruno Kreisky Commission, *Report on the Unemployment Issue in Europe* (Vienna: Bruno Kreisky Commission, 1988). See also Lester R. Brown, *Who Will Feed China? Wake-up Call for a Small Planet* (The Worldwatch Environmental Alert Series; New York: W.W. Norton, 1995).

The Zero Emissions approach—for that matter, any business approach— prescribes that the search for a sustainable solution to a demand issue on the market starts with an understanding of the demand as well as with a vision of potential sustainable supplies. The Chinese demand for paper is increasing rapidly. In view of the massive demand, the Chinese are not only cutting their own forests, but are also importing pulp, and waste paper for recycling. The government has opted for the construction of numerous additional paper mills, while also trying to eliminate the polluting practices dominant in the country's thousands of predominantly small operations. As the source of fibres from trees is very limited and deforestation has reached dramatic levels, alternative sources for pulp have been used extensively throughout the country.

The extraction of cellulose from rice straw is one of the most important input factors for the pulp industry in China. However, the use of alkali sulphates, standard practice in wood pulping, only yields some 13% of the available cellulose from the straw's biomass. The massive residues end up as waste—toxic waste. Since most of the pulping mills for rice straw are small and difficult to control, the government has decided to close all mills that do not reach a minimum volume of 6,000 tons per annum. At a later stage, the minimum size of mill will be increased to 11,000 tons.[63]

Experts advise that this is the minimum size to guarantee the economic feasibility of cleaner production technologies involving alkali sulphates, which then permit the recovery of most of the chemicals. However, the yield of 13% cannot be greatly increased because of the harshness of the chemicals used on the straw. The forced closure of the small mills eliminates the biggest polluters, while the introduction of new technologies secures the reduction of waste and the recovery of the chemicals for re-use. In line with the practice of the European and North American pulp mills, the residual contaminated biomass—black liquor—is incinerated and provides energy and steam needed in the processing of pulp.

In view of the poor yields and the pollution generated, the best advice based on standard practice in the industrialised world is to shift from straw to wood, preferably fast-growing softwoods, as a source of cellulose. Since the cellulose yield increases to some 90% of the 30% fibres available in the biomass (or 27% of the biomass up from only 5.5% in the case of straw), it is deemed more efficient, since less material is needed for more output.

---

63. Data presented by Ye Ruqin, Deputy Administrator of the Chinese National Environmental Protection Agency (NEPA), at the Ministerial Conference on Environment and Development in Asia and the Pacific, Bangkok, 22–28 November 1995 (organised by the Economic and Social Commission for Asia and the Pacific [ESCAP]).

Other experts have advised the Chinese government on how to introduce sustainable forestry management: drastically reducing or eliminating the use of chemicals, and utilising selective harvesting practices to reduce the risks of soil erosion. The best practice known in the world is being offered to the Chinese. Is it enough?

The production of pulp and paper in China is shifting from an inefficient and highly polluting process, with thousands of uncontrollable manufacturing units, towards cleaner production technologies introduced in large operations where the volume of input materials are reduced, water is effectively recycled and waste materials are converted into energy sources, which reduces the need for coal-burning furnaces generating electricity and contributing towards global warming. This trend is to be supported. It has the support of the central government, and attracts foreign investments and international financing. The problem is not exclusive to China. India, for one, can tackle its demand for paper in a similarly innovative fashion.

The Zero Emissions Approach to Paper in China

The Zero Emissions concept, building on the awareness of the opportunities to improve processes and recycle materials, proposes an integrated approach. The increased demand for paper is strong and continuous, due to the increasingly better literacy rates, as well as the emergence of the middle class in China, which will aspire to consume more newsprint and packaging. Therefore, a sustainable solution will first study all the possible options for a permanent supply of cellulose without disrupting the present and future demand streams, as well as maintaining the balance of nature. In addition, a country such as China, with limited space and tight water supply, does not possess the millions of hectares of land available for reforestation and sustainable forestry. In the short and medium term, traditional hard- and softwood resources in China will not be able to respond to demand. With 1.4 billion inhabitants, China needs to examine alternative sources of pulp. If the increasing demand is simply imported, the world market price for all grades of paper is likely to spiral uncontrollably upwards.

The two major sources that are not efficiently exploited are, firstly, rice straw and, secondly, bamboo. Straw and bamboo are the most efficient fixers of carbon, converting it through photosynthesis into cellulose, hemicellulose and lignin. Thus, while discarding straw and substituting it with wood is an option, better solutions are available. The strategy of converting the pulping source to wood and introducing a closed-loop system secures the elimination of waste from the straw-pulping process, but it does not offer a long-term solution. The production system may be cleaner, but it

Problems to be addressed	Solution	
	Cleaner production approach	Zero Emissions approach
1. Productivity	Target higher yields	Target complete use
2. Low yield of fibres	Replace straw with wood	Change technology Continue to use straw
3. Increased demand	Start sustainable forestry	Use available biomass such as straw and bamboo
4. Small-scale mills	Forced closure of small unit	Eliminate alkali sulphates Sustain small unit
5. Residual biomass	Incinerate, use as fuel	Change technology Re-use as value-added input
6. Toxic chemicals	Re-use chemicals, target closed-loop system	Eliminate chemicals
7. Water use	Reduce, re-use and recycle	3R, and make residues available to other industries
8. Cost and investment	Reduce cost up to a point	Create new profit centres
9. Number of harvests	Once every seven years	At least once per year

Table 8: *Comparison of Cleaner Production and Zero Emissions in the Case of Pulp Mills in China*
Source: ZERI Foundation, Geneva

leaves the straw unused: a massive waste-stream left to rot in the field or be incinerated (Table 8).

If the extraction of cellulose from straw is inefficient today, it is necessary to find another technology to make it more efficient, both in terms of the process and the product. If new technologies for the separation of the materials are considered, and if we take into account the upstream problems of the supply of fibres and the search for some value-added usage for discarded straw, then we conclude that alternative extraction technologies could be the way ahead. A combination of steam explosion and membrane filtration technologies offer an excellent alternative to the alkali sulphates, which are the standard on the market for pulping.[64] In addition,

---

64. 'Steam explosion' is a technique whereby wood is placed in a sealed vessel and heated to high temperatures under conditions of very high pressure. The wood becomes 'soft', as the bonds between the lignin and the cellulose start to loosen. When the high pressure is released, atmospheric pressure causes the contents to 'explode' and become physically well separated. 'Membrane filtration' is a process where a membrane of fine fibres is used to trap fibres over a specific molecular size, while allowing smaller fibres to pass through.

these new extraction technologies do not require harsh chemicals, and so do not need special processes to be designed to recover them. In fact, the demand for the recycling of toxic chemicals and the need to engineer complex closed-loop systems has been eliminated altogether!

The steam explosion and membrane filtration option increases the yield of cellulose from 13% to 83%, a sixfold increase. Rice straw is abundant and fast-growing; it is harvested a minimum of once per year and in some regions twice. Even fast-growing softwoods require seven years of growth before they are ready for harvesting. Rice straw offers revenue to the farmer in the form of rice, and a second revenue for the yield of fibres. There is no question about the economic viability, when the technologies are changed. While many rice variations have been genetically engineered to reduce the amount of straw, the technological breakthroughs described here will require the reintroduction of traditional rice varieties with extremely long straw.[65] The yield from this process is not limited to cellulose: other biomass components, such as lignin, can also be obtained in their active form, ready for re-use in related industries, as described above. Finally, the use of fibres from straw for paper will contribute to the creation of a carbon sink, urgently needed to control global warming.

The application of the Zero Emissions concept is not only valid for countries such as China and Indonesia, facing an explosive demand for paper. The same principles apply in Latin America where plantations of pine and eucalyptus trees are being grown, discarding the value of fast-growing fibre producers such as bamboo—particularly guadua, a species found in Colombia.

Bamboo as an Option

Bamboo is another renewable feedstock for cellulose. It is an extremely fast-growing biomass and generates a high quality of long fibre of such strength and performance that it even reinforces cement—as a substitute for asbestos—in the cement board produced by the Japanese company Chichibu Onoda Cement. Bamboo is stronger than steel; it is also an excellent source for paper, as has been demonstrated in India, Indonesia and China. Even when chemical krafting—separating the cellulose by burning other components away—is used, a process originally designed for hardwoods and not for bamboo, the quality pulp can be used for grade paper.

---

65. The reason for the genetic engineering of dwarf rice varieties was not to increase yields, but to reduce problems with the disposal of the straw! Another case of the *Homo non sapiens*. Rice straw was once used in the making of paper but, because of the huge paper mill closure programme, farmers were left with excess straw. This has routinely been incinerated, contributing further to China's chronic smog problems. The long straw therefore became a problem to be combated and, as no use was found, the genetic engineering option was taken.

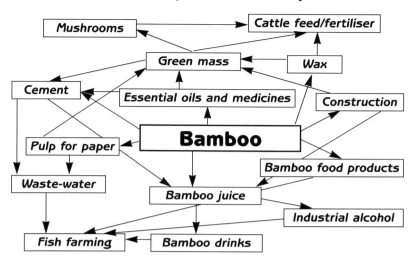

Figure 3: *The Cluster of Industries Around Bamboo*
Source: ZERI Foundation, Geneva

Applying the same steam explosion separation technologies as for rice straw—though adjusted in pressure and temperature—allows not only the fibres to be recovered, but also other components to be re-used. The hemicellulose can be converted into non-protein-based sweeteners. The lignin can either be used as a clean fuel, which does not generate O_x, NO_x or volatile organic compounds (VOCs) as the incineration of black liquor does, or it can be used as a binding agent for particle boards made from the fibres that are too short for paper production, thus offering a substitute for formaldehyde-based epoxies. While the incineration of the black liquor from the pulping is a better option than disposal through landfill or water treatments, the economic value generated in the process is very minor. The additional value generated by re-using the components as inputs for other industries is a far more productive option.

The potential of this cluster (Figure 3) is vast and goes beyond even what experts in bamboo involved in studies expected.[66] Prior to its harvest, bamboo, slated to be used for complementing cement or paper, could be tapped for its food which can then be fermented into an alcohol that offers a cleaner

---

66. The cluster around bamboo was presented at the 4th Triennial World Congress on Bamboo, Ubud, Bali, Indonesia, 19–25 June 1995 (unpublished). It has been tested by the University of Santa Rosa in the Departemento Risaralda, Colombia, between 1996 and 1998 under the stewardship of Professor Ramón Darío. Most of the elements of the cluster are now operational in Colombia.

form of energy. The bamboo, dried out and stripped of its food, turns yellow. The separation of the fibre from the other components is feasible when using the appropriate technologies, and the yields of cellulose could be high. What is most attractive is that the residues from the bamboo can provide the basic input for numerous additional industries, seldom identified with bamboo. The Japanese company Cera Rica, which supplies quality hair-wax to sumo wrestlers, has identified numerous previously discarded business opportunities and is actively developing a research and development programme to secure effective implementation.

The largest cement group of Japan, Chichibu Onoda, has embarked on an investment programme in South-East Asia, blending bamboo fibres with cement. Gunung Sewu, in Indonesia, one of the largest pineapple plantations in the world, has also started a plantation for bamboo, to be used for the making of paper. These developments offer some clues in the search for long-term solutions to the problems of how to respond to the increasing demand for pulp in a sustainable manner, while at the same time generating new sources of economic activity. They do much more than just tackle a pollution problem. They UpSize the economy and respond creatively to increasing demand. And they do not require the earth to produce more. These are the types of development we have been waiting for. The first step may be cleaner production, but the final objective is UpSizing.

Chapter 9
The Methodology of UpSizing

The analysis is clear; the science is there; the objectives have been defined: now it is time to dedicate our efforts towards how to do it. A theory has no value unless it can be applied. Even though exceptions make the rule, a commonly applicable methodology will permit the concepts of Zero Emissions and UpSizing to be implemented whenever and wherever: to schools, hospitals, housing and industry.

The objective of the Zero Emissions concept has been defined as follows:

◀   No liquid waste; no gaseous waste; no solid waste.

◀   All inputs are used in production.

◀   When waste occurs, it is used to create value by other industries.

The central mantra of the Zero Emissions concept is **value-added**. Value-added makes the economy tick; value-added secures a sustainable flow of funding; value-added is a precondition for independence and growth—for autocatalytic growth. If the recovery of the by-product or waste material is merely downcycling, elimination or re-use without offering additional value, then it is not part of the Zero Emissions concept. This is where the concept of UpSizing emerges. Many products are merely downgraded, incinerated or left as a soil conditioner. How is it possible to generate business and jobs from environmental preservation and pollution prevention when there is no added value? Politicians claim that taking care of the environment means good business: which business?

The first business is the reduction of costs. We are told again and again that the global environmental industries are booming. But pollution prevention and remediation and the adoption of cleaner technologies are part of the linear paradigm and can never succeed in eliminating pollution altogether. The business of reducing costs can succeed up to a certain point only. The second, far more interesting, business is that of generating additional revenue. That is why I define UpSizing as:

The clustering of industrial activities whereby by-products without value for one are converted into value-adding inputs for another, thus permitting the increased productivity of the overall transformation of capital, labour and raw materials leading to additional products and services for sale, at competitive prices, resulting in the generation of jobs and the abatement, eventually the elimination, of adverse effects on people and the environment.

UpSizing happens immediately when an industry has decided to target zero emissions (see Figure 4). **Zero Emissions is the final objective, UpSizing is the direct and immediate result.**

The objective of the Zero Emissions methodology (ZERI Method) is, first, to find ways of minimising the input needed in the main process, and then of achieving a maximum level of output by targeting a total throughput. As long as industry does not achieve a total throughput, and continues to discharge components of input as waste, it fails to operate at its maximum potential level. This is not a criticism: it is an indication that industrial processes still have great opportunities to improve their overall productivity. Since no industry can reach this goal on its own, in the same way that in nature no tree can take care of its own leaves, a cluster of industries that can perfectly complement each other's needs and facilitate new opportunities is necessary.

In one sector of the economy—agro-industry—zero emissions can be achieved in four-to-five years. The food-processing industries, construction

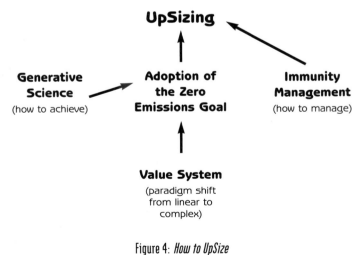

Figure 4: *How to UpSize*
Source: ZERI Foundation, Geneva

materials, forestry products and even chemicals could achieve this target in a very short time-span—perhaps within one decade. Other businesses will need longer. The textile and leather industries could very well meet the strict target within two decades. Some will require three, four or even five decades. Realising the Zero Emissions concept in the production of television sets will be extremely difficult, requiring breakthrough design innovations. Televisions are filled with heavy metals including chromium and lead for which no immediate substitutes exist. The same goes for photocopiers—in particular, colour ones— refrigerators and numerous other complex products and equipment such as cars and computers. The road to Zero Emissions will be long, but the first steps—the steps towards UpSizing—can be taken today. The methodology does not change at all: it applies the same basic approach to any business, home, university, hospital, town, island or country. There are no limits to the application of this methodology.

The Zero Emissions Research Initiative (ZERI), founded and directed by the author at the United Nations University in Tokyo, has worked out a methodology that facilitates envisioning which industries to cluster together, and how to UpSize. The ZERI Method simplifies finding answers to what, at first sight, look like complex issues. It is really a way of unleashing the intelligence widely available in a company, a region or a community, by offering a tool for focusing on a variety of objectives. Eliminating pollution, generating jobs and making economic activities more productive are key objectives all interest groups share.

The methodology has been tested with over 50 industrial sectors (Table 9), with researchers, industrialists, students and government officials on all continents, excluding Antarctica. It has been applied to islands such as Yakushima and Okinawa in Japan, Gotland in Sweden, to cities such as Mompox in Colombia and regions such as Saitama in Japan. Companies such as DuPont, Södra Cell and BP have responded positively to the ideas. All have taken up the challenge to apply the ZERI Method to their region and industries.

The business that has moved fastest from theory to practice is the beer-brewing industry. Less than three years after the first ideas on Zero Emissions and UpSizing were formulated, the first commercial operation was inaugurated in Namibia following the establishment of a test unit in Fiji a year and a half earlier. Projects are now emerging in North America, Japan, Germany, Brazil, Colombia and the Seychelles. As well as some small entrepreneurial microbreweries, some market leaders such as Guinness are also expressing great interest. These are remarkably fast developments for any new idea, which normally take decades to get a foothold—or even a toe-hold—in industry.

◀ Agro-industrial processing	◀ Construction materials	◀ Mushroom cultivation
◀ Alcohol production	◀ Cotton mills	◀ Olive oil mills
◀ Algae processing	◀ Detergents	◀ Paint palm
◀ Animal feed	◀ Energy	◀ Particle board (fibre-board)
◀ Anti-oxidants, vitamins and betacarotene	◀ Engineering services	◀ Pharmaceuticals
◀ Bamboo-related industries	◀ Enzymatic processing	◀ Pineapple
◀ Banking	◀ Fermentation industries	◀ Plantations
◀ Beer brewing	◀ Fish farming	◀ Protein extraction
◀ Cattle farming	◀ Food additives (carrageenan)	◀ Pulp and paper
◀ Cellulose	◀ Fruit processing	◀ Rayon fibres
◀ Cement and cement board	◀ Functional foods	◀ Seaweed
◀ Charcoal	◀ Furfural extraction	◀ Sisal
◀ Chemical (organic and inorganic)	◀ Furniture	◀ Sugar processing
◀ Chicken broilers	◀ Gracilaria	◀ Textiles
◀ Coconut	◀ Investment funds	◀ Tourism
◀ Colofonia	◀ Iodine processing	◀ Vegetable oil mills
◀ Composting	◀ Milk and milk processing	◀ Water hyacinth conversion
		◀ Wood processing

Table 9: *Sectors that Applied the ZERI Methodology between 1994 and 1997*
Source: ZERI Foundation, Geneva

The ZERI Methodology

The ZERI Methodology consists of **five** distinct steps, which are undertaken consecutively:

1. Total throughput models by using the input–output table
2. Creative search for value-added using output–input models
3. Industrial clusters modelling
4. Identification of breakthrough technologies
5. Industrial policy design

The Input-Output Table
The first step using the **input–output** models is based on ISO 14001 or good housekeeping procedures, such as cleaner production, to ensure that

the company has the best possible standards and processes within its particular industry. This procedure is well established and is based on the application of the input–output table. Such a table puts on the vertical axis all the inputs needed in the process. On the horizontal axis, all outputs are enumerated that are left over in the process. The inputs and outputs are quantified, offering easy reference. Table 10 offers an overview of a simplified version of an **input–output** table. The production of beer is basically the blending of water, malted barley and yeast. The output is beer, waste-water and spent grain, including residual yeast, and CO_2 generated by the fermentation process of the sugars.

This simplified version for the case of beer brewing indicates the process of inputs being converted into outputs, and the other waste-streams generated in the process. The first step, prior to searching for a use for the waste materials, is to verify that the existing production system cannot be improved, for example by reducing the consumption of water. Since breweries are massive users of water, and often compete in urban areas for quality drinking water, a more efficient use of water through the re-use of cleansing water for a second run, or the installation of electronic controls, shutting water off when not needed, could cut the amount of water needed to produce the same amount of beer in half. The result is shown in Table 11.

The drive towards increased levels of productivity of input cannot always be achieved. There are certain biological and process limits. The malt input cannot be changed; neither can the output. The taste of beer is the result of a fermentation process of the sugars from the malt. The other components of the malted barley, such as the fibres and the proteins, leave the process as a by-product. If one developed a process that used all the components of the malt, the end result would not be recognisable as beer.

The process of developing an input–output table depends on the existing knowledge of the process engineers. If they are professional, they will be able to document and quantify rapidly the details in the table. This is not a creative process: it is an enumeration of the facts, an unequivocal description of the inputs, a clear rating of the conversion rates and the quantification of the outputs, in solid, liquid or gaseous format. The search for a better use of inputs really falls into the realm of cleaner production processes and technologies. This important first stage is a necessary precursor in the drive towards zero emissions.

The Output–Input Table

The second part of the methodology is unique to Zero Emissions: the output–input table (O/I). This does require a creative approach, and is the basis

UpSizing

I \ O	Beer	H₂O	Spent grain	CO₂
H₂O	10 / 100	80 / 100	10 / 100	
Malt	8 / 100	1 / 100	91 / 100	
Yeast	–	–	–	

Table 10: *Basic Input–Output Table*
Source: ZERI Foundation, Geneva

I \ O	Beer	H₂O	Spent grain	CO₂
H₂O	10 / 50	30 / 50	10 / 50	
Malt	8 / 100	1 / 100	91 / 100	
Yeast	–	–	–	

Table 11: *Cleaner Production Input–Output Table*
Source: ZERI Foundation, Geneva

of the search for value-added in the non-used components. Here, ZERI's experience suggests that it is best to keep the process and production engineers to one side. While their input was critical in the I/O tables, it is best to draw on other, more creative disciplines available in the company to undertake the establishment of the O/I tables. The output–input process requires a multidisciplinary approach, searching for options not previously considered within the business.

In the output–input tables, the vertical axis lists all the outputs that are not part of the final product. The horizontal axis will list a creative inventory of all possible uses for these outputs. Obviously, this process is only valuable when the input–output table has been established, documented and when the company has made all possible efforts to reduce costs and improve the throughput, i.e. do more with less materials.

The outputs that need consideration must be quantified in constructive terms, i.e. detailed information on the spent grain will be necessary to imagine how best it can be reused, or which part is of value to another process. What is the moisture content? (80%); the protein content? (24% on a dry basis); the fibre content? (70% on a dry basis)? When these data are known, there is a chance of imagining a value-added use. If the waste of the brewery is described in the typical 'problem language' of environmental engineers such as BOD (biological oxygen demand), COD (chemical oxygen demand), SSP (solid suspended particles), pH level (acid or alkaline), etc., there is no chance of imagining what could be the optimal use. There is a need to obtain descriptions of the opportunities, and not detailed analyses of the problems. The descriptions of the problems are the realm of the cleaner production studies. The Zero Emissions approach requires a creative input.

A simplified version of the output–input table is illustrated in Table 12.

When a good use has been found for an output: for example, the production of mushrooms on the feedstock of dried spent grain, that process itself will generate waste. Indeed, spores will convert only 25%–50% of the substrate into mushrooms and, after several weeks of growing, there will be waste substrate left over. This must be reintroduced in the vertical axis. Waste compost from the mushrooms is then a new output for which the creative team must find a solution.

The team may decide to use the waste substrate as cattle feed. But cattle will also generate waste. Whereas cattle will convert seven kilos of this waste material into one kilo of meat, the process generates a lot of solid, liquid and gaseous waste in the process. The creative team have another output to utilise. One opportunity would be to recover the solid and liquid waste in a digester which is generating methane gas (CH_4). The gas could then be reintroduced as a source of energy for the brewery and the slurry from the digester—mineralised by up to 60%—could, after further

O I	Cleaning	Fish farm	Algae	Irrigation	Mush-rooms	Earth-worms	*Total*
H_2O	10 100	72 100	10 100	8 100	0 100	0 100	100% 100%
Fibres Protein	0 100	6 100	0 100	0 100	40 100	54 100	100% 100%
. . .							
Waste compost from mush-rooms						50 100	
Chickens							
Manure							

Table 12: *Output–Input Table Targeting Zero Emissions*
Source: ZERI Foundation, Geneva

aerobic treatment (increasing the mineralisation to 90%), be directly used as fish feed.

Each time waste is generated, it is once more reintroduced onto the vertical access. This continuous set of feedback loops allows the system to search for an ever-more efficient cluster of complementary activities. When all outputs have found a way of being used as an input for other processes or industries, then the industry under examination has attained the target of zero emissions.

In the end, zero emissions is not only achieved separately within each business, but is also realised for a cluster of industries which share—to a major or minor degree—elements of the material, gas, liquid or energy cycle. In the same way as the ecosystem around the tree deals with food and waste, it is possible to imagine the re-use of all waste to achieve the zero emissions target. The result is a major improvement in efficiency— on the condition that the outputs that became inputs do not have to be transported great distances.

A creative team will never come up with only one solution for one output. ZERI's experience demonstrates that several working groups studying the same industry will often identify the most diverse options. Thus, there is a need to select the best of the innovative solutions offered and offer convincing arguments—not only to the process engineers, but also to the financial directors—as to why mushroom farming or earthworm cultivation on site makes sense.

On the basis of the ideas obtained in the exercise to establish the output–input table, the team will have to prioritise which activities to take up. The selection criteria proposed in the ZERI Methodology are the following:

1. Determine and evaluate a market for the value-added products.

2. Establish the energy requirements.

3. Determine the capital investments.

4. Review the land space needs.

5. Calculate the job creation opportunities.

The argumentation will have to be primarily financial: how much additional value-added can be generated? On the basis of the sale price of the product generated, in relation to the cost of disposal of the original material, several areas can be prioritised. When one ton of spent grain is sold for US$20 as a cattle feed, it hardly covers the cost of transportation. However, when you consider that one ton of spent grain will cost in Japan about US$100 to landfill, then the economic case for selling the grain is clear. It is also clear that there is a strong economic case for finding ways of re-using the grain and add value. If breweries consider that one ton of spent grain can generate 250 kilos of shiitake mushrooms, and these can be sold for US$4 per kilo to a wholesaler, catapulting revenues to US$1,000 per ton of spent grain, they will conclude that such opportunities exist. The spent grain is no longer an expensive waste to dispose of but a valuable new raw material.

The advantage in the case of mushroom farming is that the mushrooms do not require major additional energy inputs—though the energy needs must be quantified, since these could entail hidden costs that change the logic of the operation. The liquefaction of CO_2 in the beer fermentation process, for example, is an interesting idea for recovering this greenhouse gas and considering it for eventual resale to producers of carbonated drinks. But the energy involved is often too high to justify the investment.

So, how much additional capital investment is needed to obtain the proposed additional revenues? If the spent grain is used for the farming of mushrooms, it still needs treatment before drying. The wet spent grain is not a suitable substrate for the mushrooms and requires a moisture content much below the 80% that it holds when it is released from the brewing process. So, to realise the figure of US$1,000 per ton, one must decide to invest in a drying tower. Several breweries have done this already, since the transportation of spent grain for final disposal in landfill or resale often requires that it only has a moisture content of only 15%–20%. Then, there must be an investment in mushroom bins. The mushroom cultures need maintenance, and the preparations require clean laboratories. Fortunately, most breweries also have these facilities as they need to keep their yeast in excellent condition.

These first four elements—the current cost of disposal; the revenue likely to be realised from the new product; the capital outlay necessary; and the expected profit and payback period—help establish a basis for a cashflow analysis and an investment decision. In the end, each decision to reserve a waste-stream as an input for another value-adding process requires a stand-alone logic. Even when the system is well integrated and highly efficient, there cannot be any form of cross-subsidisation. All processes should depend on their own financial reasoning.

However, it is becoming clear that the financial reasoning does make sense. The application of the Zero Emissions methodology can change the concept of cashflow and reintroduce opportunities for cost savings. The cashflow of beer brewing requires money. There is not a single client, supermarket chain, pub or hotel that is paying cash on delivery for its beer. This means that the brewer must wait for up to a couple months before the money is received. If it needs to wait one month, that means the brewery needs one twelfth of its annual turnover in cash to finance the operations.

But now a new type of business is introduced: mushroom farming. This business has a very different cash cycle. The raw materials are basically free, and do not require money in advance as they have already been paid for in order to get the brewing process going. The capital investment is limited, and the harvest is continuous. Since one ton of spent grain could generate 250 kilos of shiitake, it means that a brewery is generating a cash revenue each day. Mushrooms are sold for cash on the market. The cashflow of the brewery changes, since the revenue stream from the waste is different. When all these elements of each of the new processes have been integrated, the overall cashflow of the industry will change for the better.

Industry has been looking for synergies before. For example, the investment by a forestry company in a pizza parlour was inspired by the fact that one business—forestry—had a long turnaround cycle, whereas pizzas are sold for cash every minute. A corporate strategist looking for a way to generate a better cashflow may therefore make some sense from investing in totally unrelated industries. At first sight, two unrelated industries—brewing and mushroom farming—are joining forces, once more. But the reality is that, from the material cycle point of view, these are not unrelated operations: on the contrary, these are extremely complementary, and the combined cashflow is attractive for both operations. A mushroom farmer would not otherwise have access to free substrate, and the brewery would not have access to such quick cash if it were not that the company could convert a lost material that is becoming expensive to dispose of into a base material generating new value-added.

The logic of the ZERI Methodology is not limited to material cycles and re-use: it is also found in the better use of financial resources, as crystallised in cashflow, probably the most critical indicator of any business.

When all the investment analyses have been made, then comes the acid test: where can this be done? Is there land space available, adjacent or nearby to the facility where the production unit is located?

It is clear that the opportunity is only fully feasible and exploitable when land is in abundance, and readily available. This is the case in most of Africa, Latin America and Asia, but it is not so in urban areas, and not at all in Japan.[67] Therefore, the decision to implement the full or partial concept of Zero Emissions, with a detailed integration of waste as input for other

---

67. Japan does not have the domestic space to take the lead in the first schemes, but are the strongest financial supporters of the ZERI undertaking, so that, when systems do miniaturise, they will be able to implement quickly.

operations, depends on the availability of land. And the need for land will be large. The more waste that is presently discarded, the greater the area needed to convert this into useful products.[68] And the more useful value-added products we produce, the more jobs we will create.

Industrial Clusters Modelling

But, at the moment, many innovative ideas are remaining just that: ideas. The research and analysis teams need to assess the best possible clusters of processing that are to be combined. There is a need to study how these different activities can be integrated into one network, or a series of inter-linked networks.

This throws the challenge back to the process engineers. The exercise of integrating these different operations will lead to the design of a cluster of industries, based on the opportunities to re-use whatever is waste for one as an input for another. A brief look at the output–input tables offers a first indication of what may emerge, but a careful engineering study is required to confirm all the elements. It may be obvious that the alkaline water of the brewery can be used for growing algae, but is this feasible in the design of the brewery, with the land topography and existing regulations?

Search for the Appropriate Scale. The main contribution from the process engineers, assisted by biologists, chemists and physicists, is to find the best size for the unit of operation. At the integrated biosystems brewing pilot unit in Fiji, it was concluded that the ideal unit size is approximately 1.2 hectares per 2,000 hectolitres of output. This integrated system, described in further detail in Chapter 11, has thus achieved its ideal scale of operation. If the production of the main factory is higher—for example, the brewery is to produce 20,000 hectolitres—the unit scale of operation will remain 1.2 hectares, but this will be repeated + 10 times. Again, the parallel with nature offers a compelling comparison. If an oak tree grows to 50 metres, it is a sizeable tree, with fibres solid and strong enough to resist wind, wear and tear. An oak does not grow to 500 metres, even when nature provides sufficient feed in the soil. On the contrary, it provides room for ten trees, each with its own supporting ecosystem. And, since the tree cannot transport itself to the available food, it must secure a food chain

---

68. It is expected that, as experience accumulates, the system of integrating biological processes will miniaturise in the same way as the computer industry has over the last 40 years. This is an enormous new challenge for the process engineers and the biologists, who will have to go back to the drawing board with the inputs and outputs and find a way to make the financial aspects operational

around its roots, trunk, branches and leaves that will satisfy its demands and which includes a series of buffers with sufficient reserves to bridge the gaps in supply.

The industrial clustering is therefore an exercise in quantifying the ideal scale, so that the UpSizing can keep track of the flow of materials without jeopardising the economics and the efficiency of the conversion of one waste into an input for another process.

This requires a major joining of minds by the biologists and the engineers. The engineers are all too often tempted to search for higher economies of scale, whereas the biologists know that nature has many inherent limits. If, for example, a fish farm was designed with a core pond size three metres deep with a surface of 300 square metres, this would remain the ideal size, if proven so. If the supply of minerals and water were sufficient to actually build a pond ten times or even one hundred times larger, then the engineer would be tempted to go beyond charted experience and envisage such a construction. The biologist knows all too well this is not sustainable. A tree does not grow into a 500-metre-high structure simply because it becomes too fragile by doing so. The engineer may argue that human intelligence can supplement for the shortcomings of nature. The engineer will call on pharmacologists to introduce a series of antibiotics to control the illnesses that attack weakened species cultivated in large-scale closed fish farm systems. The engineers may decide to source oxygen from outside to aerate the pond and, with some additional investment in energy, offset the increased levels of eutrophication, the breaking down of organic material at the bottom of the pond, which is consuming oxygen and thus reducing the level of productivity. We would then be back to where we started from: the less-than-optimal operations of fish farms of today.

The ideal route towards UpSizing, generating overall a much larger volume of products and services, depends on the identification of an ideal unit size. Once this has been defined for a specific project in a specific region, it is a matter of duplication. At first, engineers believed that ZERI could only respond to small-scale projects. Nothing could be more wrong. The ZERI Methodology can design systems of tremendous total size by multiplying many small units.

Identification of Breakthrough Technologies
This is the fourth stage of the ZERI Methodology. In the process of engineering the cluster of industries into a system, it can become obvious that a technology is missing. Either the engineers do not have an active knowledge of available or long-abandoned technologies, such as the solid-state fermentation of the juice from bamboo into alcohol, or it is clear that a

new breakthrough technology, as in the case of furfural, is indicated. What is needed is a portfolio of technologies: a technology mix. Some technologies will be vast, others hardly visible, but all should search for the best options within the local biodiversity. The integration of numerous production systems may very well require changes in process and product technologies. For example, prior to ZERI's proposal to grow mushrooms on spent grain, no one believed it was possible, since it was not done. There was a need to establish the right conditions for growing the mushrooms, since the core element was available: the abundance of fibres. After only six months of research, the conclusions of both the Chinese University in Hong Kong and the University of Kyoto were convinced that not only was it feasible, it was operationally sound.[69] Whenever there is a technology lacking, this is not a reason for giving up, but a way of prioritising the follow-up research and guaranteeing an ongoing process of improvement towards achieving zero emissions.

Industrial Policy Design

The final step in the methodology is to summarise the approach, findings and proposals into a document that can be submitted to governments. The application of the logic emanating from the ZERI Methodology sometimes does not fit within the existing legal or cultural system. For example, there are few countries in the world that permit the setting-up of agricultural activities in industrial zoning. While beer brewing is located in an industrial zone, the material analysis cycle using the ZERI Methodology proposes to undertake agricultural initiatives next to industrial processing. The same situation applies to the neutralisation of the pH. Most countries specify that the water discharged should be pH-neutral. If, however, the alkalinity can be exploited for the cultivation of specific algae for use by other industries, it should not be a requirement to treat the water with acid chemicals first to make it neutral. This is only boosting the chemicals industry, no one else. If space is available, it should be done on-site, in an effort to avoid unnecessary transportation. The economics are obvious, but the law may be obstructive. So, when officials are informed of how the companies came to the conclusion that these economic activities should be clustered into one site, to reduce costs and pollution, there has to be a more flexible approach. Industry had been requested to isolate itself from society because it is so polluting. If it converts to a Zero Emissions approach, why should that isolation continue?

---

69. The conclusions of the research are taken up in Mshigeni *et al.* (eds.), *New Hope for Sustainable Development in Africa.*

With government behind it, the ZERI Method can enlarge its areas of application: for instance, in the design of eco-industrial parks such as the one proposed for the textile industry in Bandung, Indonesia,[70] and the application of due diligence based on the ZERI concept.

Planning for the building of infrastructure and the subsequent attraction of investments in an industrial park is a long-term investment by local and regional governments in an effort to secure economic development, the generation of jobs and tax revenues. In the past, this was a rather haphazard process. It was clear that, if no basic infrastructure in terms of water, transportation, access roads, energy and waste management was provided, no company would even consider investing. The question with regard to a ZERI industrial park is rather different: which industries to attract? Which industries can provide the infrastructure for the park?

If regional governments applied the ZERI Methodology to candidate investors, it would be relatively straightforward to identify industries which will serve as the engines of growth. As has been demonstrated, the processing of barley into beer is not only a productive industry in its own right, it provides a strong foundation for several other industries. These may or not be on the priority list, but they can be developed with minimal effort. Much as governments at both a national and local level have strived to attract car assembly plants because they would generate numerous jobs and additional investments of suppliers relocating or being established to supply the plant in accordance with the principles of JIT, so a similar approach would work with the ZERI Methodology.

If a company is a main processor of a raw material, but is discharging massive amounts of waste and by-products, the ZERI Method will permit the local authorities to study how these outputs could be re-used in other industries. The palm oil mill is a concrete case. As the analysis in Chapter 6 has confirmed, the processing of palm oil is not the only attractive business opportunity for a (partially) newly planted area such as Kalimantan in Indonesia: it is possible to visualise a cluster of at least ten different industries all centred around the plantation.

The ZERI Due Diligence

But, while governments can undertake this study to search for investors, investment groups can also apply the same logic to find good investment

---

70. The proposal is discussed by Arifin Panigoro, 'City Redevelopment: The Case of Textile Industries in Bandung', in *Proceedings of the 3rd World Congress on Zero Emissions*.

opportunities. Why is an investor prepared to buy stock at a high price? Because there is a hidden value no one has identified before. Investors will always ask for a due diligence report to be produced prior to any acquisition. This investigation studies the financial results, the technology assets, the tax situation as well as potential environmental liabilities, and it is a critical part of the decision-making process with regard to acquiring or expanding businesses. Without it, no change in the control of companies would ever happen; no capital gains would be made; no new activities would be started up. However, while due diligence is an important concept and practice, it only describes the situation today, and aims to confirm the facts. It does not offer a vision of the opportunities for the future.

The Zero Emissions concept, introduced by the author as a core element in the development of competitive corporate strategies, argues that nothing should be considered waste. All should be used in the process of manufacturing and whatever cannot be integrated into the throughput should be used as an input for other industries. The concept of waste is eliminated. The successful application of this concept, based on systems theory and complemented with a practical methodology of the output–input tables, supported by a network of scholars and researchers, is now applicable to many industries. A new element in the reporting of due diligence is necessary: ZERI Due Diligence.

When an investor looks at a business, he or she wishes to generate capital growth, either through the combination of existing investments or through the sell-off of parts of the business. While many methods are being used to assess the business's value, no one is undertaking a due diligence of the raw materials cycles to envision further opportunities. Any processing industry that is only exploiting a fraction of its materials is therefore bound to find previously unidentified chances for the generation of additional value-added. The Zero Emissions team has successfully applied its due diligence based on the material cycle to industries around the world. Some examples:

◀ The management of a Japanese cement group quoted on the Tokyo Stock Exchange wanted to increase the performance of its cement board, a high-growth construction material. Scientific research confirmed[71] that the blending of cement with long vegetable fibres would enhance the product life-cycle. Before the investment in the process was made, a ZERI Due Diligence was performed. The ZERI Due Diligence confirmed that bamboo would be an outstanding and cheap

---

71. Reported by M. Taniguchi, Senior Managing Director of Chichibu Onada Cement, in 'The Clustering of Industries towards a Sustainable Industrial System', in *Proceedings of the 3rd World Congress on Zero Emissions*.

raw material. In addition, the ZERI Due Diligence found several further value-added uses for the by-products. First, the juice could be fermented into alcohol, providing part of the energy needs of the cement factory. The cement company had originally filed for a permit to 'dump the juice'. Second, the protein residues from the washing process could be recovered and used in fish farming. As a result, a research programme was established, focusing on high value-added components from the bamboo which could be commercialised over time. The ZERI Due Diligence also revealed that the cement factory, on balance, reduces its carbon emissions, mainly thanks to the capturing of carbon locked up in the bamboo fibres, which have a life of 40 years.

◀ The board of directors of a Malaysian palm oil plantation quoted on the London Stock Exchange wished to expand operations to Indonesia. Prior to the investment, it was decided to undertake the ZERI Due Diligence. This demonstrated that the palm plantations are actually not just producers of palm oil but major production units for vitamin E: a by-product of the primary process which today is not extracted. In addition, the opportunity to produce furfural was identified in the waste, a by-product that commands a price higher than that of palm oil on the market and is used in the food and paint industry.

◀ A fresh vegetable trader and juice producer in Sweden was considered for a takeover bid. The investors studied in detail all data available and decided to undertake a ZERI Due Diligence. To their surprise, the ZERI Due Diligence report concluded that the waste discarded by the factory offers them materials free of charge which the pharmaceutical, the cosmetics and the food additives industries need. A review of the technologies needed revealed that the turnover of the juice producer could be doubled within one year, without needing to produce any additional juice. At the same time, new markets could be entered at a competitive level since the core materials—which others have to buy—are available free.

The ZERI Due Diligence is a pragmatic tool. It identifies capital growth opportunities by designing a cluster of industries, combining different businesses which are closely interlinked on the basis of their material needs and cycles. It provides perspectives for growth, profits and jobs—by identifying tremendous opportunities for the production of a wide range of value-added products—while dramatically improving environmental performance—reducing or eliminating waste to landfill and emissions from incineration while creating sustainable products—without incurring additional costs. It is a win–win–win option that has still to be recognised.

Asset Stripping versus Asset Building

The ZERI Due Diligence is a tool for the generation of new business. The analysis offers the data needed to UpSize the business by identifying new assets that can be tapped. Under the ZERI approach, the corporate raiders analysing companies for their hidden assets can become much more positive instruments of change. Instead of stripping and tearing companies apart in the search for more profits, corporate raiders will identify unique opportunities to increase their productivity by re-using materials for a variety of processing and extraction generating additional revenues on the condition that these operations are clustered together. The corporate raiders, backed by investment bankers, can then UpSize—not downsize—companies, undertake additional investments in order to extract more value, target a substantial capital growth and reap the financial benefits from the dramatic rise in resource productivity and elimination of pollution—while generating more jobs. Can we envisage a day when trade unions will not despise, but come to welcome the attentions of the corporate raider?

Conclusion

The application of the ZERI Methodology has only just begun; many more applications will emerge over time. Environmentalists see it as a tool for dramatically reducing pollution; management uses it to increase its competitiveness; investors view it as a tool for making substantial capital gains on hidden assets—making use of the methodology to identify undervalued companies that are worth taking over. Governments utilise the methodology to identify engines of growth in their region, for which a special package of incentives can be designed. And scientists turn to the ZERI Methodology because it offers a unique system to integrate various disciplines which all have a common interest in building a sustainable future, but which hitherto have found few connections to undertake a common programme.

The output–input tables offer a unique opportunity to take the reality of an industrial plant and turn it into a creative basis for the future. The key question now is: how do we manage this?

Chapter 10
Immune Management Systems

The impact of technology on society has been widely debated. Any time new production systems have been introduced, they have affected life, society and industry—sometimes for the better, sometimes for the worse. Technology has created violent resistance, or has been invited with open arms; it has created winners, and left losers; breakthrough technologies never go unnoticed or undebated. The introduction of the objective of Zero Emissions based on Generative Science and the concept of UpSizing will be no different.

Throughout history, technologies have changed society. The invention of the clock and the windmill impacted the early years of the millennium; the invention of the printing press was as important to the Renaissance as the design of the first computer chip is to the modern technological revolution. Today, on the verge of the third millennium, no industry has a more pervasive influence on society than information technology. Computers, numerically controlled systems, telecommunications and their integration into miniaturised smart systems have a profound impact. They have changed job patterns, affected the competitiveness of nations, created trade wars, facilitated massive research programmes, even changed the way children play. And we have only seen the beginning of that revolution. The home computer and the advent of the Internet have taken us into a new dimension.

New and innovative research programmes such as the Zero Emissions Research Initiative, first at the United Nations University and now throughout the world, have linked up researchers over the Internet, to draw on their expertise and design multidisciplinary solutions in order to convert process outputs into new value-adding inputs. The progress made in this research initiative would never have been possible without access to advanced computer and communication technologies. Just as old telephone switches would make it impossible for hundreds of millions of people to place a call around the world, undertaking breakthrough research by creating new virtual laboratories where thousands of PhDs gather would not be possible without the Internet. It would be prohibitively expensive today to recreate new 'superlabs' such as CERN (Centre de Recherche Nucléaire) in Switzerland or Oak Ridge National Laboratories in the USA. Governments do not have the funds available, nor the political courage and leadership to decide on bold new ideas.

The networking of thousands of scholars and the involvement of tens of centres of excellence in a decentralised and autonomous fashion used to be an insurmountable challenge from a communication and co-ordination point of view. Today, organising over 100 dedicated electronic conferences in parallel, on highly specialised issues—all part of an integrated approach to innovative industrial design, based on text, graphics and even video—is almost as convenient as switching on a television set and searching for the channel with the evening news. Who has to read the manual to switch the TV on and off? Who still needs guidance to hold an Internet-based video conference? Soon we all be empowered to do exactly that.

The Inspiration for the Future

There are many questions about the future. Where is the micro-electronics revolution leading to? How will this affect society? What will the computer networks of the next millennium look like? How will these new computer, information and communication systems affect management? What new type of management will emerge? Will this create new industries? What type of government will prevail? What sense does it make for the concepts of Zero Emissions and UpSizing?

This chapter does not pretend to offer a comprehensive answer to every question. It is only looking for a basis of inspiration: what will be the best management and organisational model to emulate? We do know that installed computer networks will force fundamental changes in the much-heralded management techniques taught by the world's leading business schools such as Harvard and INSEAD. It is clear that today's bureaucratic systems of government, designed at a time when the computer did not even exist, will have to adapt to this new environment. So, let us first study the future of the computer and information networks and find a base of inspiration to understand what the ultimate network will be. Three words will dominate: **empowerment**, **autonomy** and **decentralisation**.

At present, there is a major debate among the technology leaders of the information industries. On one side, Larry Ellison, the chairman and CEO of Oracle, inspired by Steven Jobs, one of the founders of Apple, clearly opts for the network computer (NC), which links the user to network servers.

He has a computer in mind that assumes the existence of networks and foresees the massive improvement in the speed at which telephone and cable companies can connect to transmit data and the images. His NC requires network servers, which can be provided by industry leaders such as Sun Microsystems or Silicon Graphics. His set-up requires easy-to-use browsers which guide you to the software and the information that suit your needs, as offered by Netscape and designed by Yahoo.

On the other hand, Bill Gates, president and co-founder of Microsoft, calls this 'a dumb terminal'.[72] He believes in the future of the powerful multimedia personal computer (PC). But that option is more expensive and requires extensive training. The manuals run to volumes for each software package for a multimedia PC, whereas the NC, according to Mr Ellison, will need no more than eight pages of reading to get started. Both industry leaders have their own interests to defend: Oracle wishes to sell database network software, and Microsoft aims to flood the market with more multimedia software.

When the personal computer arrived on the market, computer professionals working with the mainframe systems hardly had one word of encouragement for this under-performing machine. It was considered to be no more than just a toy. Such reactions now sound as arrogant as those of the American and European car-makers when observing the new arrival of Japanese cars on their territory in the early 1960s. General Motors and Volkswagen certainly changed their minds. Within 20 years, this 'cheap imitation' of their quality products became a formidable competitor. It is not the first time the market leaders have had to learn the hard way.

The early personal computer was cheap and functional, and responded to a need on the market. The Atari computer cost only US$500 and sold very well. The Tandy TRS 80, the Apple II and the first Mac computers certainly did not match the power and the speed of the IBM, NCR, Wang and Digital mainframe computers, but responded to demand at an affordable price. Could it now be the case that Microsoft, which was so critical to the genesis of the PC, is now starting to behave exactly like the mainframe computer executives of only 15 years ago, and the car barons 30 years ago?

The Brain and the Genes

Some inspiration for the future direction of this critical debate can be found elsewhere: in the medical sciences. A comparison of the central nervous

---

72. 'The Vision of a Heretic', *The Financial Times*, 4 March 1996, p. 16.

system and the role of the brain with the immune system and our genes may well offer new insights into the question of which computer systems will prevail in the end. But, perhaps more importantly, this comparison can offer concrete ideas on which type of management can succeed in the twenty-first century—and on which type is needed to make Zero Emissions and UpSizing happen. As we will see, it will be as revolutionary as the invention of electricity and the telephone. It will result in a full paradigm shift for management theory.

Central Management

Top management is placed at the centre of all business operations. Any corporation explaining how it is structured will put forward an 'organigram' with the chairman and the president at the top, reporting to the board of directors. The chairman or president is equated with the brain of the business. Tremendous expectations weigh on the shoulders of the leader. Linear, vertical and hierarchical structures dominate management thinking, and this approach has resulted in huge headquarters operations, numerous staff functions and co-ordinating committees, each overseeing the vast matrix of information flows and decision-making processes.

The management information system is geared towards reporting upwards and giving instructions downwards, so that decisions made on the basis of input from below can be implemented. Of course, concepts such as quality circles, empowerment and putting people first have called the management's attention to the importance of its employees but, in the end, the top-down approach has prevailed. Certainly, notions such as downsizing, concentration on the core business and re-engineering did not originate from the workers.

This centralised approach has created a lot of bureaucracy and depends on an information powerhouse—the mainframe or supercomputer—capable of processing millions of computations per second. The large mainframes and supercomputers are predominantly sold to and installed in large corporate headquarters and it is in this high end of the market that multimedia will thrive. Here, enough money is still generated to justify the investment in stand-alone multimedia computers. The central system decides what information is to be provided, when and in which format; it permits cutting across management layers, reporting through matrices and getting the job done. It has proven that it worked well in the past, and therefore it will be used in the future.

But the question should not be 'does it work?'—we know that it does. The key question should be: 'is there better?'. Competition in a free-market system is not about doing as well as your competitor: success is determined by doing better!

Mainframes and Brains

The concept of the set-up and management of a mainframe computer is very similar to that of the central nervous system. The brain and the brain cells at the centre are supported by tentacles of information lines, or nerves, which feed the central processing unit. Information is sent up, decisions are sent down. It is fast, unique and smart. The Fifth Generation Computer project, which the Japanese government funded between 1980 and 1989, had the clear objective of emulating the brain and functioning as if it were a human. It was a dream that could never come true. It required billions of research dollars, but it produced few concrete results. The Japanese computer industry prefers not to talk about it too much anymore. Not only did the Fifth Generation Computer project fall short of its objectives, worse, it failed to understand that a computer cannot emulate life.

It also overlooked the fact that the most efficient system of the human body is actually not the brain, but the immune system. If computers are to be inspired by what the human body does best, it is the immune system that should be emulated. When management needs to respond rapidly and effectively to changes in the market—taking into account historic facts, present challenges, future directions and long-term vision—the immune system provides the best model.

There is no question that much of the brain's functions and capacity is still to be discovered. But we already know that it has numerous limitations, especially compared to the immune system: its memory capacity is small and its system for data recovery is limited. A human brain can only remember parts of a person's lifetime: it does not carry the data gathered by previous generations. Who can clearly remember what they did in the first ten years of their life? And, when age advances, memory begins to fail. On the other hand—and this is something we don't fully understand—the brain has the capacity to dream and to imagine the future.

The Immune System

The distributed memory that is found in networks of human cells, full of genetic codes, offers us a superior concept. The immune system can relate to experiences from thousands of years past;[73] the cells' genetic code

---

73. Capra, *The Web of Life*.

represents an incredible network of memory. It is unparalleled. It is autonomous and highly decentralised, and each cell has a mirror version of that great historical memory: it recognises a specific virus, even if that species has not been encountered for ten generations. It processes information and compares some five billion different microbes to which we are exposed, and scans the millions that enter our body every minute when we inhale. Every minute. It considers specific bacteria as intruders, unwelcome guests to be disposed of—and treats others as allies. As soon as an intruder has been diagnosed, it will trigger the production and unleashing of antibodies. The immune system is intelligent, capable of deciding on its own: the more cells that perceive there is a potential hazard, the more antibodies are produced.

The immune system is proactive. It not only has a massive amount of information stored in the cells (the system has largely shaped the human being in the form and with the tools observed today), but, better, it provides input to the next generation on how to adapt to changing conditions. For example, because we do not need the same sense of smell as a dog, our olfactory systems are relatively underdeveloped. On the other hand, because we are adept with our hands, we have fine and delicate fingers. The brain and the mind can imagine, but it is the cells that can produce changes in the body. To paraphrase Marshall McLuhan: the tools the brain invents are always extensions of our muscles.

The immune system lives on after an individual human life. The human brain does not generate any new cells after an early age, estimated at between 21 and 25, but the immune system is capable of making thousands of cells in seconds and renews itself constantly. It does not try to preserve each cell: its survival and its strength are based on a permanent self-elimination and replacement system.

It is self-organising, and is the best example we have of highly decentralised management system. The immune system represents a recognition of the axiom that 'the more complex the challenges, the more localised the decision-making should be'.[74] In the immune system, this has been taken to the extreme: no decisions are made centrally, and all power is given to the cells. Nowhere is there a more effective autonomous and decentralised set-up.

For example, when we cut our right hand's middle finger, the immune system in that part of the body will stop the bleeding, heal the wound and regenerate the skin, without ever asking the brain for assistance. The left hand does not even have to know what the right hand went through.

---

74. John Naisbitt, *Megatrends Asia: Eight Asian Megatrends that are Reshaping our World* (New York: Touchstone Books, repr. edn, 1997).

However, while the system is autonomous, its cells are not stand-alone: it functions so effectively because of the networks that link the cells and its servers. The immune system closely co-ordinates its health-maintaining activities with the hormonal system, the glands, which secrete critical compounds such as adrenalin and hormones, and maintains a dynamic and even chaotic harmony with organs such as the liver, kidneys and pancreas—each made up of billions of cells structured in dynamic networks themselves. If we were to design a future computer system based on the immune system, the glands and the organs in the body could be considered the network servers: they would be the management hubs in a flat decentralised organisation, where everyone takes on his or her own area of responsibility.

Detailed experimental studies of cells have made it clear that the metabolism of a living cell combines order and activity in a way that cannot be described by mechanistic science.[75] It involves hundreds of chemical reactions, all taking place simultaneously to transform the cells' nutrients, synthesise its basic structures, and eliminate its waste products. The immune system maintains a continual, complex and highly organised activity based on networks of networks.

Multicast and Messaging

If the cells are structured in networks of networks, then these elements of the immune system have to operate in a coherent fashion. After all, each cell knows its area of responsibility and seems to know why it evolved from the original embryonic cells into muscles, bone marrow or toenails. The cells act energetically in cohesion with other cells, pass on vital information, receive copies of all information and secure that the complex system of networks—the human body—can function safely.

The immune system benefits from massive feedback loops, constantly sharing and receiving information. No one has to decide to share information or define the format; the system knows that its network can only survive when it shares everything that needs to be shared and comes to assistance when needed. Even more interesting is the fact that the cells of the immune system send out messages in multicast (from several to all parts of the network, with a response from all to all), while the brain sends out signals in unicast (from one to those with an antenna).

We can compare this to the multicasting over the Internet (where several can send out graphics and video to everyone, and receive responses from anyone), and television broadcasting (where only one can send a message to all, and a few can share their concerns through dedicated separate lines, the telephone, and provide feedback). The key characteristic

---

75. Capra, *The Web of Life*.

of a autonomous decentralised system is its capacity to operate in multi-cast, from localised groups (such as the cells in charge of the right finger that suffered a cut), and/or to everyone on the network in case of a major viral attack.

The immune system circulates billions of messages and copies of messages all the time to billions of senders and receivers. Our present binary computer systems would never be able to cope with such an avalanche of data transmitted over the Internet. The advantage of the immune system is that its messages are not text-based, but based on patterns. These image-based or object-based messages offer their content in a glimpse, allowing the receiver in the cell to register the overall picture. It can decide not to react, or can act accordingly. With pattern-based communication, one just has to see in order to know. Pattern-based information sends data depicting the object and its inter-relationship to other objects. This is the way the Japanese and the Chinese communicate: each ideogram tells a story. This pattern-recognition system can quickly trigger the production of millions of antibodies in the immune system; can result in the increased production of white blood cells, sugars or acids; and can enable a lower blood pressure to facilitate recovery.

When the communication system is based on patterns, there is no need to convert the information into binary codes. This would be too slow, cumbersome and impractical. If the cells had a text-based communication system, our bodies would falter and fail. This consideration of language offers a vision of the type of computer coding language that needs to be developed. Within the next 20 to 50 years, I believe that a new standard will impose itself: pattern-based, more complex, but so much faster that it will make the present types of computer based on binary codes look like dinosaurs.

Strategic Design of Information Technologies

The strategists designing the computers and telecom networks of the future must find inspiration in the immune system. It can be envisaged that a stand-alone, autonomous, decentralised, smart and visionary computer of the future will operate like a cell. It will be tiny, but will have a great memory capable of accumulating data over years, even decades, operating in a responsible independent fashion, loaded with all the necessary tools to retrieve, receive and circulate information. It will communicate, recognise, ponder and reproduce its core immaterial parts, network with billions of others, get the support of network servers for additional functions which will available to every computer—every cell—all in a matter of split seconds.

Multiple mirror versions will offer ample back-up when one computer or server is incapacitated, or is infected by a virus, and self-destructs in order to preserve the integrity of the whole system. Pattern-based communications will finally allow the breakthroughs in speed and performance that computer scientists have been searching for. We may go back to the days of the Egyptian hieroglyphic writing, or have to reinvent the Chinese characters, depicting a clear image in a few strokes of a pen; or we may just register the picture digitally and study the patterns that emerge from a time-series of images that emerge on our three-dimensional screen.

The time has come for our computer strategists to inspire algorithms on patterns and context-based information, instead of text-based protocols and computer codes that translate moving pictures into binary codes. This is a long and slow process today, even for a supercomputer. The capacity of the human being to accumulate knowledge and make judgements through a text-based system of 26 letters and around 50 characters makes only marginal use of the capacity of the brain. Patterns and pictures, in millions of combinations of colours, can be quickly recognised with sufficient visual input. As the Japanese and Chinese have proven, the brain can learn 20,000 different *kanji* or letter-signs. It gives them a unique eye for detail, and it gives them a chance to read and understand what Westerners do not and cannot possess.

There is room for a strategic initiative to design pattern- and context-based relational databases, instead of today's primitive databases. The first algorithms are on the drawing board. When these pattern- and image-based inter-relational databases are a reality, we can finally enter the era of supercomputing: an era available to all the people, not just the computer scientists with supercomputers. The reality is that the highly promoted Pentium chip cannot handle this task; and the next versions of the powerful chips from Intel, Motorola and AMD designers cannot meet that challenge either. This is not a criticism: the chips were not designed to perform that task. This requires a fundamental breakthrough in chip design, computer language, data compression systems, transmission media and networking infrastructures. And it will require transmission networks that are as flexible and fluid as the systems of peptides through which the cells communicate so effectively with each other in multicast. Pioneers such as Dan Mapes from Cyberlab in California are offering the vision that could well lead to the computer and communication structures that work from the palm of our hand.[76] Visionaries such as Kazuhiko Nishi could translate these new structures into actual businesses;[77] he did it once with the first laptop computer designs—he could very well do it again.

---

76. Personal communication.
77. Bill Gates, *The Road Ahead* (New York: Penguin, 1996).

The End of the Corporate Headquarters

When management applies to itself a vision based on the immune system—decentralised, communicating complex information to all partners simultaneously—it will mean that the heyday of the corporate headquarters is over. Instead, we will massively telecommute, while at the same time we will increase the interface with clients on a personal basis. This idea has been postulated before by such visionaries as Nicholas Negroponte and Seymour Papert,[78] but we can now see it happening. At a time when we are striving to secure total customer satisfaction—zero defections—we have to bring the company, its products and services, even closer to the marketplace. This cannot be done from the corporate headquarters. The centralisation of management functions has alienated the customer. As McDonald's knows, you have to be visible to your clients all the time. There is no future option other than reinventing the workplace, the work structure and the client interface.

Corporate headquarters could be converted into a social meeting place, where staff complement the hi-tech with the much-needed hi-touch. The employees would have far greater independence, self-organising and with a clear sense of responsibility—securing better, more profound interaction from the clients, supported from their home or car by simple network computers. Overheads would be almost completely eliminated; regional hubs would secure global coverage. For present-day management, which will want to hold onto power, such concepts remain scary. For entrepreneurs, already creating new wealth from the business opportunities available through the highly decentralised networks of the Internet, the opposite is true.

Socrates On-Line[79]

If this is the scenario to be expected from the information industries' strategy, if this is what competitive markets are offering as the next challenge, what is the role of top management? It is fundamentally different from what it is today. Management instructs and controls, must give the direction

---

78. Nicholas Negroponte, *Being Digital* (London: Hodder & Stoughton, 1995); Seymour Papert, *Children's Machine: Rethinking School in the Age of the Computer* (Hemel Hempstead, UK: Harvester Wheatsheaf, 1993).
79. 'Socrates On-Line' is a registered trademark of Environmental Dynamics, Inc., based in Chattanooga, Tennessee, offering a platform for dialogue over computer networks.

and facilitate the means to perform. In the new immunity management, it will be requested to stimulate creativity through asking questions, not by giving answers. Since the strength of the system is based on challenges, the first challenges must be posed from within. Socrates, who revolutionised thinking over two millennia ago by asking his pupils questions that guided them to the wisdom and the solutions, is to go on-line. Socrates On-Line will be the guide for cyberspace management; Socrates On-Line will incite people to think before they do something, check the alternatives, become enthusiastic, be ready to create a better quality of life, respond to the needs of others and oneself. There is nothing more stimulating than to be constantly questioned.

As any regular speaker to large audiences knows, creativity ticks when the most unexpected questions come from the floor. And as that wise professor once said, there are no dumb questions, there are only dumb answers. Powerful and centralised computers have led managers to limit themselves to control what others have been given as instructions. What management is really for is to have a vision and inspire their colleagues, and be in touch with what the customers really want.

Socrates was a true leader: the type needed today. A leader is not a charismatic person who has the answers already prepared; a true leader is the individual who may not know at all the issues that are being debated, or the interests at stake, yet succeeds in ensuring that people maintain an open dialogue, and in the end share a common vision and action plan. Of course, this does not mean that charismatic and visionary people will not have any role to play. But what immunity management needs is facilitators.

The TQM (total quality management) revolution in the 1970s and 1980s clearly taught management that, if you want good ideas—many ideas—on how to improve operations on the shop floor, ask those who spend a lifetime there. The same philosophy is now commonly used for good environmental management. While management has recognised this logic when it comes to the technicalities of manufacturing processes, it must now be prepared to adopt the same mindset for the whole enterprise. Business will then shorten its response time to changing needs; it will sense new directions or preferences as soon the trends emerge, so that the marketeers will be able to target the detailed needs of fine segments, and manufacturing systems can adapt product designs to meet those changes in a timely manner.

It cannot be done unless there are innumerable smart and responsive operators everywhere, with the most responsive multiple feedback loops that can be imagined. Everyone in the system should be considered intelligent. Not everyone may have been educated to the same levels, but intelligence will certainly be omnipresent through, for example, networked computers. This would make the free-market system strive towards perfection—because the free market can only thrive with free access to *all* information. It would strengthen democracy, of which free markets are a condition. It would require an operational structure that has eliminated all weaknesses. Competition will exploit each trace of imperfection. There is no better system for fighting possible weaknesses in marketing or production systems than the one inspired by the immune system. And the system will be best prepared if it is constantly challenged. Posing questions will help, merely providing answers will not.

Industrial Clustering

The immune system offers a further inspiration for the way industry will evolve over time—clustering into networks of networks. ZERI argues that industries working on their own can never be converted into systems that use all input factors such as raw materials. Industries have to operate in clusters or in networks if they are to utilise 100% of the input factors. The linear form of production, where the objective is to make only one specific intermediary or finished product, will always lead to waste-streams that have no further use. This book advances the argument that nature does not know the concept of waste, because whatever is of no use to one will be food for someone else. The human species is the only species capable of making things no one wants.

Industry has applied the concept of clustering and networking before when it applied JIT practices. Leading manufacturers requested their suppliers to locate close to the factory, dramatically reducing the inventory of parts, in some cases from three months of stock to just over 30 minutes. The capital unleashed resulted in a considerable improvement of return on investment.

It is no surprise that the JIT system imposed itself as a necessary requirement for survival in the competitive world economy. When interest rates were as high as 16% and even 20% per annum, it was a necessity. Today, interest rates are at an all-time low, but car companies are not relaxing their grip on suppliers. JIT is a precondition for a successful production strategy and a whole new industry—the courier services—which emerged around it. A manufacturer would go out of business today if industries did not cluster around its production units.

The same concept of clustering applies for the full use of all the materials needed in the production process. When a brewery ferments malted barley and hops into beer, it only needs 8% of the biomass; for its purposes, 92% is considered waste. When the producer of coconut oil, a raw material for environmentally responsible detergents, extracts this component, it only uses 5% of the coconut tree's biomass; the remaining 95% is considered waste. If these industries are to reduce the massive amounts of waste burdening them with additional disposal costs and society with the nuisance of smell, incineration and landfills, then a new approach must be introduced. The decentralised networks introduced to eliminate the waste of capital under JIT need to be replicated to eliminate the waste of materials.

ZERI has proved that, by combining some 40 different biochemical processes at a brewery, it is possible to convert the fermentation processes into integrated biosystems whereby everything—including the CO_2, the heat, the solid and the liquid waste—gets re-used. The research and test results for the brewing industry on the basis of the pilot plants in Fiji and Namibia confirm that the integrated biosystem can generate up to seven times more food, fuel and fertiliser than present breweries, and, critically, this system without waste generates more jobs.

The immune system offers confirmation that flora and fauna operate in an incredibly efficient fashion: clusters of billions of cells have found a way to operate in harmony, each producing a variety of products, each taking up inputs from others, each recycling as much as they can in-house, and each only discharging what other cells will absorb. The systems thinking, the networking of complementary operators in an autonomous manner, is therefore our inspiration in nature. The most efficient industries of the future can work on the same premise.

Industrial development through clustering has been proved feasible when operating profits can improve. Industry must now realise that our material cycle cannot continue in the same wasteful manner. With approximately 80 million more human beings added to the planet each year, humankind cannot expect the earth to produce more; it must learn how to do more with what the earth produces. Both nature and the cells indicate how the system works. It is up to industry to be inspired by the vision of immunity management.

Make People Happy

If management and industrial developers have to overhaul the way they look at running business, operating headquarters and manufacturing, what is left for government to do? The discontent of people with established party politics and traditional government is very clear. The mayors of the three largest Japanese cities ran as independent candidates, and won, riding the wave of aversion for party politics. And this phenomenon is not restricted to Japan. In Canada, the governing Conservative party was completely wiped out in the national elections of 1995, while, in the UK, the May 1997 elections resulted in the biggest reversal for a governing party since the Second World War. If government is overhauled on the basis of the immune system, central government will, with a few exceptions, seem quite obsolete. Local governments will be the key engines in reinvigorating regional economies and in responding to people's needs. The cities and the regions, operating as cells on the globe, will best be able to perform these tasks.

It is interesting to note that the best-performing European economies over the past 20 years have been those where regionalisation has been most advanced. The Federal Republic of Germany, with 16 quite independent states, has the strongest economy. The French economy, notorious for its centralised government and dominated by the President, and the British economy, which is only now beginning to re-empower its regions, suffered from a continuous slowdown relative to Germany. The break-away movements of the Basques and the Catalans in Spain unleashed booms in their respective job markets, overshadowing the poor performance of the national economy. The hard-earned economic autonomy of both Catalonia and the Basque country has translated these two regions into the best-performing economies in Europe. Therefore, as Europe can demonstrate, regionalisation—transferring the powers of social and economic development to the level that matches the cultural identity of the people—makes sense.

In regions without a uniform culture, such as the melting pot of America, or the Latinos in South America, people still tend to identify themselves more with their region, city or even village than with the nation-state. Only when the size of the country is as small as Andorra, or when there is a strong outside threat such as in Taiwan, will the national identify prevail. These are the exceptions, not the rule.

How can our systems of central taxation and distribution of monies ever really respond to the needs of local communities? It leads to influence-peddling, lobbying, power games and is prone to corruption. At the local level this is transparent, but at the central level it can be obscured. How can a central government decide on industrial development policies for a nation so diverse that it includes 600 languages, as in the case of India, or on investment strategies in nations such as Brazil or Indonesia? It must lead to the serving of interest groups that pretend they have jobs to lose, and not jobs to create!

After the Second World War, governments attempted to immunise their citizens against poverty, and the concept of the welfare state was born. The state would guarantee that no one would suffer a shortage of food, everyone would have the right to a job, and anyone falling sick would be taken care of. The social security system was meant to extend the concept of immunity to the level of the state. However, worldwide, the belief is growing that it is too costly for the government to provide a total safety net for all elements in society. As a result, the welfare society and its immunity system are slowly being dismantled in a number of countries. Instead of offering a detailed vision of what government could do if inspired by the concept of immunity management, I will restrict myself to recalling the end-goal of government, as described by Gabriel Garcia Marquez in *Fragrance of Guava*:

> 'What kind of government would you like for your country?'
> 'Any government that would make poor people happy.'
> Just imagine![80]

We know all too well that few, if any, governments in recent history have succeeded in making poor people happy. On the contrary, numerous governments seem to succeed in making people unhappy—through corruption, excessive taxation, lack of ethical standards, over-bureaucratisation and, most importantly, a failure to do the job they were elected to do (making poor people happy).

Is it not time to rethink the way business is run and governments are operated so that people can finally be happy? That is exactly what the immune system has been set up to achieve: to let people's bodies live healthily so that their minds can be happy.

---

80. Gabriel Garcia Marquez and Plinio Apuleyo Mendoza, *Fragrance of Guava* (English edn; Faber Caribbean Series; London: Faber & Faber, 1998).

Chapter 11
Early Success Stories
Las Gaviotas in Colombia, Montfort in Fiji, Tsumeb in Namibia, the Water Hyacinth in Africa and Gotland in Sweden

This book has reviewed the ideas, outlined the methodology and the concepts, and alluded to some cases. But where are the facts? An initiative that started only a few years ago would not attract such a following without concrete results to show. This chapter will review **five** cases. These are not the only early success stories, since initial steps have also been taken in countries as diverse as Japan, Indonesia and Brazil, but these five cases—at varying stages of implementation—demonstrate the versatility and the applicability of the concept and the methodology.

Las Gaviotas[81]

The Environmental Research Centre 'Las Gaviotas', established in 1966 and since then directed by Paolo Lugari in Vichada, in the eastern part of Colombia, provides one of the most advanced applications of Generative Science, UpSizing and Zero Emissions anywhere in the world. Whereas Colombia is facing one of the most dramatic social crises in its history, this socio-

---

81. The involvement of the author with Las Gaviotas is personal and dates back to 1984. There is no formal contractual relationship between Las Gaviotas and ZERI, although Paolo Lugari's organisation has proved to be an invaluable test site for ideas. ZERI has provided experts for Paolo Lugari and the author has jointly designed the concepts which have not only been implemented, but greatly refined by the Las Gaviotas team. In 1995, Paolo Lugari was the first to adopt the ZERI concept in an industrial process (the production of colofonia), and is a signatory to the ZERI Business Charter. Today, ZERI supplies enzyme and mushroom technologies to Las Gaviotas.

Las Gaviotas, along with Montfort Boys' Town in Fiji and Tsumeb in Namibia, has been selected as EXPO 2000 projects for the first world exposition of the new millennium in Hannover.

Vichada, Colombia

political environment has provided room for a level of initiative and innovation from which the world can learn. I have visited over 120 countries
in the world and seen many examples of radical thinking put into action
but, having had the opportunity to visit Las Gaviotas in Vichada, Colombia,
on four occasions, there is no doubt in my mind that this is the prime case
of sustainable development on the planet.

Las Gaviotas originally established its reputation with the development
of renewable energies: the use of wind for pumping water and the use of
solar for heating water. But the engineers working at this centre of creativity were operating from the standpoint of practical solutions for the
poor: their projects went from pilot phase to industrial application. Probably the largest application of solar energy for water heating in social housing in the world has been implemented in Bogota without any international
technical assistance or financial aid: it was the result of a joint initiative
by Las Gaviotas and the State Housing and Loan Corporation of Colombia
(Banco Central Hipotecario) with headquarters in Bogota.

The then-president of the Bank, Mario Calderon Rivera, demonstrated
that he not only had a vision of how social housing could really benefit the
poor, he also deliberately included renewable energies in the governmental
financial commitment. The bank funded some of the most ambitious housing

development projects, such as El Tunal and El Salitre, targeting low-income families often just surviving on minimum wages. Over the years that Mario Calderon Rivera headed the programmes, the bank constructed 40,000 apartments equipped with solar water heating. The systems are of high quality and, 15 years after the first solar heaters were installed, they still operate with similar efficiency.

Over the years, Las Gaviotas undertook numerous projects to demonstrate that not only was renewable energy economically feasible but, in many cases, it is the only viable alternative for social and economic development in both rural and urban areas. Paolo Lugari has shown that many of the innovations can be put into action with Colombian know-how, blending the ingenuity of local operators with the creativity of engineers. The introduction of the solar kitchen, operating on a semi-industrial scale with vegetable oil extracted from cotton seed and heated in vacuum tubes, was another landmark development. It offers the opportunity for remote kitchens, whether in a field hospital or a rural hotel, to cook meals twice a day without using wood, coal, turf or diesel, as is usually the case. Las Gaviotas's engineers have also designed an experimental solar refrigerator.

The Self-Sufficient Hospital

The capacity of Las Gaviotas to integrate agendas into sustainable solutions for the developing world was catapulted to the forefront with the construction of a self-sufficient hospital in Vichada, an isolated rural area a day's drive from the capital city of Bogota, or a two-hour flight in a small plane. Paolo Lugari's teams set out to design and build a hospital capable of providing the patients and staff with a facility that produces its own energy, distils its own water, cooks locally grown food, reduces humidity in the surgeon's room, provides natural air-conditioning and provides a special recovery area with hang-mats for indigenous patients who are uncomfortable convalescing in a modern bed with white sheets.

The design is ingenious, the technology simple, the applications practical, and its cost of construction and operation are lower than any other hospital. The rural hospital of Las Gaviotas was quickly recognised as a benchmark building design and selected by a Japanese architectural magazine[82] as one of the ten wonders of architectural world. The word quickly spread and visitors flocked from around the world to Vichada to see for themselves how the integrated design of the laundry room with the surgeon's room and the patient's ward provides a natural system for air-conditioning and reducing humidity.

---

82. *Japan Architectural Digest*, November 1995.

The solar panels on the roof of the hospital demonstrate how easy it is to distil water, and purify and demineralise it, without the need for non-renewable energy sources. The solar energy heats coconut and other vegetable oils in a vacuum tube to a temperature of 180°C, providing sufficient heat to cook meals for everyone, twice a day. And the food is mainly provided by the local vegetable garden. Since the indigenous families will accompany the patient to the hospital, to assist and comfort his or her recovery, the family brings local medicinal herbs and preferred food, which are planted and cultivated nearby. After just a few years of operation—the hospital was opened in 1993—Las Gaviotas can boast a unique herbal garden thanks to the wealth of knowledge provided by the indigenous tribes.

Breakthroughs on a Larger Scale

Paolo Lugari had a vision that went beyond all these marvellous breakthroughs. He believed that at Vichada—a hugely depressed area of Colombia—he had an opportunity to demonstrate that sustainable development was not only feasible, but the only way to secure long-term success. Success, according to Paolo, depends on an integrated approach and the capacity to generate value-added in the process. As will be seen, the merging of agendas, the clustering of activities and the creation of value-added are the critical components of this success story.

Reforestation and Climate Change

The fact that Colombia is logging its primary forest at a rate of 650,000 hectares a year was the starting point for an initiative to reforest Vichada. A country that today is still a large supplier of oxygen to the world is fast destroying is regenerative capacity. Las Gaviotas is committed to the most important reforestation programme ever initiated in Colombia. Reforestation is not only a way of increasing the earth's capacity to fix CO_2, it also responds to the need to recover lost biodiversity. The first agenda item, then, is part of the global challenge to ensure that the earth retains enough forest to address the problem of global warming.

It is a massive challenge to plant trees in Vichada. The soil is acid—very acid—with a pH of 4. The extreme summer conditions—with temperatures in excess of 40°C for months in a row, with a dry soil, and nearly no rainfall for several extended periods—limits the chances for young trees to survive. There is not a wide choice of trees. After a careful analysis by scientists working with Las Gaviotas, it was concluded that the Caribbean Pine (*Pino de Caribe*) would be an excellent—native—tree to plant and grow in the savannah of the Llanos in eastern Colombia. Las Gaviotas started cultivating its own trees and, after the first two years of planting, it was demonstrating that this pine species, aided by mushroom-based compost as a soil conditioner, had the right resistance for these tough climatological circumstances.

By 2000, Las Gaviotas will have planted some 11,000 hectares. Even now, with a plantation of 7,500 hectares, some surprising results and unplanned successes have resulted. The pine trees protect the soil from the harsh sun and the continuous dropping of needles is resulting in the recreation of a rich humus cap. This has improved the pH value of the soil from 4 to 5, and this in turn has facilitated the regeneration of undergrowth and the arrival of many new plants and trees. Biodiversity is being recovered. With a survival rate of 92%, Las Gaviotas has demonstrated that reforestation is feasible—even when first considered impossible. When it became known that the *Pino de Caribe* had been selected for the plantation, many people argued that the region would be covered with only one species, and that Las Gaviotas had introduced monocultures as a standard. It was considered an unecological decision. Nature knew better. According to the last botanical count, some 260 new species are found in this microclimate which cannot be found anywhere else in the savannah. The protection from the heat, the new humus and the slowly improving acidity level of the soil has regenerated biodiversity long lost due to human ignorance. The birds, the bees and the wind carry spores and seeds with them from the tropical forests located some 300 miles to the east, where the Orinoco River marks the beginning of the Amazon jungle. And with all these new plant species come bacteria, insects, birds and even mammals. The indigenous people of the Llanos, the region around Las Gaviotas, are excited, rediscovering many medicinal plants considered lost. Paradise is being rediscovered. Las Gaviotas has created a natural bridge, responding to and exceeding expectations about the preservation and expansion of biodiversity.

Development of Appropriate Technologies

Since the planting season of the pine tree in Vichada is limited to three months a year, Las Gaviotas had to design appropriate technologies. The imported planting equipment with tractors had to be adapted to the terrain, the soil and the speed with which the planters can operate. Faster planting was needed. Because the terrain is dry and has a hard soil, slightly bigger seedlings were used. Today, the team succeeds in planting nearly one tree a second, 24 hours a day, three months a year, recovering some 1,000 hectares of lost land. It is probably one of the fastest planting operations in the world.

Generating Value-Added

The pine tree is resistant to the acidity in the soil and—even better—it is productive. The tree grows to maturity in eight to ten years, and quickly produces some seven grams of colofonia a day. The colofonia can then be processed into gum resin ready for use by industry. This refined product is a prime input in the production of natural paints and glossy quality paper: products in growing demand. Today, Colombia imports 4,000 tons of colofonia a year, mainly from Honduras, Venezuela, Mexico and China, but Las Gaviotas could supply the local market with a local product refined at the premises in Vichada. The market price varies between a low of US$700 per ton (in July 1998) to a high of US$1,300 (in 1995) and, with a production capacity of 50 tons a month, Las Gaviotas has formulated an answer to the challenge of generating value-added, which will sustain the activities of reforestation, biodiversity and technology development in a open-market economy. By 2001, Las Gaviotas will process 20 tons of gum resin a day, thereby more than satisfying Colombian demand.

The search for more value-added brings with it more innovation. The packaging of colofonia used to be complex and heavy. The workers of Las Gaviotas, a team with limited formal education but with a high collective intelligence, took a close look at the packaging alternatives and designed a cardboard box with triple layers and a hole in the middle, allowing easy filling of the folded box with the hot colofonia, fresh from distillation. This innovative packaging saves the handling of colofonia, eliminates the need for cooling and secures a package of just 25 kilos each, which is easy to carry for one person. The cardboard is already recycled. This design turned out to be a major innovation—for which the producer of the board Papel de Colombia (not Las Gaviotas!) received the national prize for innovation in industrial packaging material. The team is delighted that other innovators are now operationalising their breakthroughs.

Compete with Quality

The process of reforestation would not have been completed without an investment in the production of colofonia, made possible through a donation of US$2 million from the Japanese Extension Fund for International Co-operation, managed through the Inter American Development Bank. The Colombian team of engineers carefully studied the existing facilities around the world. They designed and installed the processing unit and quickly started to improve the production process. It is now perhaps the cleanest factory of natural resins ever operated. The factory is not only clean: the first year of extraction confirms that Las Gaviotas produces the best colofonia on the market. Quality is the result of the design of every step in the process, and the dedication of all the employees. And Las Gaviotas can count on a highly motivated workforce. Las Gaviotas is not only capable of manufacturing in an environmentally sound manner—it produces with quality, and competes on quality.

From Cleaner Production to Zero Emissions

The production process has zero emissions as a target. All the polyethylene bags used to tap the colofonia are recovered and reconditioned as plastic pipes and sheets for re-use in farming. Once a month, all waste is collected and shipped to Bogota for processing. The plastic bags are collected and dried on the premises so that all waste colofonia, a mere 0.2% of the harvest, can be recovered: the residual colofonia would represent toxic waste in the soil. Instead, the recovery of this minor amount of waste amounts to one free production run per year. The waste colofonia that ends up on the bottom of the water pond is recovered and used as an ingredient in the locally produced water-resistant bricks, the main building material of the local houses. The challenge is to use all resources so that the system emulates nature, where nothing gets wasted.

Generate Jobs

The work generated at Las Gaviotas to process the colofonia and maintain operations led to 160 directly employed, full-time staff in 1998. The revenues generated today are sufficient to maintain such a payroll, which includes housing and dining facilities. This region has never seen the arrival of so many jobs because there has previously been no such initiative to generate employment. But, since the revenue-streams are based on a set of objectives which include the generation of value-added, the entrepreneurship of Las Gaviotas is proving to be a hugely successful programme. It sustains over 1,000 families.

Sustain the Culture of Indigenous People

Las Gaviotas is responding to another challenge: sustaining the culture of local people. Las Gaviotas mainly employs indigenous people, and is proud to discriminate positively in favour of them by paying them more than the white men receive. The workers stay at the pine plantation from Monday morning through to Friday afternoon, after which they return to their settlements located within a radius of three hours riding by bicycle. The locals speak several languages, with Spanish at best the second most important. Las Gaviotas is contributing to the alleviation of poverty, while providing a meaningful platform for indigenous people to sustain their culture and generate jobs.

Water and Health

The strength of the newly planted forest and its fresh undergrowth goes beyond the recovery of flora and fauna: it functions as an excellent filtering unit for water. Las Gaviotas quickly noted the outstanding quality of the topsoil water, which is rich in minerals, and purified by soil bacteria. Most of the hospital treatments are for gastrointestinal illnesses, and the leading causes of infant death in the region are related to poor water quality, which translates into diarrhoea, cholera, typhoid, hepatitis, dysentery, salmonella and *E. coli*. In fact, because 70% of the health problems in the Vichada region are directly related to water, the forest offers a new (business) opportunity. The forest of Las Gaviotas provides the opportunity to collect and bottle quality water at very low cost: a cup with 250 ml of water from Las Gaviotas only costs the consumer 62 pesos, one-fifth of the price of mineral water shipped from Bogota. The cost of transportation is prohibitive and the result is deteriorating health conditions. This is the final agenda item for poverty alleviation: secure access to clean water and the implementation of a preventative health agenda.

A New Revenue-Stream

Las Gaviotas led the world with its rural hospital, until the bureaucracy of the central government in Bogota and the legislation of a parliament insensitive to rural needs forced its closure. The parliament passed a law that stipulated that hospitals needed to have a minimum level of equipment, and that doctors had to have a certain variety of specialisations. This would make sense in a city, but in the field it is already hard enough to motivate a medical doctor to pursue his or her career in remote areas to largely indigenous clients. The law also prescribed that a hospital must be affiliated with an insurance system established with a minimum of 10,000 members. The law-makers neglected to consider the fact that the department of Vichada, the size of Denmark, Belgium and Luxembourg together, only has a total population of 26,000 and therefore could never maintain a hospital based on this public insurance system.

Paolo Lugari and his team refused to be discouraged. Since the production of clean water requires the best sanitary conditions, the forced closure of the hospital left this extraordinary building without use for only a few months. Creativity is king at Las Gaviotas. Today, this self-sufficient building provides one of the best contributions to the healthcare system of Vichada: the local production of quality water at low cost. It is hoped that this 'preventative medicine' will contribute to the original objectives of the field hospital—which hopefully can soon be reopened, providing the policy-makers come to their senses and take the reality of the rural regions into account. In regions such as Vichada, where poverty is rampant and healthcare scarce, uniform standards appropriate to a booming urban sprawl make little sense.

Harmony

Colombia is a country in search of harmony. Violence, often associated with the activities of the drug cartels, is at frighteningly high levels and corruption is rampant. But when one listens to the local music or watches local dance, it is clear that Colombians share a sense of harmony. Through their culture, music, dance and songs, the workers in Vichada demonstrate their fondness for community. It is here that one learns that changing the country for the better in a time of crisis can only be realised by break-through initiatives at the periphery. This would never be possible in Bogota. It is here where one learns that the survival of the fittest is not the answer, but that co-operation and teamwork offer the only way out of the present vicious circle of poverty.

Paolo Lugari commissioned the largest mural painting in the region. It depicts the history of Las Gaviotas and the dreams that are yet to be realised. Much still remains to be done, but one thing is certain: there is no place on earth that has succeeded in implementing the concept of UpSizing like Las Gaviotas—responding to the need for employment, healthcare, social development, economic activity, technological breakthroughs and secure water supply. Possibly the best synthesis for this planetary paradigm could be a phrase from the mural: 'The maturity of the human being is to know how to realise its dreams.' Alternatively, we could start to take seriously the words of Gabriel Garcia Marquez who, in a speech delivered in Bogota, has called Paolo Lugari 'the inventor of the world'.

Cost of reforestation	US$1,000 per hectare
CO_2 sequestered per hectare	6 tons per year
Area available in Colombia	6 million hectares
Total potential of CO_2 sequestration	36 million tons per year
Estimated potential for jobs	120,000 sustaining one million
Investment cost	US$6 billion

Table 13: *The Potential of Las Gaviotas's Approach to Reforestation*
Source: The ZERI Institute for Latin America

1.	Reforestation to avert climate change
2.	Preservation and recovery of biodiversity
3.	Generating value-added
4.	Maximising the use of your resources in a sustainable way
5.	Competing on the basis of quality
6.	Innovation and the development of appropriate technologies
7.	Total use of all resources—zero waste or emissions
8.	Generating jobs
9.	Preserving the culture of indigenous people
10.	Provision of healthy water as preventative health measure

Table 14: *How to Alleviate Poverty (not ranked according to priority)*
Source: The ZERI Institute for Latin America

Montfort Boys' Town in Fiji

In 1996, a 72-year-old ecologist named Professor George Chan met with four other men on the largest island of Fiji—one of the remotest countries on earth, lying eleven time-zones west of Peru and three zones east of Australia in the South Pacific—to plan an extraordinary experiment. Chan is an advocate of integrated farming, which in principle means using the waste of one agricultural industry as fertiliser or fuel for another, resulting in a continuous feedback loop that leaves no waste or pollution behind. What Chan planned sounded almost too good to be possible: from the sludge now being discarded by a Fijian brewery located in Suva, five healthy new enterprises would grow. What was now a troublesome pollutant would be turned into crops of fresh mushrooms, chickens, fish, vegetables and fuel for electric power.

The site of the meeting—and of the prospective experiment—was a school for disadvantaged boys, called Montfort Boys' Town, where the students traditionally have helped raise both food and funds by farming fish in ponds. With Chan were two of the school's teachers, along with Professor S.T. Chang from the Chinese University of Hong Kong, who is considered one of the world's top experts on mushrooms, and the author of this book in his capacity as founder of the Zero Emissions Research Initiative (ZERI) at the United Nations University in Tokyo, who had brought the group together in the belief that this experiment could have widespread benefits around the world.

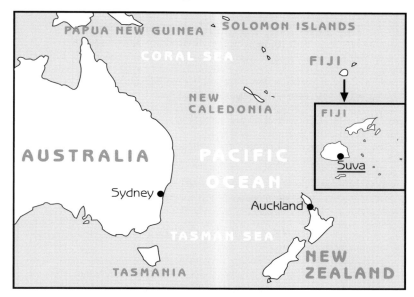

Suva, Fiji

Fiji was chosen for several reasons: it is poor, and integrated farming based on agro-industrial waste offers a way of bringing efficient, sustainable agriculture to low-income developing countries without introducing the problems—such as heavy pollution, vulnerability to pests that plague monocrop farming, loss of jobs to mechanisation, and heavy export dependence—that accompany large-scale conventional agriculture in many such countries. Fiji also had an established fish farming industry—an important element in Chan's loop—so the new business would not be entirely alien. But, most importantly, Fiji was facing a ticking clock: its largest industry is sugar, and there were signs that this industry could go into a serious decline within a few years. Fiji needed something to shore up what could be an endangered export economy.

The Montfort Boys' Town was chosen because it offered a ready environment for such an experiment. First, it has the necessary space. Montfort's students are mostly low-income (many are orphans), and the school puts strong emphasis on practical training for local industries, so many of the students were already familiar with traditional methods of fish farming. Thus, the school would provide labour in return for the infrastructural investment which would result in a continuous flow of food. The experiment would link the students' education to their country's need for a more productive, less polluting, economy.

The ZERI IBS, Industry and Island-States

The ZERI IBS set up at Montfort Boys' Town is adapted for beer breweries. ZERI has tested the system on a large number of industries, and it can be adapted and applied to any industry. In particular, this is relevant for the island-states, with a very limited supply of fresh-water and over-fishing in the sea. With prices for export produce dropping and income dollars decreasing, Sustainable Development in its broad sense, ecologically, economically and socially, is crucial, both in the short and in the long term.

The ZERI IBS offers Sustainable Development. It offers a way of creating more jobs, increasing income and producing better-quality food in an ecologically sustainable manner.

Today, attempts are made at introducing so-called 'modern fish culture', using hormone-treated, genetically manipulated fish and antibiotics. This may work in large-scale production facilities, although it is hardly a sustainable method of production. However, in small-scale economies such as island-states, affecting over 50 countries on all continents, not only is it unsustainable, it is also unsuitable for the overall structure of the economy.

The ZERI IBS adjusts the produce to what the market demands and, most importantly, to the local biodiversity. It is the respect for the biodiversity that offers the highest productivity. Biodiversity, the result of 4 billion years of evolution, offers the best basis for Sustainable Development, adapted to the conditions of each region. The mushrooms grown in the ZERI IBS are the ones best suited for the climate and available substrate. The same goes for earthworms, fish and any other part of the system. Since there are about 5,000 edible mushrooms and many thousands of species of earthworms and fish to choose from, the ZERI IBS can be applied in any climate. Wherever the system is set up, the best combination possible, offered by nature, emulating nature, is applied, generating the highest possible productivity.

Source: George Chan, ZERI Special Advisor on Integrated Biosystems

---

Beer and Mushrooms

The experiment has been set up outside the Montfort School. Chan designed the concept with the support of scientists from around the world, but mainly built on his 40 years of experience in the field. One of the elements that gives George Chan most satisfaction is the reed-thatched hut which looks like a traditional Fijian home, the kind that was common before corrugated metal and asbestos-strengthened cement board became the standard roofing and construction material on the islands. It is one-room only, with the thatch covering both roof and walls, and was built by the students of Montfort Boys' Town, using the same techniques used there for centuries: they cut structural members from mangrove trees growing in abundance on the school's land and hand-gathered reeds for the thatch. If this were a house, a family of perhaps five or six would sleep on mats on the floor. But instead of a family's meagre belongings, rows of shelves fill the hut. On each shelf, mushrooms grow in plastic tubes.

These tubes are supplied with brewery waste, a wet mash of spent grains, rich in chemically bonded carbohydrate which animals cannot digest very well, which are dried and then mixed with rice straw, sawdust or shredded newspaper. Mushrooms produce an enzyme that unlocks the processed grain, allowing the mushroom to extract its own energy for growth while leaving behind a residue that can then be used as food for chickens, pigs and other animals. Professor S.T. Chang travelled to Boys' Town twice to assess conditions and the climate for mushroom growing, and has selected three kinds of mushrooms to grow there: shiitake mushrooms (*Lentinus*), the second-highest-priced mushroom in the world; oyster mushrooms (*Pleurotus*), which are easy to grow in the tropics; and straw mushrooms (*Volvariella*), common in Vietnam. Each of the three can thrive in the wet climate near Suva, Fiji's capital. The mushrooms were cleared for cultivation on the island by the Koronovia laboratory a few kilometres away at the Fijian Agriculture Department. A native species of mushrooms would have been preferable, but none was readily available at a spore bank that would grow quickly in this medium.

The spent brewer's grain is free, of course; if the school doesn't take it, the brewery will simply offer it to the cattle farmers who basically only pay the cost of transportation. Though 'spent grain' can provide as much as about a quarter of its weight in protein, there are few marketable uses for it. According to both Chan and Chang, there are only two practical ways of breaking down the grain and making use of this protein: feeding it to earthworms and growing mushrooms. They planned both at Montfort. Mushrooms will be produced first, because they have a higher market value.

As the mushrooms grow, they derive their energy from the separation of the lignin from the cellulose, converting this into carbohydrates. In a conventional mushroom farm, the residue from this process is essentially wasted—dumped on fields where it may fertilise crops but may also overwhelm them. At Montfort, however, the boys shovel it into pails and carry it by hand to a small wooden shack, just a few metres away, which houses chickens and pigs. The mushroom residue is both nutritious and safe for animals, and so makes an excellent feed. Because they have such animals, the students at Montfort get to eat meat of one kind or another—chicken, pork, mutton or fish almost every day. This is food that almost none of them would be able to afford outside the school.

Every day or two, those animals' wastes are flushed with water into a 'digester', a concrete-and-metal contraption about the size of a waste skip like those found behind large apartment buildings in industrial countries. Inside, the natural chemicals in the wastes will separate, with each going toward either the production of energy or the production of compost. As methane gas is released, it collects in a compartment at the top of the box, while the solid or liquid wastes settle to the bottom.

The methane is captured in bottles and either taken to a gas genera-tor to power the school's lights, or used for the steaming of mushroom substrate. Later, as the volume increases, a pipeline may be built to carry the gas to the school buildings. The digester produces the equivalent of about three gallons of petrol a day, a useful amount in a school for dis-advantaged boys in a low-income country. Without the digester, the gas would be vented into the atmosphere, and its economic value lost.

Meanwhile, the solid matter left after the gas is bled off moves in a solu-tion of water through several compartments of the digester, at each stage losing some of its bacteria and some of its potential for spreading illness. When it emerges from the last compartment, this decontaminated manure is nearly converted into the same nutrients: nitrogen, phosphorous, and potash used as fertilisers on farm fields. The job is 60% done. With the help of gravity, it then flows through three algae ponds, in which bacteria, plankton and other micro-scavengers consume any residual unwanted parts of the original animal wastes and secure a further 30% mineralisation. The algae is harvested regularly and used for composting, as a high-grade fer-tiliser for the vegetables and fruit that grow on the dykes around the ponds, and as a feed for livestock. What emerges from the last pond, and then drops into a large fish pond, is a perfect fish food. George Chan has prac-tised this process in ponds in Vietnam and China and predicts that about 80% of the food needed by the fish will come from this system via the digester. The large fish pond has an ecology of its own, with seven kinds of fish, from top-feeders and grass carp that eat napier and elephant grass from the embankments, down to scum-suckers or mud carp, along with small crabs, prawns and various types of plankton.

While it is an artificial ecology, the ecosystem emulates nature and is designed to require none of the major interventions such as the use of antibiotics to fight disease or the frequent cleanings required in conven-tional fish farming. Montfort does not even have to add purchased feed. In a conventional fish farm, feed is the largest single expense. Conven-tional fish farms in Fiji are currently spending US$200–300 on grain or fish-meal food for every US$1,000 in sales. Two other major expenses for conventional fish farms are energy for water pumps and antibiotics to fend off diseases. And, in an effort to boost productivity, all fishlings are hor-monally treated so that a sex change will occur and only males will pre-vail.[83] Montfort does not need any pumps or electricity for the ponds, since it uses a gravity system, and Chan hopes this zero-emissions project will

---

83. This is a strategy pursued in commercial fish farms to produce higher yields. Females produce eggs and are less heavy and so commercial farms currently either neuter fish or change the sex to male.

not need any antibiotics because disease will be kept at bay by integrated fish farm techniques—in the same way it is kept in check by integrated pest management on fields of crops. Because the pond won't be stocked by a single, monoculture species, it will not be vulnerable to having its harvest wiped out by a simple outbreak of disease.

Some of the fish is served to the students, probably the ones worth the least on the market; the rest are sold. On top of the pond, more food is grown aquaponically. Flowers, strawberries and high-value vegetables such as golden needle are also grown at Montfort, on the banks of the ponds, so that their roots can draw nutrients from the dissolved fish waste. Most of the plants will be exported from Fiji. The plants thus provide a fifth integrated industry—and another revenue-stream for the school.

While the Montfort farm is a pilot station and a development project with both ecological and social benefits, it is also a serious scientific experiment, and so the fully integrated fish ponds operate side by side with a control group. Just a few metres away from Chan's integrated system, Montfort Boys' Town has six fairly ordinary fish ponds which have long been used to raise food and income. Each has a chicken coop on top, the wastes from which drop directly into the water for consumption by the fish and aquatic creatures—which make them already more integrated than most fish farms. However, this system does not include a digester or incorporate mushroom cultivation, and certainly does not reduce ocean dumping.[84] Nor is there a core stream of food derived from agro-industrial waste: the spent grain. The productivity of each system is tallied, and the costs and benefits compared over time. The result should be a measure of the real benefits of the integrated method compared directly with more traditional methods.

Professor Motoyuki Suzuki, the director-general of the Institute for Industrial Sciences at Tokyo University and the Co-ordinator of Japan's Zero Emissions Research Programme—the Japanese arm of ZERI—funded by the Japanese government, visited the site in February 1998 along with colleagues and installed scientific monitoring equipment. This will enable the collection of the data—the verification of the total organic carbon, phosphor and nitrogen produced by the site on a daily basis— necessary to formulate a mathematical model of the system. The hope is that not only

---

84. Fiji's islands are surrounded by exceptional coral reefs, some so remarkable that that they led Jean-Michel Cousteau to choose the Fijian island of Tavenui, the third largest, for the location of his scuba-diving resort. Yet the brewery's waste-water is highly alkaline and around 400,000 m^3 is dumped as liquid waste into the ocean each year. This is suspected to be a cause of harm both to coral and local marine life.

will the Zero Emissions concept produce outstanding results—and be replicable—but that it will also receive crucial scientific backing. On the basis of one year of data, the first indications on how the system works are due to be published in several forthcoming PhD theses.[85]

In May 1997, some 50 visitors from the neighbouring Southern Pacific and Indian Ocean Islands were invited to examine the project thanks to a grant from the United Nations Development Programme (UNDP). They came from the Solomon Islands, Papua New Guinea, Guam, Kiribati, Tonga, Vanuatu and Western Samoa. All participants seemed optimistic. With about a dozen breweries at planning stage, all consuming scarce drinking water, all dumping residues, such as the spent grain, as waste, all serving the tourists first, it is clear that the possibility of eliminating waste, generating additional revenue and making the core operations much more productive is an attractive option.

In fact, such efficiency in resource use has been practised in other places for centuries, and used to be far more common than it is today. In China and South-East Asia, people have used organic waste as a fish food for thousands of years. The Aztec civilisations of the fifteenth century had elaborate systems of canals in their cities, with fish crops living in the canal and thriving on the cities' wastes. Today's efforts in this field are, to some degree, efforts to rediscover lost techniques, as well as to use new biological or ecological knowledge to take them further and to adapt them to modern economies. The main contribution of the Zero Emissions project is to link this traditional know-how with the useful properties of discarded waste-streams from fermentation processes, such as the brewing of beer and the production of vinegar and soya sauce.

The Boys' Town project has provided not just a fine case for the Pacific islands to follow: the ZERI teams in Tokyo and Geneva believe that the scientific backbone provided by Tokyo University will provide a solid basis for further projects to eliminate pollution and reduce the need for industrial materials in countries as diverse as Latvia and Colombia.

Fiji and Sugar

But what are the implications of the Boys' Town pilot for the economy of Fiji? Can such a small-scale experiment provide solutions to the problems the island-state faces in the global economy?

The backbone of Fiji's agriculture is sugar, which accounts for about a third of the country's export earnings. Some 20% of the land is dedicated to growing sugar cane, and the crop employs a quarter of the country's

---

85. Including the author's, due for publication in 2000.

labour force. About 98% of the crop is exported. Half goes through the United Kingdom, the former colonial power of Fiji, and then on to the European Union at preferential prices agreed to under the Lomé Convention on International Trade. A small amount is also exported to the United States. These affluent buyers pay up to double the world price. Without those preferential prices, Fiji could not compete with larger countries such as Indonesia and Brazil, which, thanks to their huge economies of scale, can grow sugar more cheaply.

Now, however, there are signs that these preferential deals are coming to an end, possibly within the next eight to ten years, because of the determination of the World Trade Organisation to phase out preferential price supports. Free trade may not destroy the Fijian sugar industry entirely, but could cut its output as soon as less-expensive sugar from other countries undercuts it in foreign markets. In Fiji, as in many other poor countries, cutting back a major export industry could devastate the entire national economy. The Caribbean island-states are facing a similar fate for their banana crops. Alternatives are needed.

Many Fijians want the islands' economy to diversify, and to become less dependent on a sugar crop that may have a dim future. Some are betting on tourism to take up the slack. Tourism is growing, even though its revenues are not reaching all Fijians. But others argue that farming, with its high demand for labour, cannot be easily replaced by hotel staff and scuba-diving instructors, and that the loss of one lucrative crop such as sugar might be best replaced by agricultural diversification.

During the UNDP workshop for the Pacific regions, George Chan examined scenarios using the data from his first 12 months of operation. Capital investment, a gift of US$7,000, was provided by Japanese industrial benefactors. Chan pointed out that chickens require little space, and the structure planned for Montfort will hold 4,000 animals, generating about US$20,000 a year for the school. Two fish ponds will add about US$10,000 a year to income. The methane will sell for about US$5,400 and the pigs will sell for about US$15,000, depending on fluctuations in market prices and production costs. With US$10,000 generated from mushroom cultivation and another US$1,500 or so from the floating aquaponics gardens and fruit and vegetables, the boys and their teachers could gross over US$60,000 a year. From this, perhaps US$15,000 would go back into the costs of transport, chicks, containers for the methane, food supplements for chickens or fish, and the amortisation of the investment, leaving a net income of US$45,000. The Bank of Hawaii puts Fiji's per capita income at US$2,250 a year.

If George Chan is right, the school will receive the equivalent of the yearly salaries of 20 average Fijians to supplement its budget, and, in addition,

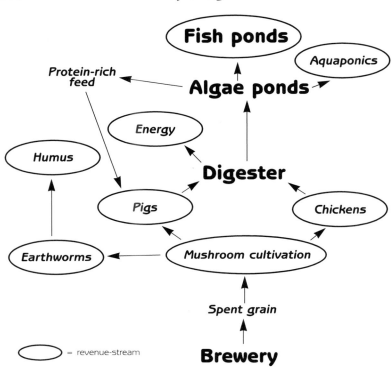

Figure 5: *The Integrated Biosystem at Montfort Boys' Town*
Source: ZERI Foundation, Geneva

the water over the Fijian coral reefs will be a little cleaner. There is more food generated in a sustainable fashion available for the students and the surrounding community. Since success breeds success, other projects inspired by this one are now on the move throughout the island-states of the remotest parts of the world, demonstrating that creativity and innovation thrive on the periphery. In Fiji, the alternative is there for all to see.

From Ideas in Fiji to Commerce in Tsumeb, Namibia

The 'brewery of the future' in Tsumeb, Namibia—which produces beer from sorghum without generating any waste, and at the same time aims to act as a protein factory for fish farming, and is already the basis of a new mushroom production unit and a valuable source of energy for the town—is

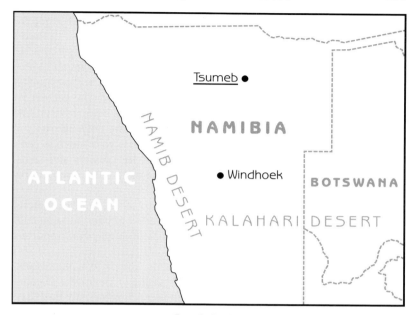

Tsumeb, Namibia

the first commercialisation worldwide of the Zero Emissions concept. Namibian Breweries adopted the Zero Emissions approach for the new brewery after the test unit in Fiji indicated in the tropics that it could be applied to the fermentation industries. In order to proceed, the company decided to re-site the brewery from the Tsumeb industrial park onto a production farm 13 km from the town in order to have space to accommodate ZERI-related activities such as the construction of two fish ponds measuring 3,000 m^2 and 4,000 m^2, a livestock pen and a biogas digester. The construction of the brewery was completed at the end of March 1996, and production commenced in May of that year. The aim is to process all waste-streams as well as partially to satisfy the energy requirements of the brewery.

The Tsumeb brewery uses a system engineered and built under the supervision of Professor George Chan following extensive research and the involvement of groups of scientists consulting on how to make best use of all organic solid wastes from the plant, particularly the spent grain solid waste.

The second implementation phase of George Chan's system is now in operation and intends to use the solid waste or 'cake' as feed for a fish farm. Farming fish also needs water—and, normally, Namibia has little to spare. But breweries also discharge enormous amounts—seven litres of water for each litre of beer, normally, and five litres in the case of sorghum brewing—so, thanks to the new brewery, Tsumeb now has water in abundance for fish farming. The water will be sent directly to the fish ponds, where traditional multicrop fish farming, as practised in China and Vietnam, is planned for introduction. The fish farms are expected eventually to reach a productivity of 10 tons per hectare per year. The project is expected to be operational as soon as permission has been granted for the introduction of fish species required to operate the polyculture.

Already, biowaste is digested to produce methane gas, which is captured and used as a fuel for the local community for cooking and heating, relieving some of the pressure on wood: the main energy source for 80% of the population of Tsumeb.

The Tsumeb brewery is the first in the world to seize the environmental and economic benefits offered by the integration of beer brewing and fish farming—and does so at a time when both problems and opportunities are growing.

Demand for beer is growing worldwide, particularly in Asia, but also in Africa and Latin America, and the issue of disposing of 'beer cake' is gaining attention, the more so as it becomes an increasingly costly business for the brewing industry to landfill or incinerate. Yet, as population pressures increase, demand for protein food rises as well.

When beer cake is used as cattle feed, it takes seven tons to generate one ton of meat. By contrast, 1.8 tons of the cake produces one ton of fish meat—and world prices for selected fish are steadily rising because of the reduction in ocean catches. Fish hatching can be increased significantly in line with the increased production of beer.

At the official inauguration of the Tsumeb brewery in January 1997, the President of Namibia, HE Dr Sam Nujoma, said:

> They believe that, to increase productivity, you have to reduce jobs. We are demonstrating that, when you focus on the productivity of the raw materials, you generate more value, more income, higher returns and more jobs—while eliminating pollution. This is UpSizing, the industrial model of the future.

Tsumeb experienced difficulties in establishing mushroom production because of the harsh climatological conditions in Northern Namibia, but with modifications made by Professor S.T. Chang, the system is now fully operational based on a substrate from the spent grain. Mushrooms are now harvested—without the use of climate controls—on a daily basis even when outside temperatures reach 40°C. A livestock pen containing pigs is also operational and produces additional biowaste for the digester, which in turn now produces enough methane gas to supply all the steam necessary to prepare the substrate for mushroom cultivation.

The application of the ZERI methodology to brewing is now receiving considerable interest throughout the world. Projects are emerging in North America, Japan, Germany, Brazil, Colombia and the Seychelles. As well as small entrepreneurial microbreweries, some market leaders are taking interest. Some further examples follow.

◀ Agreement has now been reached with the Shinano Brewery, a microbrewery in Japan, to convert their operations to a Zero Emissions facility. The Australian engineering group Burchill is supporting the effort with landscaping design, and support has also been provided by the Japanese engineering group EBARA and Tokyo University. Since Shinano is located in the Japanese Alps just 20 km from Nagano, the site enjoys the luxury of space to set up a Zero Emissions operation, a luxury usually extremely rare in Japan.

◀ Guinness has invited ZERI to apply its principles and concepts to its breweries starting with one situated in Africa. A feasibility study has revealed some interesting opportunities. The brewery is situated both next to the nation's slaughterhouse and a piggery. The effluent produced by all three facilities offers the chance to generate methane gas and CO_2 which can be converted to usable biogas. As the brewery currently imports all fuel and some CO_2 for its soft drinks operations, the brewery could theoretically reduce its costs while at the same time contributing to an improvement in the local environment. Space restrictions do not permit the application of all the options in the ZERI cycle on-site, although the compost from a 500 m^3 digester would provide a useful substrate for mushroom farming.

◀ In Colombia, an agreement has been reached with El Portico in Bogota to construct and operate a ZERI brewery in the North of the city. El Portico is a major tourist attraction with restaurants, a farm complex and an amusement park attracting around 5,000 visitors each weekend. It will provide a major opportunity to disseminate the concept of Zero Emissions and the inherent opportunities for job creation, waste elimination and value-added. It is anticipated that the brewery will satisfy all local needs and will incorporate all core elements of the ZERI concept. The Universidad de la Savannah will co-ordinate the design and implementation process.

For a concept framed only three years ago in a report by the Chinese Academy of Sciences,[86] progress has been remarkably fast. Since the projects under way are located in extremely diverse climatological conditions, the results will be analysed to improve the productivity and flexibility of the ZERI system.

---

86. Wenhua, 'Feasibility Study on the Integrated Biosystem Concept'.

The Case of the Water Hyacinth in Africa

The water hyacinth (*Eichhornia crassipes*) is a beautiful plant. Its flowers are so impressive and decorative that it was imported to Africa by settlers from Latin America to adorn the lakes and ponds. The flower blossoms continuously and the bloom is nearly permanent. The water hyacinth thrives in water areas rich in minerals and nutrients. However, this beautiful flower has now become an extremely serious problem in Africa. It is near the top of the research agendas of African policy-makers and has been recognised as a threat to the region by international donors such as the World Bank, the FAO and UNEP who have released research funds to discover ways and means of eradicating it.

The adverse impact of the excessive growth of the water hyacinth—it can double its weight in only two weeks—is being felt in the economies of all lake districts of Africa: Zimbabwe, Malawi, Zambia, Tanzania, Kenya and Uganda. The dominant plant crowds out all other water life, from the fishes to the turtles, from the algae to the benthos and plankton. The plant absorbs and uses oxygen dissolved in the water, which becomes a critical problem, especially at night when photosynthetic production of oxygen ceases. Fisherman lose their source of living: it is impossible to fish since the water hyacinth clogs up the waterways. Boat engines get stuck and the canoe becomes the only form of transportation. The flow of water to electricity-producing hydrostations is also reduced considerably, not just because of the clogging but because the plant accelerates water loss through evapotranspiration, due to the large surface areas of the leaves and their innumerable stomata. All of this adversely affects energy production. And, when the water hyacinths advance to the point where they can clog the turbines, the power generation of a whole country—as is the case in Zambia—is at risk. Tourism is also affected, and therefore countries around the world—and particularly in Africa—are searching for a lasting solution to the problems caused by this aggressive plant.

However, achievements to date have been very limited. The most common strategy for eradication is through the use of herbicides, releasing toxic compounds that are destructive to fish and other useful biota. This strategy has been called an ecological crime: the long-term impacts on the environment are poorly understood. It is also very costly. Most importantly, it hasn't worked. In Malawi, the water hyacinth took over the central lake, and spraying from the air with pesticides was undertaken as a last resort. A few months after the lake had been cleared, water hyacinths re-emerged and, in less than half a year, the plant had recovered its dominant position, while the pesticides had left other aquatic life impoverished and water quality badly affected.

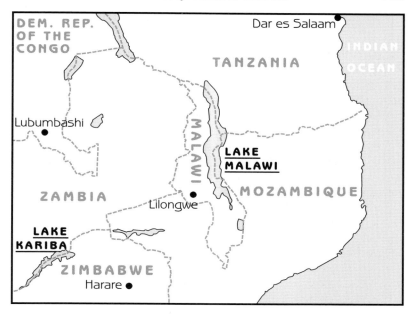

Lake Malawi and Lake Kariba

The water hyacinth in all its major varieties has one characteristic in common: its germination takes up to 15 years. This means that one can destroy the green mass, but total destruction is only successful when not only the leaves, but also the roots and seeds, have been suffocated with chemicals for a similar period. This is an implausible strategy and one that would lead to the sacrifice of all aquatic life in areas chosen for treatment. And these areas are large.

Biological methods have also been attempted. The Australian weevil beetle has been introduced in some areas. The idea is that the insect larvae eats the leaves which subsequently die. This is another non-sustainable solution, since the decomposing water hyacinth biomass will create massive organic wastes, which will consume large amounts of oxygen. In addition, inorganic minerals will be released from the decomposing plants. It thrives on minerals and nutrients washed off from farmland, absorbs them and, if killed, simply releases them back into the waterways to recreate a perfect environment for its re-emergence. There is also a big question mark over the long-term consequences of the introduction of imported insects on Africa's indigenous aquatic plants and the ecosystem in general.

Manual and mechanical removal have also been tried. In Zambia, where the situation has become critical, the army has been called in to clear the

The tree farm station at Las Gaviotas

An overview of Montfort Boys' Town, Fiji

Mushrooms growing on a substrate of dried water hyacinth

ZERI-related activities at the brewery in Tsumeb, Namibia

rivers of water hyacinths to try to safeguard the level of water flow and to keep the plants from clogging the turbines for energy generation. Around Harare in Zimbabwe, the National Parks engaged 200 full-time workers—mostly women—to remove the water hyacinth by hand. Neither approach has been successful. In Zimbabwe, when the lake looked to be cleared on Friday, the workers found the channel to the river clogged by water hyacinth on the following Monday.

The workers engaged in this uphill battle are paid no more than the minimum wage of US$1.50 per day. But, at a cost of US$300 dollars a day, 300 days a year, not to mention the cost of transporting the biomass out of the area, the cash-strapped National Parks of Zimbabwe find themselves investing over US$100,000 dollars a year just to maintain the water supply from one lake. The Kariba Lake District, in both Zimbabwe and Zambia, is worse: another US$200,000 needs to be invested simply to limit the damage, while the economic losses are in excess of a couple of million dollars.

The battle is being lost. This should come as no surprise: fighting the symptoms without tackling the causes can never lead to a lasting solution. The water hyacinth is a strong plant, but its overpowering success is a symptom of the real problems facing the affected regions: soil erosion. Whenever topsoil is washed away due to over-intensive farming or grazing, and/or the excessive use of fertilisers such as nitrates, the nutrients and minerals accumulate in river and lake beds providing a nutrient-rich environment ideal for the water hyacinth to rapidly multiply.

A different type of strategy is needed: the strategy of UpSizing.

If one considers the water hyacinth not as a problem but rather as an attempt by nature to correct the damages inflicted by humankind, the solutions would look very different indeed. After all, when all the minerals and nutrients are washed off with large amounts of nitrates, the farmland's fertile topsoil ends up in the waterways. The topsoil risks being lost forever, silting the dams, and filling the river and lake beds. The water hyacinth is nature's response to humans' destructive behaviour. It is an attempt to recover what has been lost. Instead of attempting to eradicate the 'pest', humankind should realise that the water hyacinth offers a unique opportunity to recover the nutrients that misguided actions have washed away. Through photosynthesis, and thanks to abundant access to water, the plant converts all of these lost minerals and nutrients into a biomass of exceptional quality with extremely strong fibres and a high concentration of nutrients.

When a group of scientists, scholars and deans of faculties of agriculture and natural resources met in Windhoek, Namibia, in January 1997 at the invitation of UNDP to study the potential of the application of UpSizing,

Generative Science and Zero Emissions, the water hyacinth was identified as a case study.[87]

The scientists set out to identify the best way of re-utilising this bio-mass. Knowing that the fibres are so strong, and observing that cattle and game do not eat the fresh or dried water hyacinth, the only option left was the best known option for the recovery of any fibrous material: the cultivation of mushrooms.[88]

Mushrooms and Africa

The cultivation of mushrooms on dried water hyacinth had not been tried in Africa. In fact, despite having perhaps 30% of the world's biodiversity in mushrooms, Africa only cultivates 0.3% of global output, with the major-ity of cultivated species non-native to the continent. The world market for edible mushrooms is estimated at US$9 billion, with a further sector, for medicinal use, now estimated at US$3.6 billion and growing fast. In total, this market is equivalent to the size of a traditional staple commodity such as coffee. Africa lacks knowledge of its own biodiversity and, with increasing deforestation, the natural habitats of a range of species are at risk before their true properties—whether as a source of nutrition or as the basis for pharmaceuticals—are known. There is no spore bank in Africa capable of providing base materials to farmers and entrepreneurs. Only in South Africa is commercial cultivation of non-native species practised on a large scale, resulting in Zimbabwe and many other nations import-ing to satisfy demand. Yet many African species, formerly a traditional staple for local communities, have unique tastes, far superior to imported species. Mushrooms were once a seasonal crop, harvested during the rainy sea-son, helping rural communities to secure protein-rich food. Now, because of loss of habitat, prices are high. There is a huge opportunity for rural communities to reinvent this staple using the water hyacinth as a substrate.

Feasibility Studies

While the park rangers had observed that mushrooms spontaneously spawned on the dried piles of water hyacinth awaiting disposal, commercial cultivation had not been considered. The scientists concluded that, under the guidance of Professor. S.T. Chang, a viability study would be under-taken in five countries. A group of scientists quickly reconvened after the first meeting at the Africa University in Mutare, Zimbabwe, and, under the co-ordination of Mrs Margaret Tagwira, the initiative unfolded.

The results were impressive.

---

87. Mshigeni *et al.* (eds.), *New Hope for Sustainable Development in Africa*.
87. *Ibid.*

After only 30 days, the dried substrate from water hyacinth produced a variety of mushrooms and, once harvested, it did not take more than ten days to harvest a second and even a third flush. One ton of dried water hyacinth substrate generated an impressive 1.1 tons of mushrooms, thus generating more mushrooms than base material and out-performing traditional substrates such as sawdust. In addition, since the substrate of water hyacinth is rich in minerals and nutrients, the oyster and straw mushrooms cultivated ended up enriched with potassium, magnesium, iodine and calcium, along with numerous other components that are critical to a healthy food diet. Much of what was lost in the form of washed-away topsoil can be recovered in the mushroom. Of course, the water hyacinth can also recover harmful metals such as cadmium and lead if they are found in rivers or lakes. This is a potential problem which can only be addressed by limiting the use of the plant as a substrate for mushrooms to areas where the habitat is unpolluted.

The residual substrate of water hyacinth after mushroom farming is a rich food-base for cattle. Since nearly all the lignocellulose has been broken down by the enzymes of the mushroom, the rest of the material can also be used to farm earthworms, which will convert the material into a humus. The humus that is produced in the process could then be reapplied to the soils, recovering and replenishing some of the lost topsoil. Earthworms are also an excellent chicken feed.

The cycle of biomass around the water hyacinth also allows for the production of biogas generated from the waste-streams which is needed to sterilise the substrate for the mushrooms. Cattle and chickens produce a lot of manure which can be channelled into a digester. This avoids the need to cut firewood. The upshot is a system that generates both revenues and jobs and converts a problem into an opportunity (see Table 16)

The economic feasibility has also been demonstrated. Some 60%–80% of the cost of mushroom farming is incurred in the preparation of the substrate: the purchase of the substrate and the cost of energy needed for sterilisation to kill microbial organisms which otherwise would compete with the mushroom spores. However, when the raw material—the water hyacinth—is free, and the energy cost can be limited to the purchase of a digester, then the whole process becomes extremely competitive. An individual farmer would have to invest no more than US$500 to start up an operation and, with training, the first mushroom harvest can be sold as early as one month after the harvesting of water hyacinth. Digesters designed by George Chan for the Grameen Bank[89] cost no more than US$20 and

---

89. A Bangladeshi-based micro-credit bank established in 1983 providing small low-interest economic loans to poor farmers. Fifty-six countries are now involved in Grameen-like programmes.

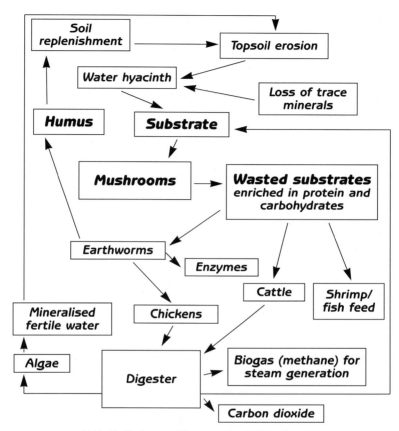

Table 16: *The Integrated Biosystem for the Water Hyacinth*
Source: ZERI Foundation, Geneva

will last for two years. A more professional and industrial unit could require US$5,000 to start up with a 10–20 m³ digester, but could achieve payback within a year. The start of such an operation is ideal for microfinancing.

ZERI, in co-operation with UNDP, has now embarked on a fast-track implementation programme, and small mushroom farming businesses have been established in both Zimbabwe and Namibia.

Sustainable Livelihoods

Africa needs a creative approach to its problems, and the socio-economic benefits of the ZERI approach should provide motivation for policy-makers. The 200 workers clearing water hyacinths around Harare on minimum wages can be boosted to perhaps 1,000 people farming mushrooms far in excess of this salary (see Table 17). The sale price for mushrooms on the market hovers around 100 Zimbabwean dollars per kilo: the opportunity to generate value-added is tremendous. If the additional advantages of earthworm cultivation, biogas production and chicken feed production are added to the loop, the total income per worker can increase further.

This is a long-term solution and it will require patience: perhaps a generation of patience. But action can begin now. The pilot project at the Africa University in Zimbabwe has demonstrated effectiveness. The people around Lake Victoria, Lake Malawi, the Akosombo Dam and the Zambezi need to be provided with education and training. Instead of depending on imported mushrooms from South Africa, Zimbabwe can consider the possibility of self-sufficiency in mushroom farming. All the components to create more income and jobs are available from a renewable resource currently considered a threat: the only missing factor is that humankind needs to understand how nature works.

According to Stephen Adei, UNDP's Resident Representative in Namibia:

Minimum wage for unskilled workers: Z$16.10 for 200 workers	**Z$322.00 per day**
Plus cost of transportation	**Z$500.00 per day**
Price for 1 kilo of mushrooms	**Z$100 per kilo**
Daily collection of water hyacinth with 200 workers	**5 tons per day**
Potential mushroom production	**5.5 tons per day**
Potential daily revenues	**Z$550,000**
Allowing for decrease in price due to increased production	**Z$200,000**
Daily potential revenue for 1,000 workers each	**Z$200**
Increasing the income by a factor of 10	
Production of earthworms on 1 ton of substrate	**100 kilos**
Production of chickens	**46 kilos**
Production of humus	**1,000 kilos**

Table 17: *The Application of Generative Science to the Revenue-Stream of Unskilled Labour in the Case of Water Hyacinths*
Source: ZERI Foundation, Geneva

The world is characterised by the irony of poverty and want in the midst of waste, inequity and insufficiency. Each day, the amount of food destroyed or thrown away in metropolitan New York . . . would feed about one million people elsewhere . . . Therein lies the power of ZERI. It proposes sustainable types of industry.[90]

The Case of Gotland

Håkan Ahlsten is a banker from Gotland. He participated in the Second World Congress on Zero Emissions which was held in Chattanooga, Tennessee, in May 1996. To him, the concept of converting economic development to meet not only the needs of the environment but also requirements for more jobs and greater productivity were extremely attractive. Gotland had made a major consultative effort to identify which kind of development the people on this island of 80,000 people—the largest in the Baltic Sea between Sweden and Finland—would like to achieve. The core elements of Gotland's economic development strategy, published in the spring of 1996, were:

1. Generate jobs
2. Develop food-processing industries based on local materials
3. Improve environmental performance
4. Increase input of know-how and technologies
5. Improve information about Gotland

Following the Chattanooga conference, ZERI were invited to look at the possibilities for the application of Zero Emissions concepts to the island. Since, to date, ZERI has mainly concentrated on food processing, those industries offered a first point of convergence. While the experience accumulated by ZERI in Africa, Latin America and Asia cannot be directly transferred to Sweden, the concept can. Gotland wishes to focus its development through small and medium-sized enterprises, which suits the ZERI approach, since smaller-scale operations are likely to realise success much sooner and are less risky: two features of great importance when innovations are undertaken.

Gotland needs to increase the number of jobs available by 5,000 by 2010. Current economic forecasts do not foresee growth of a necessary magnitude to permit such an increase in employment. The Gotland Plan explicitly

---

90. The research results and further details on the cultivation of mushrooms on a substrate of water hyacinth can be found in Mshigeni *et al.* (eds.), *New Hope for Sustainable Development in Africa*.

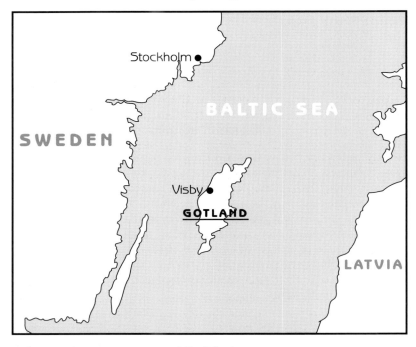

Gotland, Sweden

states that room must be made for creative and innovative ideas that target sustainable growth. Therefore, it was decided that the richest unexploited resource of the island—agro-produce and its residues—should be targeted for ZERI initiatives.

The present outline put together by the ZERI Foundation and the Biofocus Foundation of the Royal Swedish Academy of Sciences has identified a number of priority projects, including the launching of new products based on waste that is currently discarded, which can be translated from blueprint to action within a year. All initiatives start from a small scale and have limited ambitions. The programme aims to create early success stories on a minor scale so that broader-based initiatives can evolve later.

Long-term viability requires a training plan, a communications strategy and a broadening of the partnerships. While these elements are referred to here, they remain incomplete. It is only with the drive of the people of Gotland to take this concept and apply it that successes will be achieved. Such successes will motivate the islanders to convert Gotland into the first Zero Emissions zone in Europe. Some of the key proposals in the outline are now explained.

Gotland Carrot Juice

Gotland produces 15,000 tons of carrots per annum, one-third of all Swedish production. Gotland carrots are well known and considered of high quality. Up to 25% of the harvested carrots are discarded as these do not meet minimum quality standards. These carrots are disposed of as cattle feed.

The largest farming co-operative on the island takes one-third of the Gotlandic production, or some 5,000 tons per year. The co-operative has excess space, capacity and labour which could be further employed, and ZERI has proposed that this 25% waste should be used for the production of fresh carrot juice. The consumer market in Sweden is prepared to pay up to SEK30 (about US$4) for one litre of fresh juice retail (or SEK30 for one 200 ml glass in a café or restaurant). A pasteurised version will sell for SEK15 per litre.

The waste from the production of carrot juice can—in the initial stage—be used as cattle feed for easy and voluminous disposal. At a later stage, it could also be used as an additive for chicken feed, offering a natural darker colouring effect to the meat due to the presence of betacarotene. It can also be used as fish feed. Since the residue after extracting the juice includes high-value-added components such as betacarotene, vitamins and anti-oxidants, a research agenda can be established to study the technical and economic aspects of their recovery. The selection, the production of the juice and the packaging and distribution will require just three people to be employed at the initial stage. If the full programme is developed, then the juice production unit could employ up to ten.

A new business would be added, building on a current strength of Gotland. If an estimated 3,000 tons of carrots could be used for juice extraction, then approximately 1,000,000 litres of juice could be produced, or some 2,500 bottles a day if production could be spread around the year. This generates a potential revenue in the order of SEK10 million, for the juice only. Since the carrots are sold at SEK3 per kilo, it represents major value-added for both the carrot farmers and the co-operative.

As the project foresees the recovery of the waste generated as new inputs for other products and the addition of considerable value-added, it is an ideal ZERI project.

Chicken Feed Production

Gotland produces high-quality chickens. The island is totally free of salmonella, and the chickens are not exposed to antibiotics. While the quality is recognised, the high pressure on price does not permit premium pricing. There is no longer an eco-label for chickens: KF, the large Swedish supermarket chain, used to have an eco-label, but dropped it in order to be able to meet tough price constraints imposed by the merchandisers. Eighty per cent of the cost of chicken farming is the chicken feed: high-quality food results in top-quality meat. Guta Kyckling, a leading brand, produces and slaughters four million chickens a year, and the production of this quantity of chickens requires 35 to 40 million tons of chicken feed. Chickens produce manure which is an excellent basis for methane production and earthworm cultivation. For each kilo of feed, the chicken will produce one kilo of dung.

The coastline of Gotland is tainted with algae, several of which can be used as feed for chickens when blended with earthworms, offering a high grade mix of protein, fibres, minerals and vitamins. The presence of a new brewery in Gotland, due to open in summer 1998, expands the possibilities for designing and implementing an integrated biosystem that would feed the chickens all year round with local and recovered resources. The construction of a biodigester based on chicken dung (and preferably blended with other animal dung as well) would generate energy. The establishment of a test unit would enable detailed viability studies for possible construction at each of the island's 12 chicken farming sites.

The construction of a bin for the cultivation of earthworms on the basis of the chicken waste from the farm would offer an additional supply of protein to the chickens. There is a need to study the productivity and the feeding process for chickens. The launching of a pilot fish farm with feed from the slurry of the digester, in combination with other projects, can evolve with several other proposals into a broader Zero Emissions cluster of industries.

The project aims in the first place to make the chicken-processing industry competitive again by reducing the cost of feed, while at the same time increasing the energy efficiency and the revenues. The project aims to safeguard 200 jobs, currently at risk, while, through the full-scale implementation of the digesters and slurry processing, generating up to 50 more.

Algae Clean-Up

Algae are growing in the Baltic Sea. Traditional kelp has been replaced by new varieties which wash ashore and pollute beaches, thereby affecting tourism which is important to the island's economy.

Due to the low salt content of the Baltic Sea water, its algae are special—although all have the same variety of biochemical components, such as agar, carrageenan and iodine, which can be used in the agro- and food industries. Algae can be extremely nutritious and can be used as feed for cattle, chickens and pigs, either in the dried unprocessed form, or processed. The waste from the processed algae can be further re-used in the cattle feed industry. Therefore, a detailed biochemical analysis has been proposed by ZERI for the most important types of algae washing ashore.

The study is to include the use of algae as an additive to chicken feed, in particular for egg-laying chickens, assessing the impact on the colour of the egg yolk. It will also include studying the impact of using algae as a feedstock on the colour of pork meat—which is becoming increasingly pale.

The clean-up of the island could then be undertaken in a economical way. If and when it is proven that the dried algae can be fully re-used as a value-added component, islanders will see the birth of a new industry. This will generate jobs.

Fish Farming at Arla

Reports have been published by the environment ministries in both Sweden and Finland calling for the reduction of fishing in the Baltic Sea[91]—which is polluted and over-fished—and for further fish farming on land to be undertaken. Numerous opportunities have been identified in Gotland for the expansion of fish farming, using discarded water, energy and food. The possibilities identified at Arla deserve special attention.

Arla, a milk-processing co-operative on the island, consumes 160,000 m^3 of water per year. After treatment to reduce the biological oxygen demand (BOD) and to balance the pH level, it is discharged into the sewage system at a temperature of 27°C. Arla also discharges warm air from its milk powder unit, at a temperature of 40°C. Both the water and the air contain volumes of milk residues such as fats and proteins. The proposal is to convert the Arla plant into a large-scale pilot for integrated biosystems. The quality of the water, food and energy is ideal for year-round farming of tilapia, a white fish commanding a premium price on international markets: up to SEK100 per kilo in winter months. There is sufficient water, space and food to schedule three ponds of 2 hectares each. The fish farming could evolve from producing 3 tons per hectare in the first year to a full capacity of 10–12 tons per ha per annum.

A 6 ha pilot plant at Arla could therefore generate up to 60 tons of fish per annum, setting a trend and offering a fresh impetus to the fish-processing industry. If this and additional fish farming initiatives could be operationalised, an estimated 100 tons of fish could be added to overall volume. Since the fish is part of the business proposal, there is a need to quantify in detail the production results in a second phase.

---

91. See, for example, Swedish Environmental Protection Agency, *Action Plan on Biodiversity* (Report 4567; Stockholm: Swedish Environmental Protection Agency, 1996).

Essential Oils from Gotland

Essential oils are a core product in the fast-growing market of health products. Aromatherapy is a widespread practice throughout the world, with Asia the largest market for such natural products, and North America and Europe quickly catching up. The value of the world market was estimated by the Social Venture Network at approximately $1 billion in 1994 and is growing: lemon grass oil, for example, sells at US$10 per 10 ml. Gotland prides itself on its biodiversity, and numerous plants, flowers and bushes are unique to the island. This biodiversity could be converted into value-added products—such opportunities are not only restricted to the tropics. None of this is exploited today.

A proposal to establish a distillation unit for essential oils followed a botanical expedition which identified some six widely available plants on the island. The exploitation of essential oils could also be expanded to produce herbs for food and cosmetics. Since only 1% of the biomass is extracted in the distillation process, there is a lot of residue. The biomass waste generated from the extraction and selection can be used for fish feed or, if steam explosion technology is available, it can easily be converted into quality cattle food.

The initiative will reinforce Gotland's image of respect for nature and biodiversity. The project is supported by growing botanical knowledge and, since exploitation is only feasible when the harvesting is done in a sustainable manner, it is possible for the island to contemplate setting a benchmark for the practice of premium-priced organic agriculture. The planting, harvesting and distillation of essential oils and herbs generates multiple jobs. A core unit that supports a small distillation unit requires a team of 12 persons.

The revenues vary, depending on the type of essential oil. Geranium oil, extracted from a flower widely available on the island, commands a retail price in Japan of US$50 per 10 ml (or US$5,000 per litre), which supports a wholesale price of about one-third—about US$15 per 10 ml bottle. The distillation process can also be designed in an extremely energy-efficient manner, utilising solar power in the peak summer harvest.

The Gotland Brewery as a Tourist Attraction

Bolaget, a Gotlandic company, plans the construction of a new microbrewery in Visby, the island's major town. It has selected a site in the centre, well enough located to be spotted offshore when arriving by boat from the mainland. The brewery could be operational by the summer of 1998.

The new brewery could certainly incorporate elements of the integrated biosystem designed by ZERI and applied in several pilot cases to the brewing industry. Despite the fact that no pilot has yet been attempted outside of the tropics, the ZERI experts, headed by Professor George Chan, are convinced that similar initiatives can be implemented in northern countries.

However, in order to maximise all potential, ZERI has proposed a second microbrewery, sited in the harbour so that the additional activities could be accommodated on one site, thus augmenting the attractiveness for visitors who would get a complete view of the integrated system, the clusters of the industries and the remarriage of agriculture and industry. The project could very well become a major attraction for tourists—supporting the marketing of the island—while at the same time maintaining industrial and value-added production.

The breweries could establish a small malting unit in Gotland, thereby ensuring that the wheat and barley grown in Gotland does not have to be transported to the mainland and then re-imported to the island. They could also include a bottling unit for juices based on fruits and berries from the island, in order to offer a non-alcoholic alternative. The process for disposal of the waste from this activity is similar, though easier, than for beer.

The project would create additional jobs. Since most beer drunk on the island is currently imported from the mainland, there is room for expansion of Gotland's beer industry. Indeed, the name and fame generated could secure the export of beer to the mainland. The additional brewery could be operated with five to six people, while the value-adding activities, including services for tourists and the trade generated from related products, could employ up to a further 25.

The proposed ZERI brewery has a capacity of 3,000 hl per annum or approximately one million bottles per year. This is not a major volume. The sales can therefore best be complemented with other revenues such as those outlined in the integrated biosystem of ZERI.

Gotland's Biscuits and Chocolates

Gotland receives up to 800,000 visitors a year, which offers a huge potential for the sale of products linked to Gotland. A review of the products for the tourist trade has indicated that there is further room for innovation. At the same time, many of the food-processing industries operate at below capacity for most of the year, and at full capacity for only five weeks a year. This implies that a better utilisation of their capital investments and distribution networks is necessary to secure the long-term viability of the small-scale local industries.

Gotland is also a major exporter of agro-produce, and is looking for opportunities to generate value-added to these products. It has been proposed by ZERI that a new range of products should be invented, developed, tested and sold on the market. The abundance in local resources such as milk, sugar and grain, as well as excess labour during the period outside the high season, can be converted in two simple products: biscuits and chocolate. The production process of the Gotland biscuits and chocolate can be designed according to the strictest application of the ZERI concept: because the ingredients—milk, butter, sugar, cocoa and their residues—are all organic. Waste chocolate can, for example, be re-used as a flavouring for bread.

Since the production of both biscuits and chocolate can be halted during the five-week peak period without jeopardising freshness, it is possible to achieve an overall improvement in capacity utilisation within existing infrastructure and distribution channels. The residues in the process can be recovered in other processes. This will mean improved financial results.

The creation of jobs will be limited at first, since the initiative will first secure a fuller use of available labour. However, further jobs are certainly feasible in the first expansion phase. The advantage is that these are year-round jobs.

A successful operation in each of the products could lead to an additional gross revenue of SEK20 million. The design of the project according to the ZERI concept will also permit a positioning of the products at a European level in general, and Germany in particular. Both this initiative and the brewery could therefore prove to be an attraction in mobilising environmentally conscious German tourists to come to Gotland.

A Living Laboratory

The island of Gotland could emerge as a living laboratory, ready to test the ideas of Zero Emissions in a Western European environment and prepared to establish a four-tier partnership between academics, business, unions and local government. If success can be demonstrated in Gotland, the road will have been cleared for a conversion of the conservative thinking in Europe—which seems to refuse to take the employment issue into account—and show that there is a readiness to embrace UpSizing.

Chapter 12
Japan Leads the Industrialised World in the Quest for Zero Emissions

Europeans pride themselves in their advanced environmental management. European industry and policy-makers believe that environmental protection will be one of the high-growth sectors in the economy with the worldwide market for environmental technologies and services currently valued at $400 billion a year and predicted to grow to $600 billion by 2000.[92]

While Europeans in general, and the Scandinavians, Dutch and Germans in particular, are conscious about their achievements, few understand the Japanese rejection of mere preservation of nature. The Japanese prefer to lead the search for a much-needed marriage between economy and ecology. Over the past hundred years, Europe, in its drive to modernise, destroyed much of its natural capital, just as Japan has done. In Japan, however, whatever remains appears holy.[93] Perhaps it is time to reappraise the relevance of the Japanese approach for the Europeans.

The Japanese have left their mark on management principles. Successful strategies to automate the shop floor, to produce with quality, to deliver just in time or to adopt a customer-oriented strategy were all initiated in Japan. Since the oil crisis of 1973, the Japanese seem to have succeeded in breaking with the past, enacting innovative management strategies, while at the same time, at least until very recently, succeeding in taking more market share. On the other hand, the Japanese continue to consume primary rainforest, and their stance on whaling and over-fishing has been extremely unpopular around the globe.

The Japanese are capable of combining long-term corporate and national strategies with short-term targets. Already, with ISO 14001 still in its infancy, the Japanese are envisioning its successor—aptly tagged ISO 21000, or the ISO of the twenty-first century. They envisage its first approval only

---

92. Environmental Industries Commission press release, London, May 1997.
93. Shinto emphasises the importance of respect for nature.

in 2005. The idea is not only far-fetched for European industry: worse, few government officials in Europe would ever dare to put US\$10 million on the table in order to start a long-term research programme to design the management tools for the next century.[94]

This is exactly where Japan differs from Europe: putting money where its mouth is. Few Japanese would venture to explain exactly what ISO 21000 will consist of, but many Japanese would agree that the present concepts and buzz-words such as eco-efficiency, industrial ecology, Factor 4 and Factor 10 improvements in resource productivity, cleaner production and responsible care have all been around for at least a decade, but none has offered what is needed to convert the present economy into a growth economy that fully respects, protects and which even regenerates the environment that has suffered so greatly from our industrial pillaging of the past. There is clarity on the final objective: to grow the economy while doing more than simply preserving the environment.

Pollution in a cowboy economy (PCe) accumulates faster than output and wealth (OW). Pollution growth levels increase more slowly than economic output with the introduction of cleaner production (CPe). Pollution and economic growth feed off each other.

In the cowboy economy, pollution will rise even faster than economic output and, today, many governments are still willing to sacrifice the environment for the sake of job creation and income generation (see Graph 1). Indonesia's slash-and-burn policy, clearing forests to make space for palm plantations, is an unfortunate case in point. It is certainly possible that the disastrous fires of 1997, which cast a choking haze over much of South-East Asia, could be repeated. Programmes such as cleaner production aim to create a regime where growth of the economy is higher than the growth of contamination. This is not enough, and the Japanese are now stating[95] that they wish to see an economy where pollution will be reduced to zero[96] (see Graph 2). If this is a realistic objective, what tools will be required?

---

94. \$10 million has been provided by the Japanese Society for the Promotion of Science and the Japanese Ministry for Education, Science and Culture. ISO 21000 remains a novel idea, but the Japanese Management Association (JMA) has accepted the author's suggestion that the new standard should ideally be launched at the World Expo, scheduled for Aichi, Japan, in 2005. The JMA is taking a delegation of 25 executives to Germany in September 1998 to consult on the matter with the Fraunhofer Institute, Germany's largest applied technology research group.
95. Japanese Environment Agency, *White Book on the Environment* (Tokyo: Government Printing Office, 1998).
96. There are always exceptions to the rule. Corporate Japan was unwilling to sanction ambitious reductions in CO_2 emissions in the final round of negotiations on the Climate Change Convention which resulted in the Kyoto Protocol of November 1997.

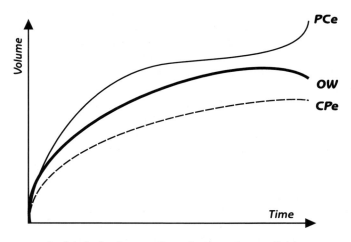

Graph 1: *Cowboy Economy, Cleaner Production Economic Model*

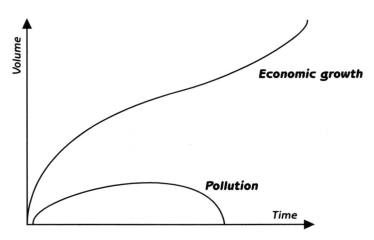

As the economy grows further over time, pollution will tend towards zero, since all waste of one industrial process will be used as input for another.

Graph 2 : *The Zero Emissions Economic Development Model*

The strength of ISO standards is that they offer, on the one hand, a set of detailed and disciplined management tools to document environmental impacts and, on the other, a clear method of communication to stakeholders that a company meets the requirements set forth. However, a close look at ISO 14001—in the design of which the Japanese played a very important role—immediately highlights its shortcomings as well. After all, a nuclear power station could apply for and obtain ISO 14001 certification; so could city waste incinerators responsible for 80% of the production of dioxins in Japan, on the condition that all emissions are well documented and within the standards set by both the company and the law.

The Japanese championed the concept of productivity. They now realise that a further increase in labour productivity is not viable. After all, after having replaced cheap labour with no labour, there is little room for improvement. There is still room for improvement in the productivity of capital, but few forecasters are predicting double-digit improvements in the years to come. The only area where double-digit growth is possible is in the productivity of raw materials.

The Japanese economy is highly dependent on imported and semi-processed raw materials. Over 70% of all food in the country is imported, with a growing proportion of this also processed overseas. Against this background, it seems obvious that the Japanese Ministry of International Trade and Industry (MITI) is keen to bolster industrial performance in material productivity. As early as 1996, the *White Book on the Environment*, published annually by the Japanese Environment Agency, stated that 'the concept of Zero Emissions is to become a standard for industry in the 21st century'.[97] Zero Emissions was defined as follows: 'all raw materials are used in the process. Whatever cannot be used will be made available as value added inputs for other industrial processes.' The 1998 edition of the *White Book* dedicates its entire opening chapter to an examination of a closed-loop economy based on the Zero Emissions methodology.[98]

Why have the Japanese embraced the concept of Zero Emissions faster than other countries? The first answer is that there is a chronic lack of space in Japan: for housing; for industry; and, crucially, for the disposal of waste. Waste disposal costs in Japan are among the highest in the world. Artificial islands have been constructed to create more capacity as landfill sites have become overloaded, but the situation remains critical. As a result, Japanese households and businesses have been encouraged to adopt sophisticated domestic recycling practices: the country aims to recycle 56%

---

97. Japanese Environment Agency, *White Book on the Environment* (Tokyo: Government Printing Office, 1996).
98. Japanese Environment Agency, *White Book on the Environment*, 1998.

of all paper by 2000. The attraction of zero waste as a solution for corporate Japan is clear.

There are also cultural reasons for the support for what is certainly a holistic target. Both the Shinto and Buddhist religions emphasise the unity of man and nature and, despite the obvious erosion of these traditional values, caused by industrialisation, they have not disappeared from national consciousness. Perhaps these values are evident in the strong support for organic produce—and resistance to the use of pesticides—in the country.

Japan also has a history of generating breakthrough technologies, and the redesign of products and processes will be a key ingredient in the Zero Emissions revolution. The trend towards miniaturisation, the need to meet stringent environmental regulation[99] and the desire to minimise wastage of precious imported products have created ideal conditions for cleaner production to flourish and in turn have provided the substrate on which the culture of Zero Emissions has mushroomed.

The statement by the Japanese Environment Agency in 1996 was the precursor of a series of new initiatives. Within a year, the Japanese Ministry for Education, Science and Culture approved a ¥500 million budget to study the feasibility of the Zero Emissions concept. The amount was quickly considered insufficient and doubled to ¥1 billion thanks to the support of the Japanese Society for the Promotion of Science. Japan is searching for a new framework for Sustainable Development and sees many advantages in advancing the Zero Emissions approach, and has therefore taken the concept and dedicated large research funds towards operationalising it, once again stealing a march on the rest of the world.

It is a commendable Japanese tradition that, when the national policy-makers get behind a new vision, industry gets organised and local authorities are stimulated to test ideas at ground level. In 1997, MITI established a co-ordination committee for local governments called the 'Eco-town Programme', urging them to develop simulations on the concept of 'what a Zero Emissions city would look like'. The objective is not to test what remains an uncertain science, but to develop management tools. From the 100 applications, four cities were selected for funding through this pioneering effort. These include Kita Kyushu, which is now offering to recover waste from neighbouring cities to separate and re-use as an input for new industries. Kamakura, the imperial city just south of Tokyo, decided to eliminate all dioxins. Plans have also been established to utilise fuel derived

---

99. After the high-profile scares in the early 1970s, such as the mass poisonings from heavy metal pollution at Minamata, the country embarked on a crash course in environmental regulation resulting in some of the most stringent air, water and noise pollution standards in the world.

from waste for power plants. In March 1997, a book, *Zero Emissions and the Economic Reality of Japan*,[100] written by the *Nikkei*'s senior editor, T. Mitsuhashi, was published and became a best-seller. It highlights cases from companies, cities and prefectures dedicated to changing the industrial paradigm of the past few decades.

A huge army of researchers are now at work in universities throughout Japan to examine priority areas in the formulation of zero-emission-oriented material cycle processes, under the leadership of Professor Motoyuki Suzuki, National Co-ordinator of the Zero Emissions Research Programme. The main objectives of the research are:

◀ To analyse the current materials flow in each production process and to elucidate the possibility of reducing emissions close to zero in each process.

◀ To study and assess the formulation of methods of production processes beyond the industrial category to reduce emissions close to zero within the local area.

◀ To develop the database and mathematical models describing the materials flow in local areas and Japan as a whole in order to estimate and/or evaluate Zero Emissions policies and technologies.

◀ Industry sectors such as steel, pulp and paper, chemicals, textiles, and construction are among those being studied. The ultimate objective is to develop proposals for zero-emissions production systems and for the technologies that will be needed for their establishment.

These are just the very first steps.

In 1998 MITI earmarked an extra ¥150 million for further projects at local government level. However, these funds are small compared to the funds reserved to encourage business to join its drive to secure concrete cases. Companies prepared to undertake pioneering investments have received major financial support. EBARA Corporation, one of the leading engineering groups in Japan, received multi-million dollar financing to support the construction of a CO_2, NO_x and SO_x-to-fertiliser conversion plant. EBARA is committed to demonstrating that the concept of Zero Emissions is not limited to solid waste, but can successfully be applied to gaseous wastes, in particular to those gases that cause acid rain and global warming. The fact that Japan is suffering from severe airborne pollution from mainland China motivated EBARA to establish the pilot plant in Chengoln, China for treatment of flue gas emitted from a coal-fired thermal power plant. It was inaugurated in August 1997.

---

100. T. Mitsuhashi, *Zero Emissions and the Japanese Economy* (Tokyo: Iwanemi Shoten, 1997).

Ebara has also developed a system that can convert industrial and municipal waste into substances such as ammonia, methane, hydrogen and gasoline. The heat created by the system can also be used for power generation. In addition, the inclusion of a low-temperature, reduced-pressure process avoids the oxidisation of metals such as iron, copper amd aluminium, allowing them to be extracted for recycling. The system will be a major feature of Ebara's planned eco-industrial park which, when completed in 2000, will aim to provide Japan with a model for a self-sustaining urban development based on Zero Emissions. The park will include factories, dwellings, shops and agricultural facilities and will fully recycle waste in a cycle of interdependence.

Chichibu Onoda Cement, the largest cement group in Japan and one of the largest in the world, invested in the substitution of synthetic fibres—in themselves already a substitute for asbestos—with natural fibres extracted from bamboo. Its cement board factory requires a 2,000 ha-sized plantation to provide sufficient bamboo fibre. Such space is not available in Japan, but is in abundance in South-East Asia. This venture is an example of how an industry responsible for CO_2 emissions can sequester them. The fibres of the bamboo consist mainly of carbon molecules which, when encapsulated in a crystallised environment by the process, permit a half-life of 40 years. More importantly, the application of the Zero Emissions concept has led to the recovery of all extracted bamboo juice, which is then fermented into alcohol and used as a clean fuel in the production process. The target of zero emissions has been pursued and funded with the assistance of MITI. This pilot project was established in Indonesia with the first full-scale plant likely to be up and running in Bangkok, Thailand, by the end of 1998.

As the consensus between business and government emerges, funds are released in parallel to undertake the research. The ¥1 billion fund involves some 42 pilot projects, employs about 50 professors and mobilises some of the best minds in the country. Networks in Japan are powerful, and can help to secure an effective interaction between government policy, business strategy and the identification of the missing links in science and technology. Still, much more is required. Whereas companies such as EBARA and Chichibu Onoda Cement are certainly large by any international standards, they do not carry the clout of giant groups such as Toyota or NEC. Their public involvement in Zero Emissions will be the real endorsement.

Let's dream a little! Toyota sponsors a Sunday-evening TV special on the concept and the application of Zero Emissions. NEC delivers a series of overseas lectures on environmental management in Japan and highlights the importance of Zero Emissions, painstakingly explaining the difference with cleaner production, responsible care, eco-efficiency, 3R and industrial ecology. The company then announces its commitment to Zero Emissions as a prime management concept, and opens to the press the first Zero Emissions factories already working in Kyushu, Kagoshima and Akita, Japan. These efforts culminate in the international promotion of a new ISO standard—ISO 21000—formally launched at the World Exposition in Aichi Prefecture, home of Toyota in the year 2005.

How much of a dream is this? Well, the involvement of Toyota and NEC is not a dream at all. On 21 June 1998 a 30-minute TV programme called *Spaceship Earth: An Amazing Farm in Fiji*, focusing on the integrated biosystem at Montfort, Fiji, was transmitted on Japanese TV. *All* the advertising around the programme was bought by Toyota, indicating that the corporation very much wants to be associated with the concept. NEC does not want to announce the operating results of its factories until 2000. However, some details are available. In April 1996, a comprehensive recycling system allowing for 'zero waste' became operational at a new fabrication line at NEC Kyushu Ltd, an NEC semiconductor-manufacturing subsidiary. At NEC Akita Ltd, the aim for fiscal 1998 was to increase the amount of pure water re-used from production processes to 74% from the 60% achieved in fiscal 1997. This, combined with energy conservation and waste reduction efforts, led to the plant being awarded the 'Superior High-Tech Facility of 1996' prize by the *Nihon Keizai Shimbun*.

Japan has always aimed to design and build new standards for business on clear-cut concepts. European scientists may have difficulties with the semantics, claiming that 'zero' is not possible as long as we do not repeal the second law of thermodynamics. The Japanese avoid such a debate. Management needs clear targets that are not only easily understood by all employees, but which can also be communicated without confusion to all the stakeholders, in particular to the public at large. Zero waste and zero emissions are aspirations clearly understood by everyone.

When Japanese cars entered the European market nearly three decades ago, the message to the customer on quality was simple: Honda offered five years or 100,000 km warranty, free of charge. The consumer did not need lengthy explanations about how this was an application of TQM: the five-year warranty said it all. The European policy-makers approach environmental issues and business in a very different manner. Europe has made a clear distinction between environmental protection and economic development. At best, industrial policies will not increase pollution. Some claim that reducing consumption, re-using products and recycling waste means good business. In reality, it is not associated with high-value-added business opportunities: such businesses have uncertain growth, are dependent on restrictive government regulations and therefore have uncertain profit margins. The remediation of polluted land, the purification of contaminated water and the scrubbing of toxins out of gaseous wastes is indeed a growing business, but it is not creating wealth for society; it is merely avoiding further damage. Its financing depends on taxation, which is ultimately borne by the consumer, either through increased prices or a reduction of disposable income.

European directives and national laws have pioneered the implementation of policies designed to reduce, re-use and recycle and promulgated the polluter pays principle as a cornerstone of that legislation. Whereas the logic is widely entrenched, it is based on the principles of engineering with little regard for biology and natural cycles.

Forcing industry to clean up its end-of-pipe act was a necessary step, but that is the first step only. The next step must go beyond the mere regulatory approach. To go beyond the regulatory framework does not imply that from here on all industry will be subject to the powers of the free market where only the strongest survive. On the contrary, it must be a market of co-operation where whatever is waste for one is shared with another in order to add value! A free market, where all actors are operating within their own closed business frameworks, driven by core business strategies and outsourcing is not the solution to the present impasse. Under these circumstances, the only option is reduce, re-use and recycle.

If Europe wishes to grow the economy, generate jobs and dramatically reduce the adverse environmental impacts created by industrialisation and the consumption patterns of modern society, then a new paradigm is needed. That paradigm is still based on a market economy, but one where the actors are not stand-alone operators, focusing on core businesses, but clustered industries where the group searches for maximising value-added to the core products and services. The power of the group is derived from the collaborative spirit within these businesses, where a network targets higher levels of total productivity than one could ever have achieved on its own.

In this framework of operation, European industry does not have many advantages over the Japanese. On the contrary, after the Second World War, Japanese industry evolved into *keiretsus* or informal holding structures of complementary enterprises. In such a network, it is much easier to cluster industrial activities whereby the waste of one is input for the other. Family-owned and -controlled enterprises, which dominate Europe, do not have the tradition of entering into such broad-based collaborative efforts. While the European Commission has consulted and tested voluntary environmental initiatives and commitments by business, there remains a good deal of distrust about whether such efforts are effective: regulation remains the favoured option. At least Europeans are not as hampered as Americans are by the culture of short-term objectives such as increasing shareholder value by downsizing and outsourcing.

The European stakeholders, which include industry, trade unions, the scientific community, governments, NGOs and the public, have to overcome their present state of romanticism for the environment. They also need to address the isolated position of the millions of small and medium-sized enterprises that largely fall outside of the legislative strategy to protect the environment. Europe should move towards an innovative but comprehensive strategy that permits the integration of two main priorities: create wealth and preserve the natural heritage.

The socio-economic reality of Europe—record post-war unemployment—should drive its stakeholders towards a creative response to the American strategy of downsizing. It is here that the Japanese approach based on the design of an economic model that prescribes economic growth, job creation and the elimination of waste on a regional (if not global) scale is offering a new vision. Whereas the model still requires time to be proven, previous initiatives emanating from the Japanese business community should convince Europeans and Americans alike that this is an option worth serious consideration. It is certainly better than the status quo based on monetary policies, which have demonstrated themselves to be capable of controlling inflation, but lack the power to respond to the social and environmental needs of the European societies: jobs and a clean place to live.

It is time for UpSizing.

Appendix
Scientific Research on Priority Areas:
Formulation of Zero-Emission-Oriented Material Cycle Processes

Selected Projects

Analysis Of Material Flows in Industrial Processes

Optimisation of heat and material cycles in the steel industry
T. Akiyama (Tohoku University)

Analysis and treatment of accumulating materials in pulp refinery processes
Y. Matsumoto (Tokyo University)

Simultaneous SO_x and NO_x removal by chemical reaction cycles
H. Niiyama (Tokyo Institute of Technology)

Key technologies for nitrogen recycle in industries
K. Aika (Tokyo Institute of Technology)

Emission structures in Japanese wine industries in Niigata
T. Kameya (Nagaoka University of Technology)

Process simulator to achieve zero emission from textile dyeing processes
Y. Hayashi (Kanazawa University)

Control of chemicals in universities
K. Chiba (Nagoya University)

Design of synthetic reaction paths and processes design for zero emission cycles
K. Funatsu (Toyohashi University of Technology)

Complete material flow analysis in pulp and paper industries
M. Akiba (Shimane University)

Control of material utilisation in semiconductor processes
K. Okuyama (Hiroshima University)

Process management and product development for achievement of zero emissions
A. Iwase (Hiroshima University)

Fluoride and water management in semiconductor processes
T. Korenaga (Tokushima University)

Recycling of rare earth atoms by membrane extraction
M. Goto (Kyushu University)

Metal recycles from waste catalysts
K. Inoue (Saga University)

Leaching process by combination of oxidatibe and reductive bacteria
Y. Kai (Kagoshima University)

Silver and polyester recovery from spent printing plates
H. Ishilawa (Osaka Prefecture University)

Material balance analysis in fish paste production processes
M. Takasaki (Ishinomaki Senshu University)

Assessment of material cycles in construction industries
K. Tanaka (Nihon University)

Recycling of wastes from photograph-related industries
A. Hirata (Waseda University)

Material flow assessment in cement/concrete industries
K. Amano (Ritsumeika University)

Zero emissions in non-electrolytic plating processes
T. Choji (Toyama Institute of Technology)

Environmental risk and cycle of construction materials
Y. Ono (Okayama University)

Construction of Closed Material Cycles within Industrial Clusters
Zero-emission process for biomass wastes
T. Funatsukuri (Chuo University)

Construction of production–circulation systems for next generation
K. Ohno (Nagoya University)

Combination of metal refinery and forestry waste treatment for total
production
                                    H. Katayama (Shimane University)
Social systems for achieving local resources recycling
                                    S. Fujita (Kagoshima University)
Electricity generation with no thermal waste-water
                                    M. Nagai (Ryukyu University)
Minimisation of waste heat from electric power industry
                                    M. Ishii (Meiji University)
Analysis and minimisation of food industry wastes
                                    K. Mutoyama (Kansai University)
Carbon recycling by carbonisation of organic waste
                                    S. Tanada (Kinki University)
By-products generation from metallurgy processes
                                    M. Tokuda (Tohoku University)
Highly selective oxidisation of natural gases
                                    T. Mizuno (Tokyo University)
Material and energy flows in cracking plants for waste plastics
                                    A. Ito (Niigata University)
Appropriate technologies for total utilisation of forestry resources
                                    T. Sawada (Kanazawa University)
Complete gasification of waste wood chips by carbon dioxide gas
                                    S. Goto (Nagoya University)
Energy-productive zero emission in *shochu* (distillery) industry
                                    Y. Usui (Kyushu University of Technology)
Recycle system by using supercritical water oxidisation
                                    M. Goto (Kumamoto University)
Carbon materials production from waste plastic
                                    W. Hatate (Kagoshima University)
Assessment of plastics recycling technologies by dynamic flow model
                                    M. Hirao (Tokyo University)

Mathematical Modelling for Complete Material Cycles
Local economy system to enhance zero wastes
                                    Y. Miyata (Tohohashi University of Technology)
Mathematical model of urban water cycles for assessment of environmental
effects
                                    H. Tsuno (Kyoto University)
Lifestyle in Zero Emission systems
                                    H. Takahashi (Kyoto University)
Consumption and circulation system for local Zero Emissions
                                    H. Imura (Kyushu University)

Management of production system and material cycles around closed water body

> K. Arizono (Nagasaki University)

Utilisation and recycling of shock manure at South Kyushu area

> S. Kanazawa (Kagoshima University)

Legal and political assistance for Zero Emissions social system

> A. Morishima (Sophia University)

Industrial cluster modelling for total environmental quality control

> S. Ikeda (Ritsumeikan University)

Total utilisation of squids

> T. Miura (Hokkaido University)

Nitrogen cycle in soil and ground-water system of vegetable farm

> K. Sakamoto (Chiba University)

Possibility of total recycling in construction business

> A. Urano (Tokyo University)

Combined farming and stock-breeding system based on field capacity of agricultural land

> A. Katayama (Nagoya University)

Construction of efficient local recycle system for organic wastes

> K. Fukagawa (Ube Institute of Technology)

Source: Professor Motoyuki Suzuki, National Co-ordinator of the Zero Emissions Research Programme of the Japanese Ministry of Education, Science, Culture and Sports

Epilogue
How to do more faster?

Today, we have poverty in a world of plenty. Inefficiency and waste are all around us. Unemployment continues to grow. In this book, I have described a methodology that can start to change things. Indeed, the first successes are there for all to see. But how can we do more faster? What are the obstacles that we need to overcome and what strategies should we pursue to leap the hurdles in our path?

The first obstacle in our path is the lack of resources we have at our disposal. The United Nations University has supported the start-up of research, infrastructure and networking towards the realisation of Zero Emissions pilot schemes. But more is needed, particularly for research. Why are businesses not being more proactive? Perhaps we can postulate that the common good of society as a whole, which, after all, is what UpSizing is all about, will not necessarily feature on the balance sheets of individual companies. The sector of society who stand to gain most from the application of the ZERI principle and UpSizing—the poor and unemployed—do not have a voice in the boardrooms where investment decisions are made.

But the strategy of downsizing is demotivating. So how should we encourage UpSizing and how can we achieve the aims quickly? If there is one resource we certainly do not have enough of, it is time. This is not an attempt to offer a quick fix or a fast solution; it is a review of some of the most effective ways to get there faster. How do we stimulate the emergence of a new leadership? What is the best way to empower the young? How do we disseminate a common educational methodology? What new kinds of partnership are necessary? Of course, the ideas are incomplete, but they are designed to help us reflect and to try to put us on the right track. In order to make it all happen, we need tremendously powerful and highly distributed intelligence networks—the concept of immunity management.

Leadership

It would be preposterous to pretend that there is only one way forward. There are always many ways to reach a goal, and a straight line is not always the easiest. When a boat crosses the Pacific Ocean, the theoretical shortest distance is a straight line. But, when one takes the wind and the sea currents—two ever-changing parameters—into account, the fastest and least energy-intensive way to get across will never be a straight line.

To succeed in the challenge of moving humankind from one paradigm to another, there is an urgent need for a new form of leadership, one that is not promising immediate results and only one solution. We should not rely on charismatic individuals: intelligence is highly distributed. A collective approach is necessary. There must be some form of ownership, some way to self-select the common vision. The leadership required to make this happen needs individuals who can ensure that people can enter into a dialogue with each other—and that, through continuous conversation and the sharing of information, this group can reach a common understanding, a shared vision and act coherently.

The new leaders will be facilitators with the skill to make all those concerned communicate, even with the 'enemy', as well as with the minorities and outcasts. This will ensure that society moves from one paradigm to the other—along the line of zero defects, zero inventory, zero defections and zero emissions and with the ultimate aim of zero conflicts. No society can sustain long periods of conflict. If the zero-conflict society is to be achieved, it will only be feasible thanks to a strong group of self-effacing twenty-first-century Socrates. These leaders have no answers to the many questions, no easy solutions to offer, but, as facilitators, they will have many questions to pose so that, jointly, we will all come to the understanding that co-operation and a shared vision are the prerequisites for society to move forward.

Of course, charismatic leaders will also emerge. Their task? To inspire, enthuse and to open up minds for new ideas. Those leaders will help overcome the fear of change and will provide the basis for confidence and belief.

The Empowerment of the Young

The largest untapped resource in this world is the creativity of the young. The young have a unique opportunity in their lives to take risks. Their drive is stimulated by their dreams, which they aspire to make come true. Thus, their intentions are pure, and they have an enormous openness to diversity and change.

The young are the antennae of our societies, the reflection of our consciences, and the translation of our dreams into realities. The young learn fast. Their desire to embrace new technologies and to absorb innovations is without parallel. So why is society not prepared to direct this bold concentration of energy into our decision-making process? We need breakthroughs in thinking and action: flexibility and openness are a precondition for success. The young are classified as dreamers, but in their dreams they can be focused. Imagining utopia is an act of creativity. We tell our children that stable jobs—jobs for life—are a thing of the past and that an air-conditioned, protected environment is a pipe-dream. We tell them that change is continuing to change, faster and faster. But these are things that frighten us not our children. We can offer the young the benefit of our experience, but we should allow them to take risks and to fail. If UpSizing is to succeed, we must be prepared to give the young their heads.

At the beginning of 1997 a ZERI convention on the island of Gotland in Sweden led to this recognition. Since then, the ZERI LINK schools programme has been established in the UK with impressive results. Education projects based on the Zero Emissions concept have been initiated in several schools. Teams of young people have then been 'given their heads' at industrial facilities run by companies such as ICI. The identification of waste-streams that have the potential for re-use is already under way. It is now planned to produce a special children's book summarising UpSizing and drawing on examples from nature.

Exposure to Whatever is Different

Humankind searches for its comfort in similarities. A European overseas searches for his familiar diet. A Japanese tourist will wish to have sushi and soba. And the Americans have exported fast food to the four corners of the earth. Humankind searches in vain for stability and continuity—even when it does not make sense, and does not respond to reality. Humankind wants more and more of the same—until we have everything of nothing! In the North we overeat, over-fish, over-harvest and over-consume everything: there does not seem to be a limit to our appetite.

It would be better if we were continuously exposed to the differences, and learned not just how to tolerate, but how to co-operate and appreciate our interdependence. The evolution theory we have replaced with generative theory earlier in this book outlines that co-operation among the most diverse varieties secures the highest level of efficiency. In nature, the most diverse combinations of fauna and flora offer the richest solutions. The wealth of the rainforests is demonstrated by its biodiversity.

The human race is overwhelmingly rich in variety as witnessed by its huge diversity of music, dance, architecture, painting, storytelling and religion.

Incest and monocultures lead to degeneration, and increased risk of bacterial attacks, so that, over time, the chances for survival are diminished. Only when genetic and cultural diversity is actively promoted will the quality of life be enhanced. Therefore, a strategy to protect diversity is insufficient: we have to proceed faster and be more focused in finding ways of increasing diversity. This goes against all the trends in agriculture, forestry and manufacturing where monocultures and cloning, standardisation and monotonous forms of consumption are the norm. Genetic engineering will not improve diversity nor strengthen the system.

The Educational Methodology

In promoting diversity, we must streamline the methodology. There is no chance of operating successfully in this complex world if there is not free access to information, and no easily understood methodology available to everyone. The only solutions are those that we find for ourselves. The only lasting solutions to complex problems are the ones that seem easy. And they seem easy because we have already invented and reinvented them. Each individual has the right to be intelligent—and he or she is intelligent, whether or not they are very well educated.

What we learn is not so important, each of us will determine our own needs, shortcomings and preferences, responding to the needs and the desires of our individual environment and culture—but how we learn is critical. Teachers should no longer download their outdated knowledge onto students expecting them to reproduce diligently what has been predetermined in government-approved textbooks. However, we do need guidance on which is the best way to learn, and how to be stimulated to learn. Without a desire to know more, there is no wish to learn.

I have often been told, after speaking at conferences, that biology and chemistry had never seemed so fascinating. When I learned to appreciate the magic of the sine and cosine in mathematics, I dared to ask the teacher what this was used for in the world. He replied that I would find out if I became an engineer and needed to build a road. I never became an engineer and still don't know the answer to my question. It seems that Socratic questioning remains one of the most effective tools: without questions there are no answers. And with the arrival of the Internet, the student can obtain so many answers, so much more easily than my teacher could ever have imagined.

Private–Public Partnerships

We never succeed on our own. There is a need for partnerships. The 1980s and 1990s have been the age of privatisation—with the assumption that things get done more efficiently when the private sector is in charge. It does not really matter who controls the company's stock: if the right environment prevails, the interest of the common good for society will be fully integrated and blended with the efficiency of the management in order to produce more with less—as a good *Homo economicus* is supposed to do. It does not make sense to consider the public sector bureaucratic and inefficient and the trade unions to be out of touch with reality. The public sector can do both good and bad, just as the private sector can behave absurdly and aggressively. Violence by the state is denounced by Amnesty International, but corporate violence should also be denounced as demonstrated in my book, *Breakthroughs*.

The private sector has advantages, and the public sector has its mission. The trade unions have a clear bias toward the interests of the workers and the scientists' towards their search for clarity. Unless the private–public– union–scientific partnership takes shape and form and co-operates towards a common vision of where we wish to be, there is little prospect that society as a whole can move forward, generate more, UpSize and achieve Zero Emissions!

The tools are available; the fools are around: it is up to the intelligent to make the difference.

Annex 1
Fact Sheet on the Zero Emissions Research Initiative (ZERI)[101]

The Zero Emissions Research Initiative was launched in 1994 by the Rector of the United Nations University (UNU) in Tokyo, Dr Heitor Gurgulino de Souza, within the framework of the UNU's Eco Restructuring Programme.

The aim was to enlist the best minds for industry to improve its environmental performance, and was a unique attempt by a UN organisation to involve the business community in the redesign of manufacturing—based on the Zero Emissions concept.

ZERI was founded to undertake scientific research, involving centres of excellence from around the world, with the objective of achieving technological breakthroughs that will lead to manufacturing without any form of waste. All inputs are either to be used in the final product, or have to be converted into value-added ingredients for other industries.

Since 1994, ZERI has demonstrated that the Zero Emissions concept works, by moving beyond the research stage and implementing a number of successful pilot projects, as well as the first commercial industrial application: a new brewery in Namibia. In the process, it has attracted growing support from the political, business and academic communities, and their active involvement in its programmes.

Political

The Japanese Environment Agency—which called Zero Emissions the trend for the future in its authoritative 1996 *White Book on the Environment*—has reserved a budget for ZERI projects. The Ministry of International Trade and Industry (MITI) has set up a Zero Emissions working group, and reserved a ¥250 million budget for Eco-town pilot projects incorporating the Zero Emissions concept.

---

101. Visit the Zero Emissions Research Initiative (ZERI) on the World Wide Web at *http://www.zeri.org*

The Ministry of Education, Science and Culture has approved a four-year ¥500 million research programme involving nearly 50 professors in Japan in developing a theoretical framework for Zero Emissions. This programme has been extended thanks to a contribution of the Japan Society for the Promotion of Science.

The Prime Minister of Sweden, Mr Ingvar Carlsson, was the first head of government to endorse the Zero Emissions concept publicly. Dr Sam Nuojoma, President of Namibia, and Sir Ratu K.K.T. Mara, President of Fiji, have given strong backing to developing ZERI activities in their countries.

Regional and local authorities—in Latin America, Africa, Europe (Sweden) and Japan—are initiating and supporting ZERI activities.

ZERI participates actively in the international policy-making forums of the UN organisations, the World Bank, regional development banks and governments.

Business

The ZERI Charter for Businesses was prepared during the first weeks of the initiative. EBARA Corporation was the first company to sign the Charter, in November 1994, and has since adopted Zero Emissions as corporate strategy. DuPont was the first US company to commit publicly to the target of Zero Emissions—and Södra Cell, the Swedish pulp maker, was the first European enterprise to do so.

The first commercial application of the Zero Emissions concept was the Namibian Breweries' new brewery in Tsumeb, Namibia, inaugurated in January 1997.

ZERI has developed the Due Diligence concept, which translates the concept of Zero Emissions into a workable and pragmatic approach offering important indicators to financial decision-makers.

Particularly strong support from the Japanese business community demonstrates that ZERI provides an excellent basis for new, innovative public–private–academic partnerships. The new brewery in Namibia is the first such partnership there. In this respect, ZERI's philosophy is very much in line with the approach of Sustainable Project Management (SPM), a spin-off organisation of the World Business Council for Sustainable Development.

Academic

ZERI has drawn on the resources of more than 3,000 researchers throughout the world, working together over the Internet, to design multidisciplinary solutions with advanced process engineering and biochemistry to convert all waste into non-polluting processes.

It co-operates closely with members of prominent academies of science: the Royal Swedish Academy of Sciences and the Academy of Engineering Sciences, the African Academy of Sciences, the Chinese Academy, the Third World Academy, and the Brazilian Science Council.

ZERI has held six international academic workshops on Zero Emissions: in Namibia in January 1997, for integrated biosystems; in Zimbabwe in March 1997, for applying Zero Emissions to the water hyacinth; in Fiji in May 1997, also for integrated biosystems; in Colombia in September 1997, again for integrated biosystems; in Brazil in January 1998, for diversification strategy; and in Tanzania in April 1998, on biodiversity.

It has developed a 40-hour postgraduate course on Zero Emissions, which has been given in 12 countries on five continents, and is currently available in five languages. Over 100 universities are now teaching the course. There is an electronic Spanish version available on the Internet, and a 20-part video version in English and Japanese. As of 1999, ZERI will be offering a Master of Science degree at universities in Latin America, Africa and Asia.

The first UNESCO/UNU Chair on Zero Emissions was inaugurated in January 1997 at the University of Namibia. The aim is to install ten chairs worldwide in the next three years.

Regional training centres have been established in Namibia (Africa), Colombia (South America), Brazil (Mercosur) and Mexico (Central America and the Latin Caribbean), and others will be set up in the Pacific, Asia and Middle East.

Organisation

The ZERI Foundation has been established in Geneva, with funding and support from the United Nations Development Programme (UNDP), the Federal Government of Switzerland and the Canton of Geneva. It will serve as an operational arm of the initiative, dedicated to the fast-track implementation of proven ZERI projects in co-operation with the private sector and local governments. Further ongoing research work will be undertaken at a number of universities, and will continue to involve scientists and academics worldwide.

Future Developments

ZERI will reinforce its research activities, in particular into material separation technologies and integrated biosystems. Training activities will be expanded. More pilot projects will be undertaken, focused on regions with the highest level of success, i.e. southern Africa, Middle America and the southern Pacific islands. Appropriate funding mechanisms will be established. Consortia of private–public–academic partnerships will be formed to implement large-scale projects.

What does Zero Emissions signify for whom?

Zero Emissions is a new vision of the industry. It reassesses the corporate role in the challenges humanity is facing and offers a pragmatic basis for research, corporate strategies, government policies considering the complexities of our time. Zero Emissions is the extension of the drive towards productivity, quality (zero defects), Just-in-Time (zero inventory) and customer service (zero defections).

◀ **For industry** Zero Emissions stands for the development of new technologies to convert production into a sustainable one.

◀ **For corporate executives** Zero Emissions stands for the dramatic increase of productivity of raw materials.

◀ **For corporate strategists** Zero Emissions stands for the development of new business sectors on the basis of former 'waste'.

◀ **For economists** Zero Emissions represents the identification of the new sectors in the world economy that are the source for the jobs of the future while offering a solution to environmental problems.

◀ **For scientists** Zero Emissions stands for a creative multidisciplinary research agenda blending traditional with innovative technologies.

◀ **For the developing world** Zero Emissions stands for an innovative way to address poverty, unemployment, health and environmental issues.

◀ **For environmentalists** Zero Emissions provides a fundamentally new approach that holds the promise of eliminating pollution problems: 'zero' equals the elimination of waste, the mimicking of nature by industry.

◀ **For politicians** Zero Emissions offers a new framework for policy-making, combining critical agendas.

The ZERI Course:
The Concept and Practice of Zero Emissions or the Search for Total Productivity

Objective of the Course

The 20- to 40-hour course on Zero Emissions or Total Productivity aims to offer a multidisciplinary overview of the new industrial activities, processes and concepts that are likely to be mainstream in the next century. The course takes the global issues into account, identifies the new trends and observes early warning systems and offers a re-applicable methodology for the design of sustainable businesses.

Who should attend?

The course is designed for a broad spectrum of university-educated people and relies on a minimum background in either engineering, economics or biochemistry. It is hoped that the interaction of at least these three core disciplines will offer the participants a vision of the new economy that is emerging and the requirements imposed on those studying today to grasp these scientific bases in order to respond to the needs of industry.

What format does the course take?

The course lasts for 20 hours and is both based on *ex cathedra* presentations, case studies and working group exercises, as well as a plenary major discussion forum. The course is ideally structured over five days, leaving time for one-on-one consultations, to engage in discussion groups and offer advise on homework and assignments. The maximum group is 40 people to permit a cross-section of disciplines and a minimum of five to six working groups.

What can the participants expect as result?

1. The participants are likely to be equipped with a methodology that will permit them to assess each industrial process and assess the viability of redesigning all product, water, gas and heat streams so that there is nothing wasted.

2. The participants will have a set of fully documented cases which permit a detailed insight on how the methodology has been applied in real life situations.

3. The participants will have a vision of the future industrial activities

that could be translated into themes for a master or a doctoral thesis or which could represent the core entrepreneurial idea for a business plan or which could form the basis for the redesign of a corporate strategy, even newly patented know-how.

The Faculty
In each country in which the course will be offered, a local tutor will secure the continuation of the discussions as well as a continuity for the further development of initiatives at the research and educational level in relation to the Zero Emissions Research Initiative of the UNU. Course experts have been trained in Brazil, Colombia, Mexico, Namibia and Sweden.

Material and documentation for Training the Trainers
The Latin American Institute for Zero Emissions has designed and developed the training manual. This is available in Spanish, Portuguese and Japanese.

Training on the Internet
The Spanish version of the course is available on Internet through the URL *www.ur.mx/zeri*. It includes an interactive video session with questions and video answers as well as full access to reading material on-line.

Training on Video
An English and Japanese version of the course is available on video (VHS-NTSC).

Original Concepts and Terminology

Zero Emissions

The re-use of all components as value-added, so that no waste is discarded. It is increasingly used as a continuation of management concepts such as zero defects (TQM), zero inventory (Just-in-Time), zero defections (total customer loyalty) and zero conflicts (consensus decision-making).

Clustering of industries

A methodology that permits the clustering of industries that were previously considered unrelated. By mimicking nature, industry can achieve the same levels of material productivity.

UpSizing

Building up economic activities through the clustering of industries which re-use the waste of one as value-added input for another.

Second Green Revolution

ZERI has demonstrated that humankind cannot expect the earth to produce more. Humankind must do more with what the earth produces. This concept has been supported by 100 prominent scientists around the world.

Total productivity

Productivity cannot be limited to labour and capital only: it must include raw materials, the third core input factor in the economy. With less than 10% of raw materials processed, there is considerable room for improvement.

Blending the impatience of the entrepreneur with the depth of science

ZERI's approach is unconventional, yet pragmatic, and based on research, experience and scientific knowledge.

Output–input tables

Economists designed input–output tables early on, whereas ZERI has designed output–input tables, allowing a creative identification of a cluster of industries based on the available resources that remain unused in a specific production process.

Zero Emissions Due Diligence

Companies undertake a due diligence procedure before proceeding with an investment. ZERI's concept of raw materials due diligence assesses what value-added is not generated due to the exclusive focus on one ingredient in the input factors—thereby identifying hidden values which could be exploited commercially.

Immunity Management

The management system for the future depends on a highly decentralised structure, with a well-distributed intelligence.

Jakarta Declaration

A commitment of heads of state, senior executives, scientists and representatives of NGOs to increase productivity, to create jobs and to reduce pollution.

Index

◀ *Steering Business towards Sustainability*
Co-edited with Fritjof Capra (United Nations University Press, English edn, 1995; Japanese edn, 1996)
A review of the ways to motivate corporations to integrate sustainable development into their core strategic considerations. Preface by Professor Dr Heitor Gurgulino de Souza.

◀ *Breakthroughs: What Business Can Offer Society*
(Spanish edn: EAFIT, 1996; Portuguese edn: PUCRS [Brazil]; Japanese edn: ASCII Publishing, 1997; English edn: Epsilon Press; Italian edn: Baldoni & Castoldi; Korean edn: Maeil Business)
A tantalising story of how business must and can generate value-added at economic, social, cultural and environmental level.

◀ *Proceedings of the 2nd World Congress on Zero Emissions*
Co-edited with Professor Dr Keto Mshigeni (English edn: United Nations University's Institute of Advanced Studies, 1997)

By the Same Author

◀ *Aurelio Peccei: The Crusader for the Future.*
A Portrait of the Founder of the Club of Rome
(Oxford, UK: Pergamon Press, 1987)
Preface by Professor Umberto Colombo.

◀ *Services: The Driving Force of the European Economy*
(UK: Waterlow Press, 1987)
A review of how the European economy can generate jobs and develop the businesses of the future while stimulating entrepreneurship. Published in English, French, Norwegian and Dutch. Preface by Gaston Thorn.

◀ *The Second Wave: Japan's Global Assault on Financial Services*
Co-authored by Professor Dr Richard Wright (Waterlow Press, UK; St Martin's Press, USA, 1987)
Review of how the Japanese are poised to challenge the leadership of the American and British financial houses using the same strategy that successfully brought Japanese industry to the forefront of the car and electronics industries. Published in English, French, German, Dutch, Italian and Japanese. Preface by Umberto Agnelli.

◀ *Doen: Dynamisch denken en doen van een Vlaamse Europeeë (Do it! Dynamic Thinking and Doing of a Flemish European)*
(Roularta Press, 1989)
Notes from his diary, travel stories, reflections on economics and the environment. Preface by the Prime Minister of Belgium.

◀ *Double Digit Growth: How to do it!*
(Pauli Publishing, 1991)
A description of the new economy, characterised by fast-growing sectors which are not taken up in national statistics. Published in English, French, German, Spanish, Swedish and Dutch. Preface by Bessel Kok.

◀ *A New Future for Andorra: The Role of Services*
(Credit Andorrá, 1991)
A description of how a small country located in the Pyrrenees could convert its social and economic future in a successful case of development. Published in Catalan and English.